EIGHTH AIR FORCE BOMBER STORIES

A New Selection

Ian McLachlan

SUTTON PUBLISHING

First published in the United Kingdom in 2004 by
Sutton Publishing Limited · Phoenix Mill
Thrupp · Stroud · Gloucestershire · GL5 2BU

British Library Cataloguing in Publication Data
A catalogue record for this book is available from the British Library.

ISBN 0-7509-3360-7

Typeset in 10.5/14pt Garamond 3.
Typesetting and origination by
Sutton Publishing Limited.
Printed and bound in England by
J.H. Haynes & Co. Ltd, Sparkford.

The aviation fraternity contains many individuals committed to restoration and research. These unselfish enthusiasts enrich aviation history and I dedicate this book to their achievements.

Contents

Preface

This further selection of Eighth Air Force Bomber Stories was born from accounts and lines of research unfulfilled when I prepared the first, now best-selling, volume, *Eighth Air Force Bomber Stories*. In some cases, the original inspired additional research to complete stories previously only touched upon. Following the book's success, I was also contacted by other veterans, family members or fellow researchers to act as an outlet for their stories, many previously untold. The result is a rich mixture illustrating courage not only in aerial combat but in other guises, featuring combatants and non-combatants alike. Their binding theme was a dedication to defeating a common enemy and preserving democratic freedoms. As will be seen, many made the ultimate sacrifice, and their stories demonstrate the risks taken by young, old and both genders fighting a malignant tyranny that had taken a cancerous hold on Europe.

That young Americans faced this tyranny in its most evil form is evidenced by a survivor from Buchenwald concentration camp. His powerful eyewitness account describes atrocities that fellow countrymen could not comprehend. The courage shown by civilians seeking to assist downed airmen is also graphically illustrated.

Revealed also are battles with the Luftwaffe, the elements and capricious fortune, all fought with courage, determination and a leavening sense of humour. The mutual respect shown between the RAF and USAAF is recounted by two radio operators – one in a Lancaster, the other in a B-17 – but bonded by events that literally entwined both aircraft.

Another tale touches on the paranormal; I offer no explanation but simply state the story and leave belief or otherwise to the reader.

Aviation archaeology is a theme for several accounts, because it inspired my first book, *Final Flights*, and fragments of fallen aircraft have come to fascinate other researchers, resulting in the unlocking of stories that otherwise would have been lost.

My apologies to those whose accounts failed to achieve publication. Their work was no less diligent, the airmen were no less heroic and the content was equally valid. It was simply that space limitations demanded wise editorial intervention and I hope to make amends next time.

Ian McLachlan
Suffolk, England, April 2004

Acknowledgements

As an author, I am privileged to act as a conduit to the reader on behalf of others also seeking to ensure that those who paid the ultimate price during the Second World War are not forgotten. This book also reminds us of many who were spared but, as time inevitably steals them from us, have now rejoined lost comrades. The ranks of survivors are thinning daily. I hope these pages will illustrate the efforts of others who, like myself, endeavour to ensure we protect the legacy left by the magnificent men of the 'Mighty Eighth'. They stood up against brutal oppression and contributed to its defeat.

Inevitably, there were stories supplied that do not appear because of space limitations, but I hope that success for this title ensures another later selection. The support from all is deeply appreciated and I hope the dedication reflects this.

I trust I will be forgiven for first acknowledging the support of my family, especially my wife Sue, whose hours unpartnered and solo efforts on many domestic duties allowed me to escape and write. Of the four 'children', Bethan's active research proved invaluable. Rowan and Jake are to be thanked for some practical spadework, while Maddie reluctantly vacated the computer.

Credit should also be given to Craig A. Fuller of Aviation Archaeological Investigation & Research – www.AviationArchaeology.com – for help with Accident and Missing Aircrew Combat Reports.

Photographs that are not otherwise credited are from the author's collection.

Finally, I would like to thank the publishing team for acting effectively as wingmen (and women) while I struggled to reach my target. (Any 'misses' are purely my responsibility.) Hilary Walford, Jonathan Falconer, Nick Reynolds, Helen Holness, Michael James, Ros Robertson and others at Sutton Publishing whose commitment, creativity, plus drop tanks full of patience, have been invaluable.

100th BG Memorial Air Museum, 385th BG Memorial Association, 390th BG Memorial Air Museum, Air Forces Escape and Evasion Society, Al Steiner, Al Tolar Jr, Alan DeHaven, Alan Hague, Alan McLachlan, Albert Demuyer, Amanda Giles, Amanda Hill, André Vandenameele, Andrew L. Ryan, Bert M. Carter, Bill Powell, Bill Varnedoe, Bob Collis,

Brian T. Jordan, Bruce Rampley, Buell S. Martin, Byron Schlag, Charles F. McCarty, Charles W. 'Chuck' Laney, Chas Reus, Chris Gotts, Christine Armes, Col Robert Steele USAF, Colin Lee, Cynrik De Decker, Cyril Rushworth, Dale Larrabee, Dan Engle, David Boddington, David S. Monroe, David Wade, Don Olds, Dr Harry Stein, Dr Julian Metcalfe, Dr Louise Metcalfe, E. Scott Mackey, E. Wickwar, Earl Pate Jr, East Anglian Aviation Research Group, East Anglian Aviation Society, Ed Beaty, Eighth Air Force Historical Society, Eric King, Ernest H. Barber, Ernest Osborne, Finn Buch, Fiona Carville, *Flypast* magazine, Francis R. Fuller, Frank McCawley, Frank Sherman, Frans L. Ammerlaan, Gary G. Gowans, Geoffrey D. Ward, George A. Silva, George Stebbings, Georgia Brown, Gerald Grove, Gerhard Bracke, Gordon McLachlan, Grace Small, Graham Herbertson, H.D. Cherrington, Hank North, Herman Engel, Herman G. Fieber, Horst A. Munter, Horst Weihrauch, Hugh McGill, Ian C. Mactaggart, Ian Hawkins, Irene Cook, Ivo M. de Jong, J.R. Spark DFM, Jack Blackham, Jack Steffen, Jacque Partridge, Jan B. Loftis, Jesse R. Brown, John C. Bitzer, John Deacon, John Derneden, John Giles, John Symonds, Ken Ellis, Kenneth L. Zeiger, Kenneth McLachlan, Lam v het Hof, Larry Grauerholz, Lee Hauenstein, Leon Harvey, Lewis A. Smith, Loren E. Jackson, Louis L. Meyer, Lucia Hutchcroft, Lucie Lepoivre, Lucien Dumont, Mark Brotherton, Martin W. Bowman, Mary Gillstrom, Mary Massari and family, Matt Sanders, Maurice Arnold, Mervyn Wilson, Michael P. Faley, Michel Doutreleau, Mick Liston, Mike Bailey, Mike Cracknell, Mike Harris, Mike Jones, Monique Hupin, Mrs Charles Guyler, Mrs Grace Dean Wood, Mrs M. Chuter, 2nd AD Memorial Collection, Mrs Mary Bowden, Newman Sanders, Nigel Beckett, Norfolk and Suffolk Aviation Museum, Norm Burmaster, Norman Leeks, Pamela Lawler, Pat Everson, Pat Ramm, Paul Collins, Paul J. Harper, Percy Chambers, Pete Snowling, Peter G. Stanley, Peter Roberts, R.W. Joyce, R. Whipps, Rachel Banham, Ralph Franklin, Ray Zorn, Rex Poulton, Robert Davies, Robert DeGrez, Robert W. Wilson, Robin Harrison, Roger A. Freeman, Roger L. Leister, Roy R. Forbes-Morgan, Russell Pointer, S.E. Harvey, Sharon McKnight, Simon Dunham, Steve Adams, Steve Peters, Steve Snelling, Steven Gleed, Stuart Wright, Sue Mayhew, T.M. Moore, Technical Sgt Mona Ferrell USAF, Tim Thayer, Tom Boyd, Tom Brittan, Tom Perry, Tom Sutcliffe, Tony Moore, Tony North, Verner Small, William A. Nicholls.

CHAPTER ONE

Haybag Annie

Unusual among creators of wartime nose-art was Anne Haywood, a young lady whose efforts adorned many B-17s flown by the 385th Bombardment Group (BG) from Great Ashfield in Suffolk.

The daughter of a farmer, Harold Douglas Haywood, Anne was the third child from his second marriage. Having lost his first wife to cancer, Harold married Anna Mitterer, an attractive, intelligent young woman from Velden in Austria, and some of young Anne's formative years were spent being educated in Austria, where her artistic leanings were soon apparent. As the European political situation deteriorated during the 1930s, Anne returned to England. These were also difficult days for the Haywood family. From a position of prosperity created by her grandfather, a Yorkshire industrialist, they fell on straitened times, with the true extent of their impoverishment emerging only after the death of Anne's father following a riding accident in March 1939. They were obliged to sell up, Anne being particularly upset by the sale of their horses, including her favourite hunter, Cubitt Boy. From a sizeable home at Coddenham, the family now occupied a small cottage at Wetherden, near Great Ashfield. These circumstances and the outbreak of war also forced Anne to relinquish plans for furthering her artistic education in Paris and she, like many women, now worked supporting the war effort. By 1942–3, Anne's mount was far from equestrian as she knuckled down driving trucks for J.H. Laing & Son. This company was busily engaged in a massive programme of airfield construction as Allied air power expanded to encompass the burgeoning US Eighth Army Air Force. One site chosen for development was a First World War airstrip between Elmswell and Great Ashfield. In June 1943 this became USAAF Station 155 and Anne's life would soon return from the artisan to the artistic and become inextricably linked with the airfield's new occupants, Van's Valiants, so named after the 385th BG's first Commanding Officer, Col Elliott Van Devanter.

American airbases required ancillary services. Anne sought work with the British Red Cross, but it sniffily declined her application on the basis that her mother was Austrian and therefore 'undesirable'. However, the American Red Cross had a more enlightened attitude and Anne's skills soon expanded from Aero Club duties at Great Ashfield to offering her artistic talents to an appreciative American audience of young airmen eager to enliven their

Anne Haywood was much in demand for decorating the popular A-2 flying jacket and is seen working on an example for a crew member on a B-17 named Remember Us. The 385th had two aircraft so named; one is recorded as transferred to the 94th BG and the other was lost in combat. (*Fiona Carville*)

drab surroundings. That summer, Anne found herself less involved in serving coffee and much in demand elsewhere. Provided with her own jeep and two service policemen, she was soon painting aircraft nose-arts, murals in buildings and the leather A-2 jackets worn with such bravado by the young Americans. As CO, Col Van Devanter officially endorsed Anne's activities and requested of the appropriate British authorities that she be allowed to stay because her efforts were such a boost to 385th morale – the men adopted and adored their

Anne was attracted to the handsome southerner, 1/Lt John D. 'Jack' Schley Jr, but fate cruelly intervened. Did Anne's emotion overrule any premonition? Decades later, a clairvoyant claimed contact with the pilot's still-troubled spirit. (*Fiona Carville*)

'Annie'. As an attractive young woman on a largely masculine airbase, Anne received much attention and, one day, was approached by the chaplain pleading with her to show some restraint. Not in any immoral context, simply that the kind-hearted Annie kept teasingly accepting offers of marriage and some of her fans immediately raced to get clearance from the chaplain! Unknown to her potential young suitors was a troubling psychic ability on Annie's part to sense those crews she knew would be lost. Only one airman seems to have crept beneath Anne's guard, a tall, debonair B-17 pilot named John Schley. Annie must have suppressed her anxieties whenever his B-17, Sly Fox, was airborne. On 16 September 1943, Schley was allocated a B-17 named Mary Ellen II when the 385th flew its nineteenth mission, the longest to date, attacking an airfield near Cognac in France. Returning in darkness, the Fortress formations faced a familiar foe, the British weather. Tired crews, low on fuel, confronted dense clouds with patchy rain reducing visibility to only 500 yards at lower altitudes. As they funnelled into a region of closely packed airfields, the order of landing became confused when lost aircrews sought sanctuary on the first available aerodrome.

Bombers from other groups were attempting to land at Great Ashfield, including some from the 95th BG who mistakenly thought they were over their own base at Horham, some 10 miles east. One of these was commanded by 2/Lt Louis S. Reno, who had seen an airfield's outer circle of lights and was in the traffic pattern following a left-handed circuit. Assuming

he was over Horham, Reno received orders from his Group Commander to peel off and, with lights full on, had just fired a recognition flare. He was also trying to contact base on the command radio while his co-pilot, 2/Lt Robert N. Moon, had control. Suddenly, from out of the murk, came another B-17, almost head on and at the same altitude. Moon instinctively hauled back on his control yoke and Reno slammed his own wheel to port. From sighting to impact took only two seconds. The other B-17, seemingly flying a right-hand circuit, also broke into a sharp, left, climbing turn. John Schley almost made it but, flashing overhead, his port wing clipped the tail position on Reno's aircraft, striking the rear guns. With the combined impact speed of over 200mph, the steel barrels cut like a knife through the lighter aluminium of Schley's port wing tip. The wing had thirty-seven ribs, with numbers 27 to 37 comprising almost half of the aileron and the wing tip. Shorn of this section and some 7 feet of under-wing skin, Mary Ellen II suffered irretrievable damage. Continuing to climb for a few seconds, Schley and his co-pilot, 2/Lt John B. Baum, fought hard to recover. Without an effective port aileron, the B-17 rolled over to the left and, from 1,500 feet, plunged into a turnip field near Rickinghall, Suffolk. Reno's B-17 lost a portion of its tail but its crew maintained control and, seeing flames glowing on the darkened landscape, tried unsuccessfully to alert Horham. Hoping the other aircraft's crew had been able to jump, Reno settled safely at an RAF station some 20 minutes later despite the failure of one engine.

Mary Ellen II had exploded on impact. There were no survivors from her ten-man crew. Whether Annie had any premonition about John Schley is not known, but, although friendly and fond of many, she never again allowed any deep entanglement with the boys whose bombers she painted. It is also strange to record that a paranormal continuation of this story occurred nearly fifty years later. I gave a brief account of the tragedy in my book *Final Flights*, first published in 1989, and was surprised to be contacted by Samantha Alexander, daughter of the renowned clairvoyant Simon Alexander. Following alleged ghostly goings-on in the Petwood Hotel at Woodhall Spa, Lincolnshire, Simon had been asked to investigate. It seems that sounds of boisterous RAF parties were echoing down the years from the hotel's wartime service as an officers' mess for the famous RAF 617 Dambusters Squadron. There were, apparently, even sightings of their leader, Guy Gibson. However, Simon made no contact with Gibson but somehow picked up the troubled spirit of an American airman named Schlow, but, with a strong Southern drawl, the name was unclear. The American was unhappy about being blamed and said it was not his fault. He mentioned 'Mary Ellen' and said 'All the Johns are here' and named crew members White and Ginger. A check of the crew list confirmed that four of the crew were named John; White was the ball turret gunner and 'Ginger' undoubtedly meant Clyde G. Gingerich, the tail gunner. All this could have been taken from *Final Flights*, but, as I had not mentioned Schley's hometown of Savannah, Georgia, I could not counter the 'Southern drawl'. It was fifteen years later that I learned of Annie's powers and her relationship with Schley, but it was then too late to obtain details — unless another connection can be established!

Like other groups, a roll-call of the B-17s from Great Ashfield invokes many names and, while there were other artists, a selection of Annie's nose-art encapsulates further dramatic

Immodesty was fortunately not an issue for Anne. Bare-backed and bare-bottomed, Dragon Lady sits astride her spine-backed beast.

wartime incidents. These stories reflect the heroism of young airmen whose brash behaviour and saucy artwork chosen to adorn their B-17s often belied many inner terrors. This chapter selects a few of Annie's bombers and her final piece of 385th artwork, completed in 1998 for the Channel 4 television programme *Time Team*.

Another example of her artwork on a 551st B-17F, 42-30836, ended up under water in heroic circumstances. Fortunately, immodesty was not an issue for the young Suffolk lass; and 'Dragon Lady', her rendition of a popular cartoon character in the Steve Canyon strip, was resplendent with a naked lady astride the fearsome creature. Dragon Lady valiantly challenged the foe on numerous occasions until slain by flak on 13 February 1944, when being flown by Lt Ed Herron and crew. That day, the Group attacked Noball 59, a V-weapon site near the coast of France, ostensibly a 'milk run' but, running in to target, the B-17 was bracketed by flak and severely damaged. Ed later recalled, 'As the Fort was approaching the

Fortresses majestic. Dragon Lady – nearest camera – and her sisters en route to a target. (*USAAF Official*)

target, bursts of flak were reported hitting the underside of the ship, and, as I turned to see the formation of the Group, and how badly they were being hit, firecrackers broke loose in the cockpit. My co-pilot, 1/Lt Walter Camp, was hit in the back of the neck and wounded severely. The instrument panel was a mass of shattered glass and small flak hit me in the hands. The No. 4 engine was evidently hit with the same barrage, for it suddenly sputtered and cut out. I feathered it and continued on over the target on three engines.' As well as both pilots, several of her crew were wounded, the radio telephone (r/t) system was destroyed and Ed's transmissions to check on his crew went worryingly unanswered from those in the rear of the aircraft. Now unconscious, Walter Camp was eased from his seat by the engineer, Staff Sgt Robert V. Savage, while Ed struggled to maintain formation. After administering a morphine shot and making his wounded comrade as comfortable as possible on the catwalk leading to the radio room, Savage slipped into the co-pilot's seat to help Ed hold the bomber level. Several control cables had been shot away and both men fought to keep Dragon Lady airborne. Homeward bound, their problems increased when the No. 1 engine, after leaking a long trail of gasoline, suddenly caught fire and also had to be feathered. Unable to hold

formation, they fell back as they crossed the enemy coast. Ed ordered the radio operator, Staff Sgt John C. Cortez, to transmit Mayday signals; these took on a new desperation when the No. 3 engine ran out of control and, despite Ed's swift reaction in hitting the button, it refused to feather. Dragon Lady skewed dangerously with the tremendous drag from now useless propeller blades spinning on the engine shaft. This snapped within minutes, leaving only one good engine. Putting this on to emergency-rich gas, Herron trimmed the B-17 for slowest descent and sent word aft for the crew to take ditching stations. The navigator, Lt Stanley V. Stodola, tried to get a bearing, but flak had destroyed his compass and wounded both him and the bombardier, Lt William C. 'Kelly' Mellillo. Courageously, Cortez continued transmitting as the Fortress slid towards the waves – he realized they would die in the icy sea unless help arrived soon. His signals might enable a better fix to be taken on their position by receiving stations in England.

Other crewmen, with only fear for company and unable to help, felt like so much dead weight and knew that impact with the sea would not be a gentle affair. Sitting with his back to the bulkhead, Kelly braced himself as Dragon Lady suddenly lost power and plummeted the last 20 feet. The 'whole damn aircraft' seemed to come apart as it slammed into the icy water. Alone in the cockpit, Ed Herron was held by his harness, which, having just saved him, now threatened his survival as he fought to snap the quick release before hauling himself out of the cockpit side window and struggling through swirling seas to the wing. This offered only a brief respite, because the Fortress was rapidly nosing under. Heaving himself onto the port wing, he balanced, staring around a bleak horizon in utter isolation – there was no sign of his crew or a dinghy. Then a raft sprang from its upper-fuselage stowage, but, enmeshed in shroud lines, it failed to deploy. Grasping his escape knife, Ed cut it free, allowing it to inflate automatically. As he clambered in, he was relieved to see several other survivors had surfaced, including the wounded, who had been assisted from the sinking Fortress by waist gunners Sgt Francis K. Temple and Staff Sgt Leonard W. Wasilewski. Both Camp, the co-pilot, and tail gunner, Sgt Juan E. Almanza, also suffering from a shrapnel-slashed forehead, had uninflated Mae Wests and were struggling to stay afloat. Using both hands Ed supported them, then lashed them to the raft, before he pulled them on board. Paddling to the radio-room exit, he found more survivors and helped them escape from the swiftly sinking bomber. Tethering Stodola to the raft, he then assisted Kelly Mellillo to the relative safety of the inflatable. Dragon Lady was going down nose first and the tail section swung high over the raft before sliding down towards it, the stabilizer threatening to take them under. Floundering in the water, Bob Savage saw what was happening and it took all his strength to push the raft away before he was hit by the stabilizer and dragged under. Shocked and powerless, the others stared at the vortex of escaping air and debris where Bob Savage had been moments earlier. Then he bobbed to the surface, spluttering and gasping for air. His shoulder had been injured but Ed jumped from the raft and grabbed him before he drifted too far. Despite his own injured hands and the freezing cold, Ed had managed to rescue six of his crew. Clambering back into the dinghy, he bailed out as much water as he could and made fast the equipment it carried before helping on board those he had lashed to the side. There were now seven in one dinghy; the

second life raft never appeared and three crew members – the courageous Cortez, with ball-turret gunner Staff Sgt A.E. Seagrove and waist gunner Staff Sgt L.W. Wasilewski – had gone down with Dragon Lady. Those uninjured continued bailing out the water and tending to the wounded, while Ed opened some of their emergency rations and allocated a small amount of drinking water and food – no one knew how long they would have to survive. Their situation was precarious; it seemed as if they would spend the night in a bitterly cold wind and open seas, their chances of survival diminishing every minute. Several were wounded and all were convulsed with cold bordering on deadly hypothermia. Ed told them to take off their shoes because contact with each other's legs as they tried to move in the confined space was proving excruciatingly painful. He dressed the tail gunner's head wound and kept up an encouraging dialogue to support morale. Strapping the Verey pistol to his arm, he put the four flares they had into his pockets for easy reach if and when needed. Darkness was approaching and Ed began planning how they might best survive the night when the sound of aero-engines caught their attention. Moments later, a formation of Typhoons from 486 Squadron RNZAF raced overhead so low that they had to have seen the tiny yellow craft, and hope momentarily assuaged something of the cold. Confirmation of their being spotted came later when two air-sea rescue Spitfires flown by Flg Offs R. Kipping and A. Gooch of 277 Squadron appeared and were soon smoke-marking their position some 18 miles south-west of Dungeness. It was now a race to rescue them before they became hidden in darkness with little chance of survival.

As the survivors clutched at hope, the RAF raced against the gathering darkness and 277 Squadron continued its efforts when Walrus X9563, flown by Flg Off J. Barber with WO Wally Butler and Sgt John Humphreys, was launched from Shoreham. Unfortunately, the stalwart old biplane damaged a float when it touched down, possibly on wreckage from Dragon Lady, and was later towed back to Dover with poor Humphreys poised on one wing to balance the aircraft and prevent it sinking. For the hapless Americans, time passed with no sign of a surface vessel. Then, with daylight and confidence fast fading, High Speed Launch 2547 from Dover hove into view. Despite their cold and exhaustion, the rejuvenated men from Dragon Lady yelled and waved excitedly at the oncoming craft. Ed allowed his jubilant crew to fire their flares but the launch had already seen them and was rapidly creaming through the seas to close with some very relieved young fliers. Throttling back, the vessel edged the last few feet; then her experienced crew adroitly took the survivors on board before, bows lifting under power, she surged off towards Dover. Ed Herron was awarded the DSC for his courage but, tragically, he was killed during the disastrous mission of 6 October 1944, when no fewer than eleven 385th B-17s were lost on the Group's worst mission of the war.

Lt Charles Guyler and his crew had flown Dragon Lady on numerous occasions, so they continued the cartoon theme when requesting Annie to adorn their next B-17 with a caricature of Powerful Katrinka. This was no curvaceous lovely but was familiar to many Americans from childhood as the robust Scandinavian housemaid featured in the 'Toonerville Trolley' cartoon strip. Protective of her young charges in the series, she was frequently called upon to perform feats of great strength, and the Guyler crew felt this was very appropriate for their Flying Fortress. Annie soon had a trestle alongside the recently assigned B-17G, and

42-31928 underwent the anthropomorphosis into Powerful Katrinka. She served the Group well during the winter of 1943–4, and it was not air combat that destroyed their plucky servant but an action unique in Eighth Air Force history.

Annie soon had a trestle alongside the aircraft. A popular cartoon character, Powerful Katrinka, was no curvaceous lovely. (*Fiona Carville*)

While airmen slept, or tried to, other essential activities continued unabated. The resourcefulness of skilled ground crews became legendary, with personnel working long hours to maximize operational efficiency. Low-level maintenance was carried out in the open, often in appalling weather, but some work required hangar facilities and, on 23 May 1944, Powerful Katrinka was in Great Ashfield's Hangar One on the southern side of the airfield undergoing battle-damage repairs. That day the 385th had launched twenty aircraft to support attacks on marshalling yards in Chaumont as part of the build-up to D-Day. Intense pressure prevailed to repair damaged aircraft in blackout conditions because Luftwaffe activities had recently increased, most notably on 22 April 1944, as described in my *Night of the Intruders*. During any nocturnal activity on the base, external lights were kept to a minimum and doused during an air-raid alert. Blackout conditions were intended to prevent seepage of light from buildings acting as a beacon to prowling Luftwaffe intruders. The 385th were preparing themselves for a maximum effort against Berlin and mission planning and briefing activities were already under way.

Outside, the Suffolk countryside was sheathed in darkness while cottage windows rattled gently to the nocturne of aero-engines high above. RAF Bomber Command was continuing its own unceasing challenge to the enemy with over 1,000 sorties flown. In retaliation, the Luftwaffe's efforts were comparatively puny, owing in part to Hitler's having previously proscribed intruder operations over the UK. However, this policy had recently been relaxed and Me 410s of KG51 were again abroad seeking to catch the unwary. On 22 May 1944 they had destroyed Lancaster NN695 of 619 Squadron at 0255 hr over East Wretham, Norfolk, with the loss of six crew. Attacks also occurred that night over Bedfordshire and bombs were dropped on the RAF airfield at Bourn, Cambridgeshire.

On 23 May KG51 was up to further mischief. It may have been only a momentary lapse in discipline or inadequate blackout precautions, but, allegedly, an open hangar door sent light shafting a beam across the concrete apron approaching Hangar One, thus inviting some unwelcome attention. At 0327 hr, an alert German aircrew seized the moment. Having passed

One bomb fell through the roof of Hangar One to explode on the unfortunate Powerful Katrinka. Cladding blown from the wall provided convenient access for firemen.

over Great Ashfield, their Messerschmitt wheeled sharply and powered back towards the airfield. Encountering no anti-aircraft fire, the intruder released seven 50kg bombs that straddled the airbase. Most exploded harmlessly but one fell cleanly through the roof of Hangar One, exploding on the unfortunate Powerful Katrinka. The blast tore sheets of corrugated iron cladding from the hangar side and lifted both sets of doors from their runners to collapse on the concrete aprons outside each end of the hangar. Fortunately, no one was killed but, within moments, flames engulfed the hapless Katrinka and threatened another B-17 just ahead.

Hearing the explosions, Staff Sgt Lawrence M. Hill, the Base Fire Station Chief, raced from his quarters to find the entire airfield illuminated by flames from the stricken building – a certain marker for further attack. Hollering at the fire crew to get dressed, Hill and his men hurtled to the scene without waiting for orders. Reaching Hangar One, the firemen faced a scene of devastation. Apart from the giant doors lying flat on the concrete, numerous sheets of corrugated cladding had been blasted from the hangar's side and bomb craters pockmarked the airfield. Powerful Katrinka, being vigorously consumed by fire fed on fuel and oxygen, was reacting very angrily to her fate as fusillades of .5 calibre rounds spat viciously from the conflagration.

Disregarding the danger, Hill ordered a line laid from his truck to the side of the hangar. Supported by his team, Sgts Don Warren and Charles L. McCarthy, with technicians Stanley

J. Lisek and Ernest A. Herndon Jr, Hill realized the torn-out cladding created easy, if risky, access, and they stepped in through the large opening blasted in the hangar side. Rapidly assessing the situation, they calculated that, if they moved fast and accurately directed their hoses, one of the two aircraft inside could be saved. Time was critical; its stabilizers were already alight. Fires also threatened a large Cletrac, just beginning to burn, and ranks of crated and uncrated Cyclone engines lining one side of the hangar. Struggling to play out their hoses, they were interrupted by an officer from Flying Control who ran up with orders from Col Van Devanter to evacuate the building. Having judged the situation, Hill was convinced they could save the second B-17 and much of the valuable equipment. Tasking Warren with persuading their superiors, Hill planned their most effective approach. He was pleased when Warren returned with the order rescinded and permission to use their initiative. All unauthorized personnel were ordered to move clear. Concluding his strategy, Hill ordered one crash truck to the hangar's rear with instructions to lay two foam lines. He sent another crew to the front telling them to set two long foam lines that required equipment providing additional pressure. Luckily, his department had already demonstrated its inventiveness in the design of a new pump, but this was as yet unproven. They had recognized a weakness in the American apparatus available, and their indigenous design cleverly combined American and British couplings, cut and welded to increase both range and pressure – this would be its first use in anger. Confident in US ingenuity, Hill called for more power. Using the fire truck at the front of the hangar with an arterial feed of foam lines branching into two capillary hoses, he gauged he could effectively strike the seat of the fire in the aircraft wing tanks. Supporting this, he had a pump feeding water along a single line drawn through a hole in the hangar wall to douse the empennage of the threatened B-17. He also positioned another trailer pump close to the rear of the hangar and two additional hoses pressure-foamed Powerful Katrinka. Skilfully using their resources and ignoring the danger, Hill and his men prevented further destruction and had the fire under control before additional support arrived.

Next morning, Powerful Katrinka was no more. Her charred and smouldering ashes littered the hangar floor, but it could have been much worse. As Dom Jordan of the 548th Squadron noted in his diary,

May 23rd 1944. I finally got my second mission in today. We bombed the railroad yards in Chaumont, France using #1000 G. P. The mission was a milk run. The real excitement was provided when a lone Jerry dropped a string of bombs parallel to the briefing area. We had just finished briefing and were in our locker room changing when we heard this ever-increasing crescendo or shriek of falling bombs. It was my first and only experience of being on the receiving end. When the shriek ended and the explosions started we were too stunned to do anything for a few seconds. Evidently the Jerry was after the personnel. He must have known our briefing time. He made a hit on the hangar with two B-17s and all the time I was running from the scene I could hear ammunition going off. He had a beautiful aiming point because the hangar was all lit up – the doors could not be closed for some reason. This was so ironic because we made sure all curtains were drawn in the

barracks. We had heard a plane buzzing around previously but thought it was one of ours. He made just one pass but it was enough. Later, one of the Brass made the remark that the bomber had been very unlucky because, although he wiped out a hangar and two ships [*sic*], just a few more yards he would have wiped out most of the base flying personnel.

Another recollection of this incident comes from the private diary of the late Master Sgt Winston Churchill Chadwick, an electronics specialist.

We, of the ground crew, figured we were in no danger from enemy action even though the British renegade, Lord Haw Haw, did say in one of his broadcasts from Germany, 'Don't worry, Great Ashfield. We'll get to you.' And they did. It was a night when there was to be a mission the next day, with take-off about 4.30 in the morning. It was Gemel's turn to work on the planes that night. I was in the sack. There was the familiar air-raid siren and then, over the PA system, came, 'Condition Red! Condition Red!' This woke me up. There was the sound of bombs exploding, followed by the sound of .5 calibre shells going off, in a popcorn popping rhythm, not in bursts as from a machine gun. Next over the speakers came, 'All unauthorized personnel stay away from Hangar One! All unauthorized personnel stay away from Hangar One!' Well, if all that noise was coming from Hangar One, you can bet we would stay away. We were already about a mile from the hangar. Come daylight, we learned what happened. As I say, a mission was scheduled with take-off about 4.30 am. The gunners had been briefed and they had gone to the planes with their guns and gear. The crew chiefs and their assistants were preflighting the engines. The rest of the flying crew were being briefed. *They* were briefed separately so they could be told where they were going. The gunners had not been told for fear some might 'go over the hill'. The briefing room was in a building right beside Hangar One. At that time, we still did not have any pathfinder planes, planes that could 'see' the target regardless of cloud cover and signal the following planes so they too would drop their bombs on the target. We were borrowing two pathfinders from another base. It was nearly time for those two planes to arrive and a plane was heard by the men in the control tower. Thinking it was the first of the pathfinders, the tower obligingly turned on the runway lights, faint rings of light outlining the runway to be used. The plane passed over once, circled and lined up for the proper runway, just as it *should* do before landing. But instead of landing, it swung over to the right, attempting to line up with planes dispersed there, and started dropping eight 250lb [*sic*] bombs. The first five, although landing close to planes, made no direct hit. On the last part of his bomb run, the German flew over Hangar One. In that hangar were two B-17s face to face, or perhaps I should say, nose to nose. We all had to take our turn at guard duty. There was a guard inside the hangar. He thought he just *had* to have a cigarette, and he had to go outside the hangar for that. Just as he took hold of the knob on the small door let into the large hangar door, bomb number six landed just outside that door.

The next instant bomb number seven came through the roof and landed squarely in the plane at the far side of the hangar. The guard was knocked flat, but was not injured. If he

A crater left by a 50kg bomb has strangely left the tent and nearby equipment unscathed. The B-17 in the background, 42-31864 Remember Us, was lost on 15 August 1944.

had had this urge for a smoke a moment sooner, the story would have been quite different. A little beyond the far side of the hangar, a crew chief and his assistant finished preflighting a B-17 and had just shut off the engines, when the eighth and last bomb landed 50 feet beyond the nose of the plane, in an unpaved area. Up until that time, when a plane went into the hangar for major repair, the ammunition was not removed from the plane. These .5 calibre shells were going off in a popcorn popping rhythm, making a sieve of the hangar walls and the remaining part of the roof. Surprisingly, no one was injured. About a third of the group's planes were damaged, most of them by air blast and flying pieces of bomb. All the planes that were intended for the mission were loaded with twelve 500lb bombs and the fuel tanks were topped off. If the German had made a direct hit on one of those planes, it would have made quite a mess. Gemel told me that everybody in the area where he was dived for the ditches, expecting the German pilot to do some strafing after he dropped the bombs. He didn't. After the end of his bomb run, he passed right over a gun emplacement. There were no anti-aircraft guns on our base, but we did have these two positions where there were what we called 'pea-shooters', .5 calibre guns. Either the two guys, who were supposed to be manning the guns the German flew over, were asleep (though I don't see how they could have been), or they were afraid of drawing his attention, for they did not even attempt to bring him down. We learned later, however, that the German did not make it back home. The word was, 'We got him, Great Ashfield.' The incident let us know that the Germans had some very accurate information about our base – the time of take-off, the fact that two planes would come from another field and also the exact time of their arrival.

On a lighter note, a healthy trade was soon under way in bartering bomb fragments as airmen filled in the craters. Technicians assessed damage to other aircraft as minimal and Gen Le May called personally to see if the 385th could mount the day's mission. Undaunted, they still mustered twenty-three aircraft for the assault on Berlin.

While one of Annie's creations lay consumed by flames, others still carried her own form of defiance to the enemy. 'Mr Lucky' had long adorned a multi-missioned B-17G, serial 42-38035, of the 550th Bomb Squadron. The name proved apt on 1 March 1945 for 19-year-old Sgt Joe Jones, tail gunner on 1/Lt Charles J. Armbruster's crew. Now, nearing the end of the war, this was group mission 260 to marshalling yards in Ulm. For Joe, it was his twenty-second sortie and looked set to be a milk run as thirty-eight 385th B-17s climbed steadily away from England then over Belgium, hidden by ten-tenths cloud. Joe was happier riding in the tail and had won the slot that morning when a good-natured dispute between him and another gunner, Sgt Arthur W. Harold, was settled when Chuck Armbruster told them to flip a coin. As it spun, Joe called 'heads' and won – Wendy Harold now squeezed himself into the cramped confines of the ball turret. At 13,500ft they were scudding amid cloud columns and, as the bombers made a shallow right turn, Joe was fascinated by the brilliance of alternating sunlight and shadows as their silhouettes danced across the cloudscape below. Nothing about the sparkling iridescence seemed malevolent but the turmoil of air contorting within seemingly innocent clouds foreshadowed a disaster.

Mr Lucky was flying number three position in the lead squadron, and opposite him was 1/Lt Louis Winter, who later recalled,

> I was flying the right wing of the lead ship opposite Armbruster that day. We were in an SOP [Standard Operational Procedure] climb at about 14,000 feet. The leader made a shallow turn to the right then levelled his wings. A matter of seconds later Armbruster's ship pulled up abruptly and collided with Rusecky, who was flying above and close in trail. The following is my diagnosis of the accident: Armbruster's ship did not correct soon enough when the leader levelled his turn to the right. He kept closing on the leader, then when he was about to hit the leader, recognized his mistake and instead of correcting to the left, he hauled back on the stick . . .

Others in the formation that day felt that, as Armbruster's B-17 clipped through the peak of another cloud, it possibly hit a shaft of turbulence, causing it to surge upwards. Armbruster had over 700 hours of piloting experience, but the air can be a treacherous, unforgiving environment, and a moment's lapse in concentration could prove fatal. During basic training in October 1942, he had been partly responsible for a mishap when his BT-15 collided with another student's aircraft as they were landing. Fortunately, both pilots escaped uninjured, although Armbruster's ship suffered damage to its landing gear and flaps. The incident in 1945 would prove much worse. When the B-17s emerged from the cloud-cap, aghast eyewitnesses were powerless to prevent what happened. Mr Lucky, perhaps bouncing on a column of turbulence, surged abruptly upwards into the path of the number four, high-

Annie at work on a chill winter's day creating the nose-art for 42-38035 Mr Lucky. Note the absence of mission symbols.

Twenty-one mission symbols later, the veteran Mr Lucky. The swastika beneath the first bomb denotes an enemy fighter claimed by her gunners.

element lead ship (43-38273) piloted by 1/Lt Alexander Rusecky, also of the 550th. Rusecky had no time for avoiding action and Armbruster, with co-pilot, 2/Lt Robert W. Davis, had lost control of Mr Lucky. Chewing into Mr Lucky, the propellers on Rusecky's port side cut the B-17 in half at the radio room while numbers three and four propellers on Mr Lucky slashed through the nose and cockpit of Rusecky's aircraft. Technical Sgt Neill G. Duell was manning the top turret of Lt Eugene Vaadi's Fortress and later recalled,

We were just behind . . . when they collided. We sustained considerable damage flying through parts of the exploded planes. Due to the alertness of our two pilots who peeled us off straight down in a dive and then pulled us out . . . we survived this one. We had lost a lot of skin from the radio room back and oxygen lines ruptured. We got the leaks stopped and had the tail gunner and ball gunner's positions both out, both gunners having to go on walk around bottles but Vaadi said the ship still flew OK so we elected to climb back up and join the tail end of the bomber stream and finish the mission . . . We knew both crews from the ships that went down . . . A good friend of mine named Clabaugh was flying togglier, having been a sole survivor of another crew and had been through so many close ones they were going to finish his tour a mission or two early. I was surprised to hear his name called that morning.

Pilot 1/Lt Joy H. Dunlap stated,

At about 14,000 feet we encountered a layer of middle clouds. I was flying in the lead squadron, low section number six. As we climbed I was in and out of the peaks of the clouds so pulled off to the left of the formation and climbed individually until breaking out. I picked up the formation to my right and a few seconds later saw the two ships collide. Number three plane of the lead pulled up sharply in front of number four high element lead. The left engines of number four cut into the fuselage of number three at about the radio room. Number four tried to pull up but number three fell off to the left hitting the number four plane on the left wing. Number four's left wing broke off just outside No. 1 engine and number four started to spin to the left and dropped into the overcast. Number three plane broke up and dropped into the overcast. Lt Davis who was flying as co-pilot in number three plane had flown with me the previous day. His formation was well forward but very unsteady in lateral position. He had a tendency to over-correct and sometimes to pull up abruptly. It is my opinion that being bothered by the overcast he might have pulled up to get out of the clouds. I seemed to observe one parachute open just after the two ships collided and then catch on some wreckage and collapse.

Watching from his navigator's position on another B-17, 1/Lt William Varnedoe was stunned.

I thought I saw the radio man blown out into space without a chute and then I saw the front end of Mr Lucky slowly tilt to the left, and I could distinctly see Chuck Armbruster

Left to right: Chuck Armbruster with his regular co-pilot Howard A. Muchow and navigator Howard M. Tripp. Tripp was renowned for liberal use of his .45 automatic seen in its shoulder holster and frequently put holes in the barrack ceiling. He drank quite a bit. 'On several occasions, when he overly imbibed, he had difficulty finding the latrine – mistaking dresser drawers and adjoining occupied beds! In the middle of the night, when we would be awakened by a tremendous outburst of profanity, we knew he had baptised a bunk mate again.' (*Lewis A. Smith*)

looking over his left shoulder, trying to see what had happened. The airplane then went into a sudden spin and disappeared into the clouds. The crash, the flying debris and metal flying back into the slipstream – it was one of the most eerie moments of my life. Two of our aircraft shattering each other, metal tearing itself to pieces and here, in the nose section of our B-17, it seemed to be in total silence. The drone of our own engines suppressed all outside noise.

Concentrating on the front of Mr Lucky, Bill Varnedoe had not seen Rusecky's disintegrating aircraft vanish into cloud rapidly followed by the torn-off tail section from Mr Lucky tumbling earthwards.

Inside that severed tail, Joe had no idea that the entire front of his aircraft had vanished but guessed something catastrophic had befallen them. Their regular co-pilot, 1/Lt Howard A. Muchow, had been ill and had been replaced by 2/Lt Robert W. Davis. He heard Chuck yell sharply at the substitute to 'PULL OVER – we don't want that guy's wing in our lap'. To Joe it suddenly 'felt like being hit with a sledge hammer' and he was thrown violently around his cramped compartment. Looking up through the perspex, he was aghast to see at very close

quarters the bomb-bay section of another B-17. The feeling in his ears told him he was falling but, oblivious of the true situation, he tried desperately to raise his pilot on the r/t. 'Tail to pilot, tail to pilot?' Nothing. Losing the courtesy of discipline, Joe finally hollered, 'Damn it Chuck, answer me!' Then he realized with absolute horror there was not even the sound of engines! Like a living nightmare, Joe felt himself falling, falling, falling – not straight down but feathering back and forth with increasing speed. Grabbing his chest-pack parachute, Joe made for his emergency exit. Pulling the release achieved nothing, so, grasping an overhead strut for balance and leverage, he kicked hard but the hatch stubbornly refused to open and a further kick only overbalanced him into a tangle of ammunition belts. Now really scared, Joe realized he was trapped. Sickening gyrations and the terrifying falling sensation told Joe, now in utter panic, that he had little time. Abandoning efforts to release the hatch, he struggled forward for the main entrance, only to find his path blocked by linked ammunition and other debris. His mind hit overdrive. Remembering recent experiments using parachutes to slow down an aircraft upon landing, Joe thought he could adapt the technique to slow his descent. Crawling aft to his seat, he released his parachute and tried stuffing folds through one of the shattered windows, but this clearly would not work – the parachute had no chance of deployment in time. Giving up, he resigned himself to die and braced himself against some armour-plating. Calmer now, he felt an overwhelming sadness for his mother, who would soon receive the dreaded telegram – she had wanted him to enlist in the Navy. There was nothing else he could do. Steadying himself within the now-spiralling tail section with the wind howling through the torn-off fuselage, he managed to light what he felt would be his last cigarette. Inhaling deeply, he quietly awaited the end and his own inclusion in the war's grim statistics.

Henri Ryjkeboer and his family tore at the wreckage to reach the airman trapped inside.

On the foggy Belgian landscape near the town of Slijpe, Gilbert Deschepper was cycling to work along a country lane when he heard the collision and the dreadful sound of an aircraft crashing nearby. Pedalling through the mist in the general direction, Gilbert came upon the torn-off tail unit surrounded by spectators afraid to go too close for fear it might explode or catch fire. Undeterred, Gilbert inspected the tattered remains; his inspection revealed a body, bent double and pinned inside. Feeling for signs of life, Gilbert was filled with hope. Miraculously, the young airman, bleeding badly, was still alive, and it seems as if the falling-leaf motion of the severed tail section had impacted at the lowest and slowest point in its trajectory. Urging others, including farmer Henri Ryjkeboer and his five daughters, to help, Gilbert tore at the wreckage – the airman inside was unconscious but seemed otherwise uninjured apart

from lacerations around his ear and a cut tongue. Unable to bring Joe round, his rescuers carried him to the nearby Ryjkeboer home, while Gilbert hurriedly cycled 6 miles to the home of a local doctor, a pro-German who needed some forceful persuasion to accompany Gilbert to the wreckage. Following preliminary treatment, Gilbert then confiscated the local bus and took Joe to a British field hospital in Ostend, where it was found the American was suffering from internal bleeding; had almost severed his own tongue and had a broken vertebra in his neck. Gilbert could do no more – it was now in the hands of the Lord.

Joe Jones could remember nothing between his last cigarette and waking up in hospital. Of all those on board, Joe was 'Mr Lucky'.

The Report of Aircraft Accident erroneously described Joe as having 'successfully used parachute but extent or nature of injuries is unknown'. Three days later, Joe regained consciousness – he could remember nothing between his last cigarette and waking up in hospital. His injuries were expertly treated apart from, as he discovered years later, hairline fractures to his teeth! Joe was soon introduced to Gilbert Deschepper whose daily visits began a lifelong friendship. He was the only survivor from Mr Lucky – the eight others all perished when the B-17 exploded on the Kamiel Glorie farm some 900m away from the tail section. Tragically, all but one of the Rusecky crew died and the survivor, Sgt Stanley J. Lejowski, was so emotionally distraught he was later invalided home. The care given to Joe ensured his recovery and he was back at Great Ashfield attending a Red Cross dance six weeks later. Joe's experience was published in the Ripley *Believe or Not* series and this 'Mr Lucky' dedicated his life to the service of his nation until he lost a long battle with cancer on 13 January 1994.

Anne's endeavours on behalf of the group earned her the distinction of having a B-17 named in her honour; but 'Haybag Annie' seemed a somewhat backhanded compliment, albeit accepted with Annie's innate good humour. When the natural-metal-finish B-17G, number 42-97280, first landed at Great Ashfield and taxied to hardstand 20 by the 550th Squadron's maintenance hut, someone had already adorned the starboard cheek with a crudely captioned 'Haybag'. To this, the mischievous ground crew under Master Sgt Ed Hallisay added the name 'Annie'. This was in affectionate recognition of Annie's regular travels taking hay to her two beloved horses, reminders of better, pre-war days when the family had had a string of mounts and she had indulged in amateur racing. Not so innocent of the double entendre, Anne was further persuaded to add a self-portrait, and the warplane soon sported a caricature complete with her characteristic lapcap – headgear that hailed from Lapland, offering fold-down flaps for ear protection in East Anglia's biting easterlies. In self-mimicry

Annie's endeavours earned her the distinction of having a B-17 named in her honour but 'Haybag Annie' seems a somewhat backhanded compliment. Annie's self-mimicry soon adorned the B-17.

Anne also added a paint pallet, paints, a mug of coffee and a word-balloon with 'Good Ole Gal', a common rustic expression of endearment. During the ensuing months of bitter combat, Haybag Annie led a charmed life, and mission upon mission mounted with no casualties and, to the credit of Ed Hallisay and his men, no aborts either during nearly 1,300 flying hours and 105 missions. The last five credits for Haybag Annie were spam cans alongside the bomb symbols to recognize the food missions flown to Holland. On 19 June 1945, operations orders were cut stating that 'The following aircraft and personnel assigned thereto will proceed via the best available air route to Bradley Field, Windsor Locks, Connecticut . . .'. The 385th was going home.

Assigned to Haybag Annie were pilot 2/Lt Robert G. Gunn and nineteen other personnel under projects denoted as 'Green' and 'White'. Essentially, the movement of over 2,000 White aircrew and aircraft would be accompanied by Green personnel, often those who had maintained the aircraft or excelled at scrounging places. Uncharacteristically, as Haybag Annie was being readied to leave for the last time, a problem arose with the hydraulics and a junior member of the ground crew was hastily dispatched to obtain some necessary parts, which were soon fitted. Take-off was not a problem and Haybag Annie settled into formation

for the short hop to RAF Valley in Wales, where tanks would be replenished for the next stage of their journey.

Arriving over the RAF's Welsh coastal airfield at 1715 hr, Gunn called the tower for landing permission and was instructed to orbit: the airfield was very busy. After circling for 15 minutes admiring views of the Holy Island and Caernarfon Bay, they were advised that landing was to be to the north on runway fourteen. This touchdown would complete the first leg of their journey home and the 6,000 feet of asphalt offered plenty of room. There was no indication from Haybag Annie that she would soon demand every inch and then some! Gunn gained clearance and entered the traffic pattern to the east, edging Annie lower as he followed other aircraft in to land. The undercarriage descended with reassuring rhythm and thunked into place. Peering left he reported aloud 'Down left' and co-pilot, 2/Lt Richard D. Ettling, confirmed 'Down right'. The tract of water shimmering cheerfully below seemed to shine of peacetime – follow it west far enough and, discounting Ireland, you were home – exactly their intentions. Ettling continued through the familiar checklist including the hydraulic pressure gauges – the fluid was level and pressure registered a satisfactory p.s.i. Haybag Annie was burdened not by bombs but by airmen and many accoutrements acquired during their stay at Great Ashfield. All told, the Fortress weighed some 52,800lb, steadily descending at 130mph. Conscious of passenger comfort, Gunn had no weather worries, a gentle 5mph wind posed no discomfort as he eased gently over the threshold and touched down delicately some 100 yards further on. Letting the B-17 settle, he dabbed the brakes, felt the bomber's speed decrease, then released them to let her roll. No hurry – nothing untoward – plenty of runway left. Ettling initiated the post-landing checks. Opening cowl flaps, neither pilot noticed that only those on the port side were actuated, an indication of hydraulic pressure problems. They were about to become alarmingly aware of this issue. About 2,000 feet had elapsed since touchdown and Gunn judged the need for further braking because Annie was veering to starboard and required adjustment. He applied the brakes again. Nothing! No diminution of speed and the aircraft continued swinging to the right, off the runway. Pressing hard, he yelled to Ettling, 'We have no brakes!'. The hydraulic pressure gauge now read zero! Hoping for a miracle, Gunn continued pushing hard on the left brake and opening throttle on the starboard engines to correct the drift. Energized by the urgency in his pilot's call, Ettling vigorously operated the emergency handpump, striving to accumulate sufficient pressure for effective braking. Gunn kept both feet firmly on the pedals. Mocking their efforts, the pressure gauge needle still sat stubbornly on zero p.s.i. – the brakes were useless.

The B-17 had now swung off the asphalt and was bumping rapidly over grass towards the edge of the aerodrome. A crash seemed inevitable unless they risked ground looping, a last, desperate gunning of engines and metal-tormenting torture on the undercarriage to swing the bomber left, away from a grass embankment and ditch looming ever larger in their windscreen. Urging the port throttles forward, Gunn intended to curve the errant Annie to the left, but it was too late. Bounding over the perimeter track, the aircraft swept on towards a knoll and ditch bordering the airfield. Seeing their predicament, Capt F.H. Schott hastened

Slithering on her belly, Haybag Annie seemed determined to bathe in the Irish Sea.

Detail of her mission symbols – each one a story in itself.

forward between the two pilots and pulled the mixture controls to cut-off as Gunn turned off the switches to lessen the fire hazard. They could do no more.

Still under momentum, Haybag Annie surmounted the knoll at around 40mph and fell 6 feet into the ditch. The left wheel sheared off in a spume of soil causing the right undercarriage to collapse, slamming the wheel into its nacelle. Slithering on her belly, Haybag Annie seemed determined to bathe in the Irish Sea but, her energy gradually exhausted, the gallant old bomber slewed to a halt in scrubland some 100 yards from the runway's end. Thankful to have avoided an impromptu dip, a flurry of activity saw airmen hastily vacating their hapless bomber. Luckily, Haybag Annie kept her casualty record almost untarnished. Only three men were injured: Capt William K. Dery was hit in the side and back with the left cheek gun; waist gunner Sgt Arnold L. Walker suffered a cut finger on his left hand, and Sgt Michael S. Elliott was thrown against bulkhead number six and injured his shoulder. Dery and Walker were X-rayed but had no injuries worthy of hospital detention. In the event, their misfortune cost some delay but all eventually reached home safely. A report on Haybag Annie at least spared her the ignominy of the Arizona desert:

An investigation of the aircraft after the accident revealed the following: Two of the batteries were checked and found to be serviceable with specific gravity readings of 1250, the other battery was damaged upon removal from the aircraft at the time of the accident, but from external appearances is presumed to have been serviccable. Examination of the fuse

panel proved that neither the hydraulic switch fuse nor the hydraulic pump fuse was blown. The hydraulic system was operated and found to be functioning properly. The electric pump was run, the handpump operated and pressure and fluid obtained down to the brake deboosters on both main struts. The hydraulic system was intact as far as the brake deboosters after the accident. Fluid was obtained from the lines connecting from the deboosters to the wheels. The flexible hose connecting the debooster and wheel on the right gear was believed to have broken as a result of the wheel coming apart from the shock strut; hydraulic fluid was obtained from the ruptured hose line. The flexible hose line on the left wheel was damaged at the disconnect fitting. The brake expander tubes were not ruptured on either wheel. Because the landing gear was badly damaged as a result of the accident, the Aircraft Accident Investigating Committee was unable to determine whether or not there was a leak or a broken hydraulic line prior to the accident. Although this could not be definitely determined, it is the most probable explanation for the brake failure.

Interestingly, an account given years later by a veteran crew chief cited the fact that, to cure the pre-take-off problem, a B-17F part was found and fitted even though the hydraulic connections differed from the B-17G. Perhaps this officially unrecorded error accounted for the mishap? Haybag Annie ended her career at Valley but her namesake could be proud of this Flying Fortress centenarian.

Anne had witnessed B-17s return riddled with holes, red flares signalling wounded on board – young men dying or rapidly ageing with combat fatigue. Now they, like she, began returning to lives interrupted and for ever marked by war. She waved them off, happy for their futures and, as Great Ashfield slid into dereliction and demolition, the evidence of her craft in the buildings disappeared and the B-17s themselves became history. After the war she met David Gordon, a Commander in the Royal Navy, and they married on Gibraltar in 1948. When David was at sea, Anne lived a somewhat bohemian lifestyle on a yacht and, although adored by the Admiral, was considered somewhat risqué by other, starchier naval wives. She finally returned to her interrupted art education and was awarded a scholarship at the Ruskin School of Art on the strength of her work, including a pencil study of US airmen at prayer. On completion of her course, she won another scholarship to the British School in Rome, but her marriage was disintegrating and circumstances saw her moving without David to Henley-on-Thames, where the American connection continued when she regularly hosted rowing crews from the USA during the famous regatta. Her work naturally included numerous rowing scenes, but she developed and diversified to include landscapes, portraits, book illustrations and modern art, often sold at exhibitions abroad. Her early work on Flying Fortresses was all but forgotten.

The 385th had been disbanded in 1945 and its achievements became part of a proud legacy soon to be invigorated thanks to the drive and initiative shown by a former crew chief, John C. Ford. Until John's involvement, 'Van's Valiants' – now the 385th Bombardment Group Memorial Association (BGMA) – had held occasional reunions in America, but John felt the group's heart rested on that crumbling old airbase now blending into the tranquillity

As Great Ashfield slid into dereliction and demolition, the evidence of Annie's craft in the buildings disappeared. A cheeky piece of artwork over the bar in the Officers' Club. (*Milt Taubkin*)

Snack bar in the Aero Club – long since demolished. Annie's artwork is much in evidence: silver wings and four squadron badges to the right, a group insignia and a jiving couple on the far wall. The airman nearest camera has an A-2 with 'Round Trip Ticket III' and at least 25 mission symbols. (*Fiona Carville*)

Annie's pencil study of US airmen at prayer was instrumental in helping her achieve a scholarship at the Ruskin School of Art. (*Fiona Carville*)

of the Suffolk countryside. Like many veterans, John wanted a final pilgrimage while health prevailed. In 1976, their planned UK reunion rapidly expanded into over 300 veterans and families visiting Great Ashfield. Knowing how strongly their history was entwined with that of Anne Haywood, John traced their 'Haybag Annie', inviting her to join the reunion on a visit to their long-abandoned airfield. On Tuesday, 7 September, following a service in All Saints Church, Great Ashfield, four coaches swung onto the crumbling remains of the old airbase and convoyed slowly to the intersection of the runways. The doors hissed open, disgorging dozens of veterans and much emotion. Waiting to greet them were villagers from Great Ashfield and their own, special artist. Anne was overwhelmed by the cheerful, tearful, middle-aged men, and names of long-vanished aircraft soon echoed over the empty hardstands. Many of those attending were, like the writer, from the post-war generation given peace and democracy by these now ageing warriors. It seemed, also, that there were others whose presence could be felt but not seen, a greeting of ghosts still haunting former flight lines and cheered by the return of their comrades.

Reflecting on this eeriness, I felt empathy for two particular crews even though they died before I was born. Eleven years earlier, as a young Air Training Corps cadet, I had found the wreckage of buried bombers that turned out to be B-17s of the 385th. For display during the

reunion, I had items from these aircraft in my car and it had not gone unthought that these parts had, at last, made it home. Eventually, the tragic circumstances surrounding the loss of these aircraft inspired *Final Flights*. Over two decades thereafter, the book itself triggered what would be Annie's last 'nose-art'. From the 1976 reunion, as Anne rekindled old friendships, I embraced new ones and cemented a bond with the 385th BGMA that evolved into becoming its UK historian.

In 1997, I contacted the television archaeological programme *Time Team*. Being an ardent fan, I felt an opportunity existed for a programme in the series embracing aviation archaeology that, if handled carefully, would promote the subject to a wider audience, develop a new theme for *Time Team* and create some fascinating television. More importantly, it would honour the twenty-one young airmen who perished in a wartime tragedy.

On 21 February 1944, Capt John N. Hutchison and his crew were to fly their twenty-fifth mission, the completion of their tour. To publicize the event, a young photographer, Sgt Frank L. 'Bud' Creegan, would accompany them to cover the mission and their jubilant homecoming from an attack on the aircraft depot at Diepholz, north-western Germany. Their mission successfully accomplished, the crew were already celebrating when tragedy struck at 15.39 hr over Reedham Marshes, Norfolk.

Hutch was leading a V-formation of three Fortresses as they descended through cloud. In those grey confines, the aircraft flown by his number three, 1/Lt Warren J. Pease, inexplicably went out of control and spun earthwards. Recovering control just as the aircraft broke clear of cloud, Pease pulled up into the path of Hutchison, his flight leader. Hutch had no time to avoid the collision and his aircraft, 42-31370, severed the tail of 42-37963 flown by Pease. Too low for anyone to escape, both bombers plunged into Reedham Marshes.

Salvage crews retrieved the bodies but much of the aircraft sank into the marsh and facts surrounding events submerged into the archives, leaving only rumour and local legend. Following up this folklore led to my appearance in 1964 searching for 'German' bombers reputedly still buried near Reedham. As related in *Final Flights*, I began piecing together the story and my endeavours focused on 42-31370 and the Hutchison crew because there was more wreckage extant. Following publication of *Final Flights*, new material emerged, including contact with Hutchison's brother, who kindly gave me some original letters written by Hutch to his family. In one dated 18 December 1943, Hutch said, 'I have a "Sleepytime Gal II" now. The first one [my second ship] is in a sad shape. The new one is a G and a most sweet handling job.'

The aircraft flown by 1/Lt Warren J. Pease inexplicably went out of control. (*Guy de la Bedoyère*)

On 21 February 1944, Capt John N. Hutchison and crew were to fly their 25th mission. *Rear left to right*: 1/Lt John E. Epps, navigator; 2/Lt Charles G. Curtis, co-pilot; Capt John N. Hutchison Jr, pilot; 1/Lt Edmond J. Gamble, bombardier. *Front*: Technical Sgt William J. Dukes, radio; Staff Sgt Emilio M. Corgnatti, left waist gunner; Jim O'Malley (not on board); Staff Sgt Joseph J. Carpinetti, tail gunner; Joe Fulgieri (not on board); Technical Sgt Roy C. Kitner, top turret. All those on board perished in the tragedy.

Both bombers plunged into the marshes. These are the mangled remnants of B-17 42-37963. Over five decades later this would be the scene of *Time Team*'s first programme on aviation archaeology.

It is probable that Annie did the artwork for his first Sleepytime Gal but uncertain whether his second aircraft had any nose-art or 42-31370 was the plane he intended as his second Sleepytime Gal. For the television production, it was agreed that Anne would feature in the 'cameo', a section of the programme linked to the main theme but branching out from pure archaeology. Previous cameos included crafting pottery, constructing furnaces and even sword manufacturing. For the 'Bombers' programme, Anne would re-create the nose-art Hutch might have had on his Sleepytime Gal.

My original proposal to *Time Team* had been to include recovering wreckage of both aircraft but preliminary planning excluded this approach based on budget and a potential lack of clarity for the audience. Television celebrity Tony Robinson fronts the programme, and to have him breathless between sites recovering similar finds risked baffling viewers. Months before the programme, metal detector surveys were conducted, with both sites providing strong readings. Each had benefits and disadvantages but discussions drew down on the Pease site because it had seen less prior digging.

Time Team genuinely does what it claims when Tony dramatically asserts 'and we have only three days to find out . . .'. However, in advance of the shoot, there is considerable preparation and even the excavation of only one bomber looked set to be one of their most expensive programmes ever. The site near Decoy Carr on Reedham Marshes is a Site of Special Scientific Interest (SSSI), so great environmental care was essential. A series of permissions was required and the absence of any one would be a showstopper. Landowner's and tenant's consent, Environmental Agency, Drainage Authority approval, English Nature, English Heritage, Ministry of Defence licence, Health and Safety Executive, insurance – all essential before disturbing one blade of grass. Several meetings were held and correspondence accumulated along with costs. Roadblocks were encountered and surmounted, including the requirement for an expensive hydrogeological survey, conducted in May 1998 by Hydrogeological Services International Ltd. The thirty-page report stated in part:

Environmental organisations, including English Nature, have indicated that they have no objection in principle to the recovery of the aircraft. However, they have expressed concern that changes to the hydrology and water chemistry as a result of the excavation could cause the immediate or longer-term damage to the flora and fauna associated with the dykes in the area. The site investigation comprised: the digging of five trial pits to a maximum depth of 5m; lithological description of strata penetrated; measurement of trial pits inflows; measurement of field physicochemical parameters and water quality sampling of trial pit and dyke waters; and dyke surveys . . . Inflows of water into trial pits were recorded at two main levels: the upper level was at a depth of less than 1m from the Upper Peat, where it rests on clay; the lower level was from within the Middle Peat, at a depth of about 4m where upwelling of water from depth was observed . . . Dewatering of the aquifer during excavation might induce flow from the dykes, due to the change in head gradient, although water loss from the dykes is expected to be small. During trial pit construction, the vertical walls of most of the pits were found to collapse over time site.

Disturbance of the strata surrounding the dykes during excavation probably presents the greatest risk to the integrity of the dyke walls, and therefore of loss of water from the dykes. In view of this, as a precaution, it is recommended that the excavation should be at least 4m away from dykes . . . In addition, iron and manganese concentrations of the peat waters are significantly higher than those of the dyke waters. Discharge of these waters directly into dykes from dewatering during excavation will temporarily change the hydrochemistry of the dyke waters and may adversely affect the ecosystem, and is therefore not recommended.

This recommendation eventually entailed commissioning, and erecting on site, a specifically designed water-storage lagoon with oil-extraction absorption booms. Taking water 400m to the lagoon involved hiring three special Sykes Wispaset-silenced diesel pumps. Added to requirements from the hydrogeological survey, a risk-assessment survey was carried out, ultimately requiring acceptance signatures from all attending the site. This assessment cited the risk of .5 calibre ammunition and warned, 'test pits have demonstrated the extremely unstable nature of the marsh stratigraphy which effectively prohibits the use of shoring below 2m'. Anyone who fell in would vanish into a quagmire likened in texture to chocolate mousse. Additionally stipulated were the dangers from heavy plant and, for the dig, *Time Team* had hired two tracked Hymacs, one of 35ft reach and the second with an incredible grasp extending 75ft. Reassuringly, St John's Ambulance staff were to be on-site.

Finally, its budget off-scale, 'Bombers' got the go-ahead for three days of filming from 29 June 1998. In their hotel on the evening of Sunday, 28 June, *Time Team* conducted a 'pre-mission' briefing opened by programme director Simon Raikes, describing the programme's background and the obstacles already addressed. This military tenor was further enhanced by Flt Sgt Don Borritt of the RAF's Explosives Ordnance Disposal (EOD) contingent from 5131 (Bomb Disposal) Squadron, Wittering, who alerted all, and alarmed some, with a discourse on the dangers of unexploded ordnance that I hopefully alleviated by outlining my previous crash-site experience and survival thus far. Nevertheless, I endorsed the need to respect any ammunition we found. Apart from the RAF's obvious command structure, television personnel came under Simon Raikes and series production director, Tim Taylor. Less stringently in this chain of command were the *Time Team* personalities led by Professor Mick Aston, with Phil Harding and Carenza Lewis backed up by other archaeologists and technical support staff. Also present were Air Crash Investigator Bernie Forward and former USAAF crew chief Bob Spangler, with experience of the B-17's anatomy. I was 'leading' a team of enthusiasts representing several East Anglian aviation museums, and the blending of all these disparate forces would encounter some friction. Rising magnificently above such issues, and capable of puncturing the most pronounced ego, was Haybag Annie, now in her 70s, rather more corpulent but still with a boisterous spirit. She was the only one present likely to have known the airmen involved in the tragedy that drew us purposefully together, determined to discover what still lay hidden in the marsh.

Next morning witnessed more activity reminiscent of military operations as a command centre sprang to life in the office of Gary Gray on Hall Farm. Soon, a convoy of vehicles set

Still with a boisterous spirit, Haybag Annie on the *Time Team* dig.

off for Decoy Carr and shuttle buses were established for stragglers. Tony Robinson was on high ground approaching the site giving his introductory piece to camera against the vista of wide Norfolk skies and verdant grassland below. 'What exactly happened? We have three days to shed some light on the mystery . . .' I soon found myself similarly set upon by a film crew and was suitably 'wired-up' with a back-pocket transmitter, wires under my shirt and a tiny microphone attached to my collar. Clearly, I would have to be careful – any utterance would be instantly picked up, expletives no exception! My first scene, the opening, set a soon-familiar standard as we filmed three or four variants. Not being paid for my participation, my only stipulation was to credit *Final Flights*, so I was delighted to have it featured briefly; but I would soon learn that what gets filmed frequently fails to survive the editorial scissors, including my promised book 'plug'. Most other footage followed a similar pattern and I rapidly realized that nothing in the pace of TV-land proceeds as swiftly as programmes pretend. Scenes were shot then re-shot – not forgetting 'continuity' – did I have my gloves on or off when we started – where had I stood? Soon I understood the dreaded phrase 'take it from the top', which caused both amateurs and professionals to wince as we once again recreated a scene. Progress on-site was painfully slow as the traditional archaeological approach took precedence. Scrape and trowel, while two giant machines stood idle. This was fine for stratification and dating, but we knew the date, and the turmoil of subsequent recovery operations by the USAAF to retrieve bodies, plus my own and other previous efforts in the 1970s, confounded any benefits derived from stratification.

Eventually, the opening scenes were shot and 'in the can' – the anticipatory excitement of a *Time Team* programme owes much to the craft of camera and cut. A geophysical survey ('Geofizz' in *TT* speak) for both ferrous and non-ferrous metals had triggered a shower of anomalies, with several still extant despite depth adjustment to filter out lighter debris near the surface. Providing a panoramic view of the site, *Time Team* scaffolded a tower and platform from which cameras gave viewers an appreciation of the site layout. As Geofizz perambulated across the marshland with its wheeled detector, wittily christened 'Molly Malone', Flt Sgt Don Borritt was on camera dispensing suitable wisdom and warnings about the .5 ammunition. 'A pretty dangerous piece of kit', remarked one of the *Time Team*.

Hutch wrote home 'they have the prettiest girls in England'. This picture was returned with his belongings. Beautiful, mysterious and still unidentified.

Later, in the incident room, Guy de la Bedoyère and I outlined the mission flown on 21 February 1944, our fingers tracing that homeward journey by the 385th. Hutch and his crew were so close to the joyous completion of the tour and Tony captured to camera the words on Hutch's last telegram to his mother, 'Am OK. One to go. Love Johnny'. Lost hopes held for ever in simple words. This aura transmitted itself down the generations, eventually reaching millions as *Time Team* demonstrated the professionalism that emerged in their adept and sensitive treatment of the topic.

Nearby, Anne and Carenza had commenced the cameo, a re-creation of 'Sleepytime Gal'. Supported on a metal frame was a large, olive, drab panel simulating the fuselage curvature of a B-17. Carenza was illustrating the curvature of a young lady but was more earthily clad as Anne set about illustrating a diaphanously attired Sleepytime Gal.

Rejoining the dig, I found my team totally demoralized. Trench one had been opened after two and a half hours of inactivity but only eight bucket-loads had been removed before Phil called a halt. The machine had scraped over a sizeable piece of B-17, which he was tackling with his famous trowel. The spoil heap, mostly clay, had already been thoroughly searched by a miniature army of detectorists and every morsel extracted. Trench two, tracking a Geofizz 'hot spot', revealed only a few rounds of ammunition before readings ceased and it was closed. In trench one, Phil was now teaching trowelling techniques to clear earth from a large piece of screw-threaded metalwork, which Bob Spangler initially identified as the tail-wheel retracting screw. This created consternation, because all evidence to date confirmed that the tail had been severed from the fuselage. Bob later revised his opinion – we had found the port main landing gear retracting screw. Indicative of the crash and chaotic aftermath were shreds of parachute mingled with the undercarriage debris. From the spoil heap came another

confusing find – a battered piece of aluminium with a condom snared to it. Cameras rolling, I clarified for Carenza that, far from maligning the crew in that wretched cliché 'overpaid, oversexed, over here', gunners sometimes used the prophylactic as a protective measure over gun barrels to prevent moisture ingression. In a lighter tone, I related the allegorical tales assigning another technique of peeing in the condom while the plane was climbing, then detaching and knotting it to freeze at altitude before launching the 'missile' over Germany. Quite what enemy bomb-disposal experts thought is not on record! This was another scene edited out and rightly so because it detracted from the programme's purpose and could be misinterpreted as lacking respect. Admiration for the courage of those young airmen was a common denominator for all excavation participants and none wished for any detraction.

As day one slipped towards sunset, a compromise was achieved between traditional archaeological techniques and the desire to dig deeper, faster. We were learning from one another. Trench three, a foray triggered by Geofizz on the dyke's far bank, found only more ammunition and the remains of a broken, rusting hawser, possibly discarded by the wartime recovery crew. *Time Team*'s Stewart Ainsworth had also forsaken technology and was using the Mk 1 eyeball and wartime photographs looking for evidence of the crash in undulations on the pasture. His attention focused on an indentation in the otherwise straight-edged dyke banks, perhaps created by the bomber's impact. Day one closed with discussions on the proposition of wreckage extant deep in the dyke itself.

Day two opened with further dialogue on exactly where to dig: Geofizz had determined further hot spots, so two more trenches were opened. One yielded the base of a reinforced concrete gatepost and the other just a few fragments. Elsewhere, topsoil was scraped away as we chased additional detector readings but little of significance emerged. It was becoming apparent that the focal point of activities would be trench one and the dyke itself. The trench initially measured some 3.5m wide and 6m long and the topsoil had been removed to a depth of 1m, exposing a layer of debris and a large, curving line cut through the natural clay layer. This cut contained a mixture of mid- and dark-grey clay mingled with large patches of blackened clay, aircraft debris and pockets of aviation fuel. It was considered that this cut indicated the original impact crater. This, plus study of wreckage by Bernie Forward, verified a steep, high-speed impact and total disintegration, discounting eyewitness accounts describing moments of hope in a shallow approach, with the aircraft slithering over the marsh to explode when it hit the dyke. Wartime photographs discovered since the excavations strongly support Bernie's deductions. Later, additional evidence would allow him to firm up his theory of events that fateful day.

The unsung heroes working on the spoil heaps continued, adding to the items retrieved. Combined with finds taken from the crater, an array of debris slowly accumulated: fragments of fuselage and main spar; a current inverter; the base of the navigator or bombardier's seat; a section of armour-plating from the pilot's seat. Reminders of the young men themselves also emerged: a throat microphone; remains of a flying glove; the peak from an officer's cap; a crumpled boot; half a leather flying glove. Carenza was especially touched by the poignancy of these finds. They were not as remote as discoveries on medieval digs but came from men who, as she sadly commented, should be still with us.

Working into trench one had now taken us to a depth demanding great caution and the erection of a warning barrier. I was again becoming impatient and, thinking such concerns should be off-air, made a discreet interjection, but Tim Taylor would have none of it. A dash of ire made for good television, so a scene was filmed to catch my frustrations. This would be the last opportunity I had to probe deeper and discover whether or not wreckage lay beyond our 1970s excavations. Back then, we had made some interesting finds, some illustrated in *Final Flights*, but, after a propeller was found, our excavations came to an abrupt end when the digger submerged into backfilled quagmire and the mystery of what, if anything, lay deeper would be solved only twenty-two years later, if we got a move on.

Another 'discreet' aside to digger driver Vic Doughty revealed that he had found further wreckage during dyke clearance. He felt that we should probe as far into the dyke as possible. We also needed to exhaust trench one, so continued during the afternoon until the finds petered out on Geofizz. However, walking across the clay, Simon Dunham still got a reading on his Fisher detector. We were now over 2m deep and knew that, beneath the remaining skin of clay, lay the dangerous morass of unstable peat; and the risks were emphasized when one of the Geofizz team got stuck and had to be extricated sans wellies, which were then retrieved to great merriment all round. However, conditions were clearly too hazardous to allow further access – was there anything there or not? Penetrating clay into the peat could create an engineering disaster as the edges of our excavations caved in, creating an ever-expanding crater. With suitable drama, Tony announced, 'Tomorrow, we're going down!' At last.

1 July 1998. All were aware of this being the final day. Redundant trenches were closed, our efforts concentrated on probing the dyke, but, despite the bucket disappearing optimistically ever deeper, our spirits drained with every empty load. After we had penetrated over 15m and met no metallic resistance, it was evident that the dyke held no submerged debris and our hopes focused on trench one. From this emerged the cockpit armoured glass, then, further in the soluble peat, the machine exposed a piece of piping, instantly recognizable to my team-mate, Pete Snowling. A *Time Team* crewman did not believe him and a hastily placed bet kept all agog as the digger swooped back on the now sunken find. Moments later, Pete was £10 better off but, better than this, the bucket had neatly scooped out a prime-condition .5 calibre machine gun, one of the classic weapons from the Second World War. Carrying our trophy made fine television and a cheerful demeanour was further brightened when a second superb specimen appeared; but there was no evidence of any further remains, and throwing the EOD's Forster detector head in on an extension lead produced no more signals. Trench one was devoid of debris. A final spasm from Geofizz saw us open trench five on their last hot spot, and this revealed itself as an aileron mass balance buried 3m deep and undoubtedly undisturbed since the crash. This discovery helped Bernie align the angle of impact and he concluded that the aircraft had gone in almost vertically at over 200mph. But why?

To enhance the programme, the producers had requested the availability of major finds from previous excavations. Two propellers remained off-camera until Tony trundled into view with them on the back of Pete Snowling's 1943 Diamond T. Wrecker, a superbly restored

The bucket had neatly scooped out a prime condition .5 calibre machine gun, one of the classic weapons from the Second World War. (*Mick Aston*)

example of the type undoubtedly used on site during the original USAAF recovery operations. The propellers' appearance as if 'just discovered' proved controversial following the broadcast, but one propeller proved invaluable when Bernie quickly noted that its blades had been feathered, a feature previously overlooked. It was felt that Pease and his co-pilot had lost control in cloud, perhaps been disoriented – and here was a possible cause. Bernie theorized that, during their descent through cloud, Pease had lost an engine and, while preoccupied with the feathering process, his attention had been diverted and control lost. Emerging from cloud in a steep dive, he pulled up to avoid crashing but climbed into the path of Sleepytime Gal, with disastrous consequences. We now had an expert opinion, made possible only by *Time Team*'s involvement, so, while little wreckage had been located, a sense of satisfaction permeated activities. Channel 4 had a good programme; *Time Team* and the enthusiasts were now teaming well, each learning from the exchange. To acknowledge our success, Mick Aston, celebrating his birthday, was allowed by EOD the honour of detonating a charge of plastic explosive used to destroy the substantial pile of unexploded ammunition accumulated during the dig.

Anne's cameo role was complete and the re-creation of Sleepytime Gal stood as backdrop to our finds in the programme's folding moments. Typically, three or four options for ending

A superbly restored wartime Diamond T recovery truck provides the stage for filming a debate on the bomber's demise. *Time Team* were pleased with their first foray into aviation archaeology.

Producer Simon Raikes arranges finds for the closing scene. Annie's last 'nose-art' is in the background.

Time Team and a temp. Tony Robinson, Mick Aston, Carenza Lewis, Phil Harding and the author.

were filmed and the simplest of these ultimately chosen, with a rearrangement of the programme's boisterous theme tune into softer tones for those lost souls as the concluding credits rolled. Fifty-five years to the day, the broadcast attracted the programme's highest-ever audience ratings. The programme had its detractors and, while a flurry of e-mails to its forum debated the dig's purpose and the 'attitude' of the enthusiasts, many viewers were supportive. 'Totally compelling viewing.' 'Whatever the merits of *Time Team* doing this dig – it's been worth it as it seems to have made us all stop and remember.' '*Time Team* learn a great deal every time they venture into uncharted territory like this. I feel they are to be congratulated on taking such a risk and producing a programme far different from the norm. It has clearly been far more thought provoking than traditional archaeology . . . many of us are privileged to know World War II airmen and last week's programme called their experiences to the forefront of our minds . . .'

Anne did not like her rendering of Sleepytime Gal because it was not one of her original designs and time constraints had not allowed her to satisfy her standards. However, it was donated, along with most of the wreckage, to the Norfolk and Suffolk Aviation Museum. But what about the remains of Hutchison's aircraft, his Sleepytime Gal II still extant on the marshes? My thoughts turned to this and a final memorial to both aircrews. In 1997, our redoubtable digger driver, Vic Doughty, had been clearing Mill Dyke, adjacent to the Hutchison crash site, when his machine struck something large and very solid. Further probing revealed the cylinders of a Wright Cyclone radial engine; but Vic's role on this occasion was dyke maintenance, so he reburied his find for a future occasion. *Time Team*'s decision to focus on the Pease site added to our knowledge of events

and cleared the aircraft; but the Sleepytime Gal II site was tantalizingly unfinished. Television had proved instrumental for the Pease site, but working in full view of 5 million people imposed restrictions not required for planned activities on Hutchison's B-17. Even so, compliance with landowner's requirements plus licensing, insurance and pollution control delayed excavations until September 1999. Funding this time would be from our own pockets, although the Norfolk and Suffolk Aviation Museum generously donated £100 towards costs.

Saturday, 18 September 1999, was blustery but warm, and, travelling to the site, we saw the local hunt and sympathized with the fox. Our hunt had its own challenges, and wind whipped wavelets the length of Mill Dyke as our pumps surged into action, draining water between two earthen dams built to segregate the crash site. Our metal detectors had provided one powerful reading at the dyke's edge where Vic estimated the engine lay 15m down. We had a second, strong reading a short distance into the meadow beneath a shallow depression, which was all that remained to indicate previous unsuccessful efforts a decade earlier. Underneath, the terrain here was friendlier, with deeper and more tractable clay – hard to hand-dig but less dangerous than the layer of peat at Decoy Carr. Customarily scraping aside topsoil, we worked slowly, penetrating deeper in drier conditions than on any previous occasion. Adept sloping of the crater's edge negated the need for shoring and the absence of flooding provided unimagined visibility. Early discoveries included the inevitable ammunition; perspex; personal equipment – oxygen masks, throat microphones and an extension cable for an electrically heated suit. Testimony to the intense heat near the surface was a light bulb in which the glass had not broken but melted. Yet, nearby, a small morphine bottle lay intact.

Probing deeper, we once again exposed the engine cylinders some 5m deep and realized the propeller was still attached. Gingerly clearing the clay, we attached some strong webbing and began to ease our find from its 55-year-long entombment. The propeller slid neatly off the engine shaft to be hoisted steadily skywards, its dark, twisted blades grotesquely symbolic against the skyline – a realm they once dominated. Clearing the propeller facilitated removal of the engine and careful manœuvring of the digger bucket nudged the Cyclone on board. Soon it was on the surface being enthusiastically hosed down ready for transportation to the workshops of Harleston Engineering for renovation by Pete Snowling as part of an exhibition piece featuring his Diamond T recovery truck.

Following retrieval of the engine, we traced another reading and located a second propeller towards the dyke. Conditions were difficult and access to the crater entailed journeying in and out on the digger bucket because the slopes were too slippery to climb. We were now below the bed of the dyke and securing this propeller proved arduous; but determination prevailed and its long sojourn was broken. However, the marsh god still had one trick to play. As the Hamilton Standard came free, we found only two blades attached, but those closely involved with its recapture were convinced they had felt a third still attached. Further probing failed and, if it existed, it remains to this day as an offering to the marshland deity. Deep excavation now terminated to allow expansion of the crater into seams of debris exposed

A propeller hauled heavenwards, its blades grotesquely symbolic against the skyline – a realm they once dominated. (*Eastern Daily Press*)

in its banks nearer the surface. One line of detritus led into the compacted and burnt remains of William J. Dukes's radio compartment. Crushed and shattered remnants of wartime electronics and bunches of anti-radar chaff were bagged for sorting and subsequent museum distribution. Slowly, we began the process of back-filling. Searching the spoil for items overlooked still produced detector bleeps like a chorus of aliens. My son Rowan gave up using his detector and was feeling for finds when one innocuous lump evidenced a solid centre, so he began carefully to dig it clear. Then he called me over, visibly excited. I was puzzled for a moment, but it suddenly dawned on me that I was looking straight into the lens of Bud Creegan's hand-held K-20 camera: nearly six decades earlier, the last images flashing into that eye had been of a bomber crew celebrating, almost home, their tour complete. Protruding from the edge of our discovery was a fragment of film. Was it just possible that a few haunting frames survived? Clamping clay over the camera's back, we hopefully prevented further exposure of any film inside and dared not look to confirm as we bundled it into a black plastic bag. This required specialist handling.

The last images seen by this camera were of a bomber crew celebrating – almost home. Was it just possible that a few haunting frames survived? Michael Nice from the 100th BGMAM considers its condition.

I had been visiting this site for thirty-five years, excavating first by hand and later with machinery, so I experienced both sadness and a sense of 'mission accomplished' as the land was now levelled for the last time. We set a simple British Legion cross of remembrance on the site and held an impromptu service in memory of the young men who had perished here so long ago. In age, they would have been my seniors when I started; now they were nearer to my son's age. At least my efforts had achieved recognition for them and items found over the years were now displayed in both British and American museums. There was, however, still one action outstanding – the memorial.

Next morning found Rowan and me hurrying with the camera to Duxford's Imperial War Museum, where Stephen Brooks and Andy Anderson swiftly conveyed our bagged lump of muck into their immaculate darkroom. Excited aspirations of historically dramatic images faded to disappointment when delicate cleaning under infrared revealed only one piece of film. The back of the camera had been gutted and the cassette ripped away, leaving only burned morsels. The lens was intact but the images taken on board Sleepytime Gal II had vanished in flames for ever.

For thirty-five years I had sought to perpetuate the memory of the twenty-one airmen who died over Reedham. To maintain a commitment made during the *Time Team* programme, a memorial was being planned. One intention was to ask Anne to the dedication. It was not to be.

Cameramen from the 385th BG photo lab. *Left to right*: Tony Kosierowski, Bud Creegan, Clifford Peek. They dealt with all bomb-strike photography and flew missions for functional and PR purposes. Clifford Peek was shot down with the Rosener crew on 15 August 1944 to become a POW.

On 31 October 1999, Anne died following surgery for cancer. Her contribution to 385th BG history had concluded with Sleepytime Gal, but she remains an integral part of their achievements. Thanks to support from *Time Team*, 385th veterans and Reedham Parish Council, memorial costs were covered and discussions on design under way. Original intentions for incorporating finds from both aircraft proved impractical to maintain in perpetuity, so, to honour these fallen 'guests' in parish history, Reedham Parish Council Committee allowed the establishment of a memorial alongside the existing village memorial, so the sacrifice of these allies would for ever be a shared remembrance during the villagers' annual homage to their own fallen.

On 17 June 2000, some seventy 385th veterans and their families attended a service dedicating a grey marble plaque inscribed with twenty-one names. With my books, the television programme and the unveiling of the memorial, I felt these young flyers had been rescued from historical anonymity. As I said to a reporter from the *Eastern Daily Press*, the afternoon was like 'the end of a chapter'. I only wish Haybag Annie had been able to share it with me.

The author speaking at the Memorial Dedication Service, 17 June 2000. Rescued from the risk of historical anonymity, the names of those who died share an honoured place alongside the village war memorial. (*Art Driscoll*)

CHAPTER TWO

Buchenwald

Some place names will for ever send chilling messages into the history of mankind and none more so than those associated with the evil of the Holocaust. One such place, opened on 16 July 1937, was Konzentrationlager Ettersber, which lasted only a short period in this guise before adopting the infamous name 'Konzentrationlager Buchenwald' (KLB), a place paramount in the ranking of Third Reich atrocities. The grim legacy of Buchenwald casts a long shadow over immeasurable human suffering. Within its ghastly portals, a heavy toll was taken of peoples incarcerated in this hell on earth and subjugated beneath the Nazi jackboot. It is little known, and belatedly acknowledged, that some Gestapo 'guests' in Buchenwald were captured Allied airmen – British, Canadian, Australian, New Zealanders and some from the US Eighth Air Force. These men came to fight an air war and most knew little of the politics and issues facing the peoples beneath their wings. William 'Bill' Powell, a navigator with the 385th BG, was typical and later recalled, 'Flying a B-17 at 25,000 feet is rather an impersonal way to fight a war. Sure, you are exposed to flak and fighters but you have no idea of what's happening below.' Bill was destined to find out.

Bill's family migrated to America from Rochdale in the north of England, and he was their first child born on US soil, in Philadelphia, on 9 January 1917. His father died when he was still young and his mother moved to Waterbury, Connecticut, where Bill grew up. His formative years through high school included an early interest in politics, but his own right-wing leanings were democratically balanced, unlike the extremist views being expressed within the political darkness now creeping sinisterly across parts of Europe. Moving on to the University of Nebraska in Omaha, Nebraska, his charm and good looks more than matched his Hollywood namesake. This undoubtedly assisted his political aspirations when active support for the Republican Party became an early step in a potential political career as a party representative. This would be interrupted by his entry into the military and Bill later encountered at first hand the risks of allowing democracy to fail.

Trained as a navigator, Bill eventually found himself flying combat missions with 'Van's Valiants', the 385th BG from Great Ashfield. On 29 January 1944, his group undertook its fifty-sixth mission and contributed forty-one aircraft in 'A' and 'B' groups to attack targets in Frankfurt. Enemy resistance was fierce and the 385th was attacked by an estimated 125 Me

'Flying a B-17 at 25,000 feet is rather an impersonal way to fight a war . . . You have no idea what's happening below.' Some of those in this crew were destined to find out. *Front left to right*: 2/Lts Ralph H. Palmer, pilot; Ryall L. Skaggs, co-pilot; William Powell, navigator; Frank W. Wieczerak, bombardier. *Rear left to right*: Technical Sgt Arthur M. Pacha; Staff Sgts Allen D. Patterson, right waist gunner; Robert J. Piarote, radio; Sgt Leo J. Reynolds, ball-turret gunner; Staff Sgts Elmore S. Loveland, tail gunner; William J. Williams, left waist gunner.

109s and Fw 190s. Bomber crews also observed an Me 410 and Junkers 88 cavorting in the distance to decoy US fighters, while the single-engined red-nosed and yellow-nosed enemy interceptors took classic advantage of the sun. Ferocious combat raged in heaven as men reduced God's empyrean majesty to the basics of kill or be killed. Bombers culled from the defensive cohesion of their formations were mercilessly slaughtered. American fighters, mostly P-47s, fought vigorously to protect their charges, but packs of German fighters sometimes overwhelmed the escorts. Three crews from Van's Valiants were among the twenty-nine bombers lost that day. So close did German fighters press their attacks that one Me 109 collided with, or rammed, the aircraft flown by 1/Lt Raymond E. Notestein and split the B-17 open.

Crews in aircraft nearby were horrified to see airmen thrown from the broken bomber, some, without parachutes, flailing helplessly as they fell from view. The co-pilot, 2/Lt Earl R. Follensbee, was fortunately wearing his parachute when the Me 109 impacted and threw him

Bill's exposed position offered a mind-numbing panorama through the perspex nose of Hustlin'
Hussy – B-17F 42-30354 of the 549th Squadron.

from a hole torn through the cockpit. 1/Lt Robert L. Bostick's aircraft, 42-97506, hit by
fighters, was last seen heading for France and was apparently put on autopilot as the crew
bailed out. Commenting on the loss of their third B-17, the 385th BG Statistical Officer,
Capt James R. Hamilton, could only state, 'Aircraft 42-30354 of this Group was lost due to
reasons unknown. This aircraft was last seen at 11.30 hours near Rally Point with No. 4
engine feathered under control and dropping behind formation. No chutes were observed
leaving aircraft.' Only now do we have details behind the fate of this aircraft, navigated by
2/Lt William Powell.

Bill's exposed position offered a mind-numbing panorama through the perspex nose of
'Hustlin' Hussy', a veteran B-17F recently inherited from the Verne Phillips crew. Bill
calculated this to be their thirteenth mission and the auspices looked bleak when flak
silenced their No. 4 engine on the bomb run. The pilots, 2/Lts Ralph H. Palmer and Ryal I.
Skaggs, held Hustlin' Hussy steady and 2/Lt Frank F. Wieczerzak was able to release his
bombs on target. As they cleared Frankfurt, Hustlin' Hussy's crew knew full well the fate
awaiting them. Unable to hold formation, the protection of the herd rescinded until the
ailing B-17 was alone. The cruel savagery of air combat did not spare the weak and wounded.

Dragging onward like a wounded bull sensing the wolf pack's presence, the B-17 crew readied themselves for their final combat. It came in a series of attacks as German fighters seemed almost to toy with their victim. Cannon and machine-gun fire lacerating the Hussy inflicted further damage. Incredibly, none of her ten crew had suffered serious injury and there appeared to be a lull in the combat as their adversaries determined another plan to bring down the still-battling bomber. Bill saw the *coup de grâce* coming in the shape of a powerfully armed Junkers 88 and further fighter attacks.

Unsuited for combat with American fighters, the Ju 88 fighter had been spawned from an original bomber design and proved formidable against British night bombers. When circumstances allowed, its heavy armament, including rocket-carrying capabilities, was effective against American heavies, and a badly damaged B-17 provided an ideal opportunity for some target practice. Keeping out of range of the bomber's guns, the Ju 88 simply 'lobbed rockets into the B-17'. Shrapnel from one salvo shredded through the Hussy and the crew were then hit by further cannon fire. The right waist gunner, Staff Sgt Allen D. Patterson, was hit by 20mm cannon shells in the head and neck. His companion on the left waist, Staff Sgt William J. Williams, was wounded, and hot metal shards also hit the radio operator, Technical Sgt Robert J. Piarote. Bill Powell hastened aft to see if he could help, but, examining Patterson, he realized the gunner had been killed outright. Ralph Palmer, now captain of an airborne sieve, realized that Hustlin' Hussy was finished. She had valiantly held together until they were beyond the German border and her crew now stood a better chance of falling into friendly hands. Ordering his men to bail out, Palmer continued piloting the bomber until all had departed and the Hussy held only the body of their fallen comrade.

Bill's parachute deployed and he was relieved to see other parachutes descending nearby. Fears for their safety swelled with the approaching roar of aero-engines and he witnessed further vindictiveness as enemy fighters strafed the area. Bill's parachute dropped into woodland at le Bois de Gabelle, near the small Belgian town of Lobbes, and, although hurt in the landing, he hastily concealed himself, because German search parties were in the vicinity. So, too, were members of the Underground, and Bill was quickly located by partisans and found himself whisked into the home of René Croquet and his wife. The rest of his crew were also spirited from woodland hiding places into the town and secreted in the homes of courageous Belgian families. A doctor in the Resistance was called and Williams had two bullets or pieces of shrapnel removed from his arm while Piarote also received treatment, all this beneath the noses of German patrols. Being rescued by the Resistance could be a long, dangerous process for all involved and no words can adequately express the heroism demonstrated by those in occupied Europe who risked their lives aiding Allied airmen. War fought at this level was a clandestine activity cloaked with forged documents, false papers and names concealed to protect those along the 'line' who moved evading airmen from one safe house to the next. Every journey was hazardous, and German intelligence, aided by sympathizers and collaborators, sought to penetrate Resistance cells and break the line. Betrayal, or a word out of place, could mean torture and death or deportation to a concentration camp. Always in peril, the men, women and children who helped fallen fliers

were unsurpassed in heroism, but sheer courage alone would not always combat cunning, collaboration and treachery.

Ralph Palmer held Hustlin' Hussy aloft long enough for his crew to escape and he parachuted clear a few miles further on into the hamlet of Fontaine L'Evêque. Good fortune once more intervened and Ralph was lucky in his choice of homestead: his anxious tap on the door was answered with a swift beckoning motion and he slipped quickly into the farmhouse of Eugene and Janne Hupin with their 7-year-old daughter Monique. Several days elapsed while Eugene, not, apparently, connected to the regular Resistance movement, tried to help his guest. Alone in a strange land, Ralph was very nervous, despite the kindness shown by the Hupin family. Communication was difficult, and Monique giggled at the tall stranger's mistakes with language as her father painstakingly pointed out words in his small French–English dictionary. Always agitated, the American struggled to translate the correct intentions – it might have been funny had the situation not been so dangerous. Some two weeks elapsed, with Ralph remaining concealed but becoming increasingly concerned because he knew the risks being taken and he feared for the Hupin family. However, Eugene's contribution to the Allied cause did not stop at concealing airmen, and one evening he left the farm for nearby Charleroi, where, in a small bar, he met some shadowy contacts possibly able to help him obtain some heavy weaponry to protect his American visitor. Who had plenty of these? The Germans! Whether his movements were premeditated or opportunistic is not known, but Eugene was tipped off about the presence of a German ammunition truck and had soon slipped surreptitiously beneath the tarpaulin. Emerging with quiet triumph clutching a machine gun, Eugene found himself confronting the muzzles of a well-armed German patrol. It was a trap. A set-up. Eugene was dragged savagely homewards and the patrol burst into the Hupin home to search for more weapons. Instead of guns, they captured the bonus of an American airman. It was a terrifying ordeal for Monique – angry soldiers, her father already beaten, her mother being manhandled and insulted by these brutal intruders. After the house had been ransacked, Monique's parents and the unfortunate pilot were hauled away to the notorious Gestapo cells in Charleroi jail. Monique was cared for by kindly neighbours, who knew the little girl might never see her parents again.

Within the grotesque confines of Charleroi prison, Ralph Palmer and Eugene Hupin were brutally beaten and despicably tortured for day upon tormented day. Janne Hupin also suffered degrading treatment as their inquisitors cruelly extracted what little information the trio had. Palmer should have been treated as a prisoner of war under the Geneva Convention, but such niceties were ignored by the Charleroi prison regime, as were any guidelines to an occupying power on its treatment of civilians. After some fourteen days Monique's mother was inexplicably released, but her father and the American remained with the thugs, who were determined to degrade and destroy them, both physically and mentally. Then, on 25 April 1944, a high-ranking SS officer was visiting the prison, and, to 'honour' their guest, ten prisoners were randomly selected for the firing squad. Thirty-nine-year-old Eugene Hupin was one of the ten and Ralph Palmer was dragged from his own cell and forced to watch the execution. This further reduced the American's morale, and his own barbarous treatment

A high-ranking SS officer was visiting the prison, and ten prisoners were randomly selected for the firing squad. Eugene Hupin paid the ultimate price for assisting Ralph Palmer. (*Monique Hupin*)

continued until, no longer of any value to the enemy, he was shipped to a POW camp. Returned to his family in California during 1945, Ralph Palmer was a broken relic of the eager young pilot whose ambition had been to fly even after a narrow escape in an AT-17 Bobcat during training. Aged only 25, his life had been ruined by the agonies inflicted on him and the burden of self-imposed guilt over Eugene's fate that for ever haunted him. Traumatized by this and his treatment from the Gestapo, Ralph spent the rest of his life in a veteran's mental institution until his death in the early 1980s. In later years, Janne and Monique Hupin wondered why their pilot had never made contact, but, in a sense, the Nazis had also executed him back in 1944.

Bravely facing such risks, other Belgians continued to resist, and several members of the Hussy's crew remained concealed in Lobbes, completely unaware of their pilot's fate in the nearby prison.

Bill Powell and the other seven crewmen who had avoided capture remained undiscovered thanks to the citizens of that small community, then boasting a population of some 5,000. Bill had been successfully transferred from the Croquet household to that of Mr and Mrs Gaston Gilbert and their daughter Renée at Entreville. Of necessity, Bill's life became furtive, but as the weeks elapsed he and Bill Williams, always vigilant, were allowed to emerge and even helped out on the land. But Bill Powell had not enlisted to hoe weeds. The only weeds he wanted to eradicate were strutting on the soil, not growing in it, and he was anxious to resume a more active role. Gaston Gilbert counselled his impatient young guest to remain in the town and let the war come to them, but Bill's frustration drove him to activity and his determination to return to combat prevailed. Passed along the line in April to Gondregnies, 16 rue du Marais, he was next sheltered by Charles and Sylvie Lepoivre with their three children, Lucie, Carmen and Marcel. The following month Bill Powell, Bill Williams and the radio operator, Robert Piarote, were taken to Brussels by Resistance operatives Victor Screyeu and Odette Grysfont. It was a walk of many miles, every step accompanied by fear. Superficially, the Americans might have blended in, but any false movement or non-European gesture could prove fatal. The simple slip of eating American-style in a café, a careless utterance or an accustomed military stance risked instant exposure. For the airmen, it usually meant a tough interrogation and shipment to a POW camp, but their escorts courted the cruelty of the dreaded Gestapo. It was a long chain, with a cellular structure to reduce risk, with cells functioning in isolation as far as practicable, but not all the links were robust. Members of one cell would not know others, but communication

required couriers, and brave Belgians of both genders and all ages quietly endangered their own lives shepherding airmen to freedom. They felt indebted to these fliers fighting on their behalf and this was the least they could do to help defeat the Nazi menace.

Bill Powell's journey down the line found him with false papers living, ironically, at 56 rue Américaine with Melle Flebus. While the secret army sought to move him safely on, it also provisioned for him, and records held by the famous Anne Brusselmans show that she covered his transport costs and some minor pharmaceutical expenses from 26 February until he left her section of responsibility several weeks later. Anne was later awarded the Belgian Croix de Guerre with palm leaf plus the British MBE for her role in rescuing Allied airmen. Born of a British mother and a Belgian father, Anne was fluent in English, and she played another prominent part in the Belgian Resistance. Papers passed to me by Larry Grauerholz of the Air Forces Escape and Evasion Society show that she interviewed Williams, Powell and Piarote to verify their accounts. It was not unknown for enemy agents to infiltrate posing as downed Allied airmen. The Hustlin' Hussy men were accepted, but several weeks elapsed, and it seems the intensity of enemy

Brave Belgians of both genders and all ages quietly endangered their own lives shepherding airmen to freedom. The Gilbert and Dumont families helped the airmen from Hustlin' Hussy. (*Bill Powell*)

activity and congestion or flaws further down the line made it too dangerous for them to remain in Brussels. On 1 June 1944, Bill Williams and Bill Powell returned to the countryside, but not to the Lepoivre family, whose home was full. Another aircraft had been shot down in the vicinity of Lobbes, so they had courageously sheltered seven new arrivals. With the Lepoivre home overcrowded, Bill Williams and Bill Powell were secured in the home of the Dumont family at Gages in the province of Hainaut.

Momentous events were about to unfold. On 6 June – D-Day – the fist of freedom punched a hole into Festung Europa's northern defences. While troops fought their way ashore with superb naval support and Allied aircraft secured supremacy over the beachhead, Bill's jubilation was tempered by impatience, but he was obliged to continue waiting. Four weeks went by – the British were capturing Caen and, far across the world, Japanese forces on the Marianas were being mopped up as Bill moped, still eager to rejoin the fray. Allied policy in Europe frowned on the return to operations of fliers who had been assisted in evading capture for the very sound reason that recapture jeopardized those that had assisted them. This was not applicable to fighting in the Pacific theatre, and the more Bill saw of the Axis powers the greater became his motivation to contribute to beating them. He would soon

experience the very core of their evil, but meanwhile his contribution to the war effort saw him whiling away the hours constructing a model of Hustlin' Hussy for 12-year-old Lucien Dumont. By now the Germans were jittery, and moving the evaders was extremely hazardous, but Bill's wishes were at last granted; he would be moved to Paris in preparation for transition to Spain or through the lines towards advancing Allied forces.

Leaving the kindly and intrepid people of Lobbes, Bill and three others of his crew were moved into Paris unaware that the Germans, supported by French traitors, had broken the line. On 3 August, the Gestapo swooped and all four were captured: Bill Powell, Bill Williams, Technical Sgt Arthur M. Pacha, the top-turret gunner, and Sgt Leo J. Reynolds, the ball-turret gunner, suddenly found themselves neatly netted, with no opportunity to resist or escape. Penetrating the line in numerous places, the Germans caught dozens of airmen and many of their gallant helpers. Victor Screyeu was captured; the entire Lepoivre family was arrested with the exception of Carmen. Rolling up the Resistance forces was a coup for the enemy and a devastating blow for those on the threshold of freedom – Paris was less than a month from liberation.

Bill found himself with scores of others in the notorious confines of Fresnes prison, a dauntingly ugly medieval-looking edifice in Paris where his claim to be an Allied airman and POW was completely ignored. Without a uniform and papers, he was regarded as an enemy agent and treated accordingly. Thrown with six others into a cell measuring only 6ft square, they were deprived of sleep and repeatedly dragged off for brutal interrogation. The constant clanging of heavily barred gates was punctuated by the frequent accompaniment of screams echoing down long, bleak corridors at any time of the day or night. Sanitation comprised an open bucket per cell and the scant food received was barely fit for human consumption. Their captors made their status as spies and saboteurs abundantly clear and their vermin-ridden existence was designed to deprive them of any human dignity, spirit or value. This was viciously emphasized by the constant crack of rifles. Every morning, they were made to watch other prisoners, men and women, being executed by firing squad. Some of the airmen endured their own executions, only realizing as fear evacuated the bladder that the breechblocks of the rifles that had just been 'fired' were empty. The message conveyed was simply and sadistically 'Your turn may really be next'. Bill Powell never reached the front of that grotesque queue. The frequency of Allied air raids now regularly shook the building, but hopes of deliverance vanished when, after about eight days, they were told they were leaving Fresnes – the prison was being evacuated. The airmen felt sure their destination would be Germany for interrogation and transfer to a standard prisoner-of-war camp. It was to be worse than this. Much worse.

Some 2,000 inmates of Fresnes, mostly French civilians, were to be transported to Germany. Frightening rumours circulated that they were bound for a concentration camp from which, many realized, they stood little chance of returning. Ensnared within this misery and despair were the Allied airmen. Bill feared for their future. Controlled by heavily armed guards, they were crammed into railway wagons, a press of humanity struggling to breath with more than ninety souls squashed into wagons that would have been 'full at thirty'. For rations on a

journey of unknown duration to an unknown destination, they were each allocated three meagre slices of bread and a 4in length of sausage. There was no latrine. Prisoners had no alternative but to urinate and defecate where they stood, so the stench soon became unbearable as the train clattered on through the midsummer heat. When stops were allowed, the Nazi mentality devised further methods of dignity deprivation. The locomotives would draw into German towns, where men and women were obliged to perform their ablutions in public, to jeers and taunting from the local populace. Further 'entertainment' saw prisoners callously beaten or whipped. Others were simply shot and their bodies discarded down the railway embankments. The airmen's hopes of interrogation at Frankfurt and the comparative safety of a POW camp vanished. Whatever their destination, they were clearly not to be prisoners of the Luftwaffe, and the horrors of the journey were about to be exceeded.

On 20 August 1944, the engine drew into a station before shunting its cattle trucks and their cargo of some 2,000 people – deprived, dirty and fearful – backwards down a siding towards a railway platform that presaged the entrance to hell. As the engine hissed menacingly to a standstill, the wagon doors were slammed aside by a reception committee of SS guards wielding guns and wooden staves or pick-axe handles. They were screaming at the bewildered, light-blinded incumbents 'raus, raus' (out, out) as their snarling dogs bit any prisoner in range. Within seconds it was bedlam, as the first blows fell upon those not moving fast enough to form the required columns. Soon, as these lines of ragged humanity approached enclosures through an entrance, mockingly almost ornate, Bill was shocked by the pathetic, semi-skeletal figures shuffling behind the barbed and electrified wire fencing interspersed with machine-gun towers. An atmosphere of despair permeated from within, and hopelessness slid like shackles around their souls as the gates swung shut.

Buchenwald was initially a work camp providing cheap labour. Ultimately, it was developed into a killing camp with all the heinous apparatus, processes and logistical arrangements for massacre and disposal of the bodies by cremation. Extraction of the resources was not overlooked. Fat was rendered into lubricant for greasing the Wehrmacht's wheels or those of the wagons delivering more 'material' into this demoniacal supply chain. Hair was saved for being woven into draperies – bones were crushed and pulverized for fertilizer. The Nazi 'culture' did retain some art-forms – tattooed human skins were stretched into frames and kept with a collection of shrunken heads and other specimens for the amusement of visiting dignitaries. The machinery of mass murders required for Hitler's 'Final Solution' demanded planning and transport, and later the resources directed to perpetuating this evil continued even as the Reich imploded.

Bill's political background was at the other end of the spectrum from this barbaric sanity created by an ideology in which cruelty was boundless and genocide a perverted policy. This, he realized, was the cost of abrogating democracy and basic human rights as enshrined in the US Constitution. He was now at the mercy of the evil he had been fighting. Now the enemy sought to further divest them of their respect and pride as soldiers serving in the armed forces of a nation defending freedom. Bill, like the others, had already been humiliated; they now faced further debasement and possible extermination. After all, who knew they were there?

All the new arrivals were stripped and their bodily hair was roughly shaved. Frightened, naked, surrounded by creatures accustomed to cruelty, the new arrivals were forced towards those notorious concentration-camp showers. Jammed in at gunpoint, Bill swallowed his own terror and felt that of others surrounding him. They knew the innocuous shower heads, visible in the dim, overhead lighting, might either spout water or be a macabre ruse while the deadly Zyklon-B gas was prepared, submitting them to the final torment. A mass of choking, convulsing, writhing humanity being asphyxiated, clawing upwards into that desperate pile of dead and dying for the last vestiges of air. Seconds passed as the final victims were forced in. The doors were closed. This could not be happening. Stark pipework along which would flow – what? The showers were turned on . . . pipes shuddered . . . it was water.

Moving on, they were issued with some threadbare clothing but no shoes. Further indignity transformed Bill from a 2/Lt in the USAAF, where he accepted his number with pride, into *Polizeizeihäftling* number 78296. Pacha was 78288; Reynolds 78292; Bill Williams became 78294. The numbers were not tattooed on their forearms as with other inmates – *Polizeizeihäftling* literally meant 'prisoner of the Gestapo'. They were not regarded as prisoners of war and lost even the little protection offered by that status. Given one blanket between four, they found themselves assigned to the 'Little Camp' in Horsestable Barracks, but they were not given any individual quarters and slept in the open, rotating in turns into the barracks. Buchenwald is located in picturesque woodland, cynically situated near the German cultural centre of Weimar, whose citizens would one day be forced to confront this embodiment of Nazi erudition on their doorstep. Even in August, the nights could be bitter and, as winter set in, the cold claimed many souls emaciated by lack of sustenance. Food was 'practically non-existent', with their daily ration comprising two slices of ersatz bread and a small bowl of soup in which it was not unknown to find human teeth. They had to adapt, and one group of fliers concealed a body for three days, duping the roll-call, simply to get his rations. Diarrhoea was prevalent and Bill's weight fell from 187lb when sheltered by the Belgians to around 118lb in his first four weeks in the camp.

Technically, the Konzentrationslager was still a work camp providing labour for nearby industry. Prisoners were cheap and disposable – they could be, and were, literally worked to death supporting the Reich's war economy. Factories located nearby made small arms ammunition and parts for the V2 rocket, but their output did not go unnoticed. On 24 August 1944, First Air Division B-17s raided Weimar, and, even though the casualties included slave workers, the Air Force inmates felt a palpable sense of pride. They knew the falling ordnance could not distinguish friend from foe, but the Americans were proud of those shiny Fortresses, embattled but resolute and majestic in the skies overhead. Heavy bombs crumped into German factories and blasted the SS barracks. The only damage to the camp was a shower of incendiaries setting the mess hall alight. After the attack, rumour held that the camp commandant's family had been killed. Reprisals were expected and, as the rumble of engines overhead rescinded, all the Air Force prisoners were forced to line up, fully expecting the Germans to exact revenge. Strangely, this did not transpire: they simply wanted a disciplined group to help extinguish the flames. Risking retaliation, the Allied

airmen hesitated but then realized that the lack of a mess hall only punished themselves and other even harder-pressed prisoners, so the *Polizeizeihäftling* helped douse the fire.

As *Polizeizeihäftling* was one category of prisoner, there were others denoted by coloured triangles sewn on their clothing. Yellow was for Jews; red for political prisoners; green for criminals; pink for homosexuals; purple identified its wearer as a Jehovah's Witness and black as 'anti-social', whatever that meant in the twisted minds of those in authority. Whatever the colour coding, the treatment was callous, but one class was specifically denoted to have no mercy shown and was selected for pitiless treatment. These were people decreed by Hitler in 1941 as 'Enemies of the Reich' and were marked in camp as *Nacht und Nebel* (night and fog). Men and women who wore *NN* were often partisans, Resistance workers and captured Special Operations Executives. Their heroism and courage cannot be lauded enough, and the sadistic treatment they suffered during Bill's period in the camp included several being bound then hung on butchers' hooks from nooses made of cheese wire. Their deaths were agonizingly prolonged before they were cut down and the corpses or those who were nearly dead were hoisted into the crematorium.

Bill knew that one of those netted in the penetration of the line assisting him included 35-year-old Victor, a father of three who had been his contact in Brussels, where Bill had gone to collect an identity card so he could travel. Victor, as an *NN* prisoner, fell victim to some of the most inhumane, sadistic treatment ever inflicted by members of the human race on fellow human beings. In 1941–2, at Buchenwald, Doctors Genzken and Mrugowsky, under the malevolent physician Dr Ding, distorted the Hippocratic oath and began medical experiments on helpless prisoners to support the needs of the German army. Buchenwald specialized in trials of unproven vaccines for various diseases faced by the Wehrmacht, particularly on the Russian front. These included typhus, smallpox and cholera, with hundreds of prisoners being murdered in these ghastly trials. The method used was to select a batch of prisoners, inject some with the vaccine but infect them all with typhus and study the outcome. Further despicable treatment saw some inmates given typhus for the sole and sickening purpose of using their bloodstreams as a 'bank' for storing the virus. Human life was of a value lower than the germs required for their experiments. During 1943, the Buchenwald-based perpetrators of these horrors were commended and their 'research station' became the 'Department for Typhus and Virus Research' headed by SS Sturmbannführer Dr Ding. Victor was selected for use in the typhus trials and deliberately infected. Somehow, Bill managed to see his friend in the so-called hospital. 'His legs were a mass of sores from the typhus being induced so as to test a medicine for curing it. In a few days Victor was dead but not before they had amputated his legs so further experiments could be conducted.'

Another form of torture was less complex and Bill never forgot the camp roll-call. 'This was the time the SS could show their cruelty. [The roll-call] lasted a minimum of three hours but often six to ten hours . . . We witnessed punishment to half-dead inmates for various petty crimes. The punishments consisted of hangings, whippings and others.' Some of these were simply too brutal for Bill to recall, but records of what the airmen witnessed come from other sources. One describes a prisoner kicked and beaten to death over a protracted period

simply to amuse the guards. It took the man twelve hours to die. This inhuman treatment saw him shuffling hopelessly away from his taunting tormentors, clutching his belly and trying to retain his intestines where they had literally kicked open his stomach. Bill did record other events.

One night a train arrived from Magdeburg with 400 Rumanian Jews. They had been in the boxcars for six days with very little food. At least 40 per cent of them died in the cars. A good many of them did not have the strength to leave the cars. Many more died when the SS turned the dogs loose on them. During roll-call that lasted three hours many more dropped by the wayside.

He continues:

In the fall of 1944 so many died that bodies lay in the open. The SS seemed powerless in the face of mass dying. There were 57,000 prisoners killed at KLB. Nature's call was answered atop of naked dead bodies. Savage struggles to death took place over the pitiful daily ration. It was almost impossible to get out of the crowded barracks at night time. The human mind is unable to picture these horrible scenes. To picture camp life you must understand the corruption and the intrigue in the prison hierarchy. It was a cut-throat, every man for himself atmosphere. The struggle to keep alive and avoid killing work details obsessed his mind. Remaining alive depended on one's physical condition, inner attitude and politics. You can imagine with only about 120 SS guards, the Germans used the prisoners to supplement their work. The Nazis with their peculiar minds provided leisure time as well as torture. Inmates assigned to easy work were in good enough shape to play soccer. The SS thought this was good advertising and provided impressive uniforms. In addition the SS set up a canteen mostly dispensing beer and some food. This was not free as they collected the small wages they paid some workers. There was also a brothel set up by importing women from Ravensbruck. The brothel was set up to further corrupt the prisoners and it worked on some . . . We are not sure how we were finally released from KLB. We think that Hermann Goering, head of the Luftwaffe, was helpful. Goering as well as many of the German heads of government had a villa at KLB. We think that he heard a BBC broadcast stating that there were airmen in KLB and not wanting to put his own fliers who were POWs in any danger of retaliation, he wanted us out.

On 19 October 1944, Bill and most of the other airmen were transferred to Stalag Luft III. Sagan, Stalag Luft III, in eastern Germany was a standard prisoner-of-war camp for fliers, where conditions, although severe, did not include the systematic torture and killing that were the hallmark of Buchenwald and the other concentration camps. However, like Buchenwald, its name has sombre associations following the cold-blooded murder of fifty Allied airmen after the 'great escape' in March 1944. Bill stayed at Sagan only three months, because, on 27 January 1945, the POW camp was evacuated. Prisoners were forced out on

foot into the teeth of a howling blizzard, thus beginning another challenge for survival. The Russian army's swift advance was threatening to overrun the camp and Germany did not want thousands of fighting men released as a resource for its enemies. There now commenced an infamous series of marches, with thousands of Allied POWs joining multitudes of refugees fleeing the Red Army. Already weakened by concentration-camp conditions, Bill found himself struggling within an enormous column of other frail, diseased, half-starved POWs. His circumstances were dire, but nothing matched the deprivations and depravity of Buchenwald. At one point, some of the former concentration-camp contingent baulked when pressed by their guards towards buildings with an ominously tall chimney. This time it was the simple sanctuary of warm straw on the floor of a brickworks, not a crematorium. Day after day, the lice-ridden, dysentery-stricken soldiers and airmen slogged westwards until another railway yard was reached. Once more, facing those feared box cars, Bill's spirits sank. Crushed in again, they endured another fearful journey. Again, there were disgusting unsanitary conditions, with one bucket to a wagon full of diarrhoea- and dysentery-sufferers. Added to this was the nightmare of being killed by one's own side, as Allied fighters foraged for German troop trains and marching columns. Tragically, the train was strafed, killing and wounding a number of POWs, but Bill's luck held, at least for the time being.

On Sunday, 4 February, their locomotive hauled slowly into Nuremburg, the south German city once a much-vaunted pillar of Nazi propaganda but now being steadily pounded by both British and American bombers. For the next eight weeks, this bombing simultaneously stimulated morale and terrified the prisoners, because the camp housing them, Stalag XIIID, was in perilous proximity to many targets and they suffered the constant

Bill Powell's POW identity card after his transferral to Stalag Luft III. (*Bill Powell*)

fear of 'friendly' bombs. Ordered to move again, the prisoners found that their next destination was Stalag VIIA at Moosburg, further south in the ever-shrinking Reich. Rail movement was now extremely hazardous, and the senior Allied officers simply refused to entrain. This stance risked provoking adverse German reactions, but there was no doubt that rail travel did indeed risk lives, and it was accepted that the prisoners could walk. Rumours now ricocheted like stray bullets – the POWs were marching south to become hostages in the last bastion of Hitler's power. They would be pawns to bargain with as the Allies drew closer. Whatever the truth, the situation was precarious, with many guards fanatically loyal to the Führer, and some prisoners were badly maltreated, even murdered, during this last weary and dangerous trek. Finally, the column struggled into Moosburg, now overflowing with a seething mass of mixed humanity facing appalling conditions, but Bill's determination to survive strengthened in what he knew was the denouement of a deadly regime. On 29 April 1945, following a heavy skirmish between the SS and General Patton's 3rd Army, it was over. The camp's swastika, a symbol of suppression and monstrous evil, succumbed to the fresh red, white and blue flag of freedom – a star-spangled banner. A few weeks later, Bill at last went home, but almost immediately went to a B-29 navigational school in readiness for transition to the Pacific theatre. He was en route in Oakland, California, when two other B-29s unleashed weaponry that even the fanatical Japanese were not prepared to confront further, and hostilities were quickly concluded. Bill could now begin rebuilding his life and, like other survivors of the camps, strive to sublimate the horrors of Buchenwald.

Bill Powell married, had children – he remained in the USAF until 1960 – became an accountant, built a successful business career and was an ordinary family man with an extraordinary tale hidden in his background. His three children, William, Pamela and Sharon, were raised far beyond the shadow cast by Buchenwald and, while proud of his achievements, were barely aware of the details behind his wartime imprisonment. Bill, like the other airmen confined to Buchenwald, kept these hidden for many decades. He was glad to be an American, but it saddened him that, in time, his democracy did not recognize that he and other American airmen had even been there. He later recalled the disbelief and denials encountered, such as an occasion when *Life* magazine carried a major feature on Buchenwald and Bill, sitting in his local barber shop, overheard dialogue doubting it had ever happened. This was dangerous, because doubts helped pave the path towards repetition. Concerned by this, Bill joined an exclusive group, following contact from a Canadian former inmate in the late 1970s. The Canadian had located a list of all Allied airmen incarcerated with him and initiated club KLB (Konzentrationlager Buchenwald) to vocalize more effectively the fact that 168 Allied airmen had been imprisoned in that horrific establishment. This included eighty-two American citizens, a situation not recognized or officially acknowledged by the US government. Joining KLB helped prompt Bill to undertake in 1984 a long-overdue pilgrimage to Lobbes, with his wife Yvonne, to thank its citizens for their valiant efforts. Instead, the stout-hearted people of that community turned the tables, and the modest American found himself fêted as the hero. At a luncheon in his honour, Bill made a short speech to the gathered townsfolk and Resistance veterans:

Your contribution to the winning of the war was tremendous. Many American and Allied fliers can attest to that. I can personally vouch for your contribution on my behalf. The sacrifices made and the dangers faced by the people of your town, and especially Mr and Mrs Gaston Gilbert and their daughter Renée, were multiplied by thousands of other Belgians who fought and sacrificed in their own way to help the cause of freedom in the world.

Bill also carried a letter from President Reagan, which he presented to the Burgemeister:

Forty years ago, the United States and Belgium fought a common enemy with heroism and sacrifice.

On January 29, 1944, an American B-17 bomber was badly crippled while returning from a mission over Germany. The crew was forced to bail out over German-occupied Belgium. At grave personal risk, the citizens of Lobbes took these airmen into their homes and into their hearts. The people of Lobbes were willing to sacrifice their lives for the freedom of Belgium and the continent of Europe. As a result, these eight crewmen survived the war. Your efforts helped secure the freedom of Western Europe. Today our countries are also engaged in the fight against forces that would take away the freedom our nations value so dearly. Your dedication to that freedom serves as a guiding light for all the world to see.

I salute your tribute to some of this world's bravest citizens. I pray that our continued commitment to freedom may some day make the world a united community of peace.

Twenty years later, the enemy has changed, but those words are sound guardians of a fundamental truth. Bill hoped that the President's endorsement would ensure that, at last, governmental recognition of the American presence in Buchenwald would follow; but official acknowledgement still took until the mid-1990s. Then, Republican Senator Tim Hutchinson introduced legislation in Congress to honour a unique group of American veterans, now dwindling in numbers. Bill also spoke more openly of his experiences and sent the author a recording of his recollections that has been a primary source for this insight into one of the most horrific episodes of modern times. Within this chapter we have witnessed the most despicable form of human behaviour, but counterbalancing this are the selfless acts of courage shown by ordinary people who risked and often gave their lives assisting Allied airmen. Their joint cause was the elimination of a cancerous creed and we of later generations are indebted but should never forget the lessons of history. The message conveyed to us by Bill Powell's Buchenwald memories should be a warning and we ignore it at our peril. Bill did not seek recognition of his experiences for personal benefit but simply to remind us to guard our democratic freedoms, often taken for granted, and to assist others in achieving them.

Bill Powell died on Tuesday, 5 August 1997. This chapter is dedicated to him and his crew, to the Resistance and to the memory of the countless others for whom the world must always weep.

CHAPTER THREE

By Day and by Night

Dawn on Dunsfold aerodrome in Surrey that March morning revealed a strange
spectacle. Sitting forlornly on the field was the USAAF B-17, serial 42-38124,
'Passionate Witch' of the 728th Bomb Squadron, 452nd BG. In a grotesque parody
of two giant insects exposed mating, an RAF Lancaster had seemingly attempted to mount
the American bomber. The force of impact had sheared some 20 feet from the Boeing's
starboard wing and knocked the No. 4 engine completely off its mounting to droop wearily
on the grass. Eighth Air Force photographer Russell J. Zorn photographed the scene and
pondered on events leading to this strange encounter. His images of two battle-damaged
bombers still symbolize the dangers faced by Allied aircrew, by day and by night.

Sgt George A. Silva had already flown seven deep-penetration missions to Germany and
would have welcomed a milk run, but, on 20 March 1944, the crew of Passionate Witch was
cursed with ten hours to Frankfurt. George did not know his fellow crewmen well. A slip on
the ice at Presque Isle, Maine, had changed his fortunes. Originally assigned to 2/Lt Charles
C. Young Jr's crew, George had trained with them at Moses Lake, Washington, before
heading overseas in December 1943. Stopping over at Presque Isle, the crew were told to
collect their subsistence allowance from Hangar One. As they trudged through fresh snow, it
was inevitable that their boisterous spirits would see a snowballing opportunity, and
moments later the air was thick with 'flak'. Dodging an incoming snowball, George slipped,
crashing headlong onto the ice. Luckily, two Air Force nurses were on hand to tend the 'shot-
down' hero. Had George not felt so dizzy, their ministrations might have been quite
pleasurable, but the nurses were punctilious on Air Force regulations, one of which dictated
five days' hospitalization for head trauma. His protestations were defeated by the bruise
demonstrably increasing in size on his head. So, while George was detained for observation,
his crew departed for duty overseas. They kept his personal kit, assuming he would soon
catch up, but three weeks elapsed before George arrived in England at Deopham Green, the
452nd's north Norfolk airbase. His crew, already operational, had been obliged to secure a
replacement radio operator.

George made one mission with them as a waist gunner, then 1/Lt Robert M. Cook's crew
also required a replacement radio operator and George was assigned. Unfortunately, their

1/Lt Robert M. Cook's crew. *Rear left to right*: Staff Sgt Richard L. Thayer, waist gunner; Hubert Roughton (not on board); Technical Sgt Gerald H. Poplett, top-turret gunner; Staff Sgt Carl H. Blichmann, ball-turret gunner; Staff Sgt John C. McLaughlin, tail gunner. *Front left to right*: 1/Lt Robert M. Cook, pilot; 2/Lts Ronald J. Casey, co-pilot; John F. Osswalt, navigator; John A. Rowland, bombardier. (*Tim Thayer*)

bivouac was full and some distance from his Nissen hut, so this curtailed much of the customary camaraderie and bonding between crew members. The crew had already named their B-17G 'Passionate Witch' from the humorous novel of the same name by Thorne Smith. His main character, a young, fun-loving white witch, looked after the man in her life, so the crew hoped their witch would do likewise, plurally. Not having been involved in the early days, George did not feel entirely assimilated even after six missions, and now, flying his eighth, he reflected that he had flown over 68 hours in the black witches' cauldron of German airspace. Today, events were not proceeding as planned. Their defensive formation had been loosened by strong winds and clouds towering to 27,000 feet. B-17s, dispersed by weather conditions, lost their mutually defensive firepower, and scattered ranks thinned the cover available from their fighter escort, creating gaps for enemy interceptors. Rendezvous

Fighting like a demon, spent casings clattering to the fuselage floor, Dick Thayer leapt from left to right waist gun, aiming repeated bursts. (*Tim Thayer*)

arrangements failed and many bombers abandoned the mission, thus further depleting defensive coherence.

The 452nd had struggled on but adjusted its ambitions to the secondary target, Frankfurt. Reaching the initial point (IP), the 452nd turned to begin its run in. A flurry of aggressive flak bracketed the aircraft at the IP, but eased in quantity if not accuracy over the target. Freed from the burden of her bomb load, Passionate Witch set course for home amid the caverns and canyons of cloud – beautiful, but deadly for being ambushed. Passionate Witch lost the formation in the overcast, so Cook, ordering extra vigilance, turned the weather to advantage as they slid warily through the concealing cloudscape.

In the vicinity of Paris their protection evaporated, exposing the lone B-17, and Passionate Witch was soon discovered by a pack of prowling Me 109s and Fw 190s. At least eight enemy fighters pounced, and, as the intercom crackled with terse warnings, her crew knew they needed every spell in the witch's armoury. Guns were primed, ready to mete out their own unpleasant potions as gunners tracked their swiftly incoming assailants. Moments later, the B-17 shuddered as the first punishing exchange occurred. Tracer flashed defiantly towards the enemy as German shells lacerated the bomber, savaging the fuselage in their first pass. Left waist gunner Sgt Hubert C. Roughton was severely wounded when an exploding 20mm round hit him in the chest. Saved only by the density of his chest-pack parachute, he fell back into the fuselage with the ruined parachute now useless. His companion, right waist gunner Sgt Richard L. Thayer, was also seriously wounded, but, ignoring the severe pain and blood gushing from leg wounds, defiantly manned both waist guns. Fighting like a demon, with spent casings clattering to the fuselage floor, Dick Thayer leapt from left to right waist gun, aiming repeated bursts. Numerous vicious attacks were deterred, but Passionate Witch still suffered additional punishment despite her vigorous riposte. In the mêlée of a desperate battle, her gunners claimed two enemy fighters destroyed and two damaged during a succession of attacks. Determination, skill and courage kept them aloft as Lt Cook and his co-pilot, 2/Lt Ronald J. Casey, even used fighter-type tactics, banking the big Boeing into the oncoming enemy aircraft, forcing them to break off their attacks or collide. Despite their efforts, further cannon and machine-gun fire raked through the fuselage, now wounding their tail gunner, Sgt John C. McLaughlin, in the back. Sweating and working hard at their controls, both pilots knew the odds: the outcome was inevitable unless they could evade their adversaries. Their only hope was the sanctuary of cloud cover and they fled in a desperate, diving, running fight, snapping back when cornered, then running again.

In the radio compartment, George frantically broadcast SOS messages, pleading for friendly fighter protection to remove these fiends assaulting the Passionate Witch. Clinging on, he flinched instinctively when enemy fire hammered home and, demonstrating the ferocity of combat, a piece of still-smoking shrapnel embedded itself in his radio table, having narrowly missed him. Then the blue world of violence vanished as they slid into a cloudbank's grey haven. Teamwork, discipline and sheer determination had carried the day – so far. One engine was now useless, air shrieked through punctures in perspex and aluminium, but the rugged bomber kept going. Ceasing transmission, George went aft to assist the ball-turret gunner, Staff Sgt Carl H. Blichmann, clamber from his claustrophobic

confines into the fuselage. They had shaken off the enemy but home was still more hope than reality as navigator Lt John Osswalt calculated their course, distance and chances.

Cautiously descending from cloud, they knew that safety dictated staying low, hiding in the contours and using their olive-drab camouflage to best effect. Crippled or not, the crew were tired of being on the receiving end, and gunners used this hedge-hopping opportunity to deal a few blows. Barely above the tree-tops, George joined in as they machine-gunned a radio station and delighted in catching off-guard one of the hated flak towers. Other beneficiaries of this leaden largesse were a steam locomotive and a tugboat. Over France, they received countless gestures of support from farm workers toiling below, and their exchanged victory signs offered mutual encouragement. Cresting one hill, they flew over a gun battery, whose less welcoming gesture smashed a shell clean through the bomb-bay catwalk, but still the witch's magic kept her airborne. Then, at last, the coast lay just ahead. Following an estuary, Passionate Witch exchanged fire with the coastal defences; then, as the battered B-17 crossed seawards, dipping to wave-top height, huge geysers erupted from heavy-calibre shells exploding in the sea. At one point, the B-17 punched through a wall of water thrown up in her path. The shock of hitting it almost wrested control from the pilots, but, shaking water off like a dog on the beach, Passionate Witch emerged and stubbornly kept going. Leaving the French coastline, the bedraggled bomber, carrying three wounded gunners, had one engine feathered, an aileron shot away, holes in her wings, fuselage and tail, unserviceable hydraulics, some control cables almost severed and no intercom. The gallant witch had a touch of magic keeping her aloft, but only just, and the crew now began discarding any excess weight. Machine guns, ammunition, flak jackets all tumbled seawards, as they limped home. They needed an airfield, but miles of water slid by uncomfortably close before the English coastline hove into view and they edged gratefully inland, searching for an airbase. South-west of London, the RAF aerodrome at Dunsfold was a welcome sight.

Cook ordered his crew to their crash positions as he eased Passionate Witch lower. No hydraulics meant no brakes and he needed every blade of grass the airfield had to offer. Lowering the undercarriage, Cook committed himself to landing and prayed the landing gear would not collapse through battle damage. Crossing the boundary, he dropped smoothly and felt the B-17 touch then settle to rumble unsteadily across the aerodrome. Lacking brakes and steering, the B-17 meandered wearily onwards before drifting nonchalantly off the runway and rolling to a halt. The three functioning propellers juddered to a standstill as the bomber decanted a grateful crew and RAF medical personnel clambered in to assist the wounded. Those uninjured gaped disbelievingly at the condition of the aircraft and began to count the perforations. Large holes, tiny punctures – the number kept climbing until they gave up and estimated some 2,000! Staying airborne must have been witchcraft – Passionate Witch had woven a spell fit for the angels. Now, her job done, the crew felt guilty abandoning her to the Repair and Recovery crew for assessment to repair or salvage. Whatever their decision, the battle-scarred bomber testified to Boeing's rugged design and manufacturing prowess.

Returning to Deopham Green, George Silva could be forgiven for thinking his original crew assignment might have been safer; but destiny rations luck. Three days later, the

It was the fourth sortie for the crew of RAF 103 Squadron Lancaster ND 572 PM-M, M-Mother. Photographed on the morning of 24 March 1944. *Left to right*: Sgt Jack Spark, wireless operator; Plt Offs Ron Walker, navigator; Norman Barker, bomb aimer; Sgts Arthur Richardson, flight engineer; Fred Brownings, pilot; Ken Smart, mid-upper gunner; Bob Thomas, rear gunner. *(Jack Spark DFM)*

roulette wheel of life in the Eighth Air Force turned once more when the Charles Young crew were attacked by fighters near Rodenbeck. Their B-17 exploded in a sickening fireball vomiting the remains of men and aircraft earthwards in ugly, smoking tendrils of twisting, burning debris. There were just two survivors. George realized that a slip on the ice had probably spared his life – but fate had only forestalled events for 39034221 Sgt George Silva.

While George contemplated his future, or lack of it, another radio operator was preparing to take the night shift. It was the fourth sortie for the crew of RAF 103 Squadron Lancaster ND572 PM-M, M-Mother. Leaving their airfield at Elsham Wolds, Lincolnshire, they faced a gruelling haul to a target feared by bomber crew in both daylight and darkness – Berlin, the capital of tyranny. Sgt Jack Spark sensed his crew's disquiet, noting with concern the loss of their customary exuberance and pre-flight banter. From his radio operator's seat, he felt an unwelcome premonition permeating all 69 feet of fuselage; but duty prevailed as each man suppressed his fears and busied himself for take-off and the dark journey ahead. M-Mother's four Rolls-Royce Merlins lullabied her into the night sky at 2130 hr and sang sweetly over the North Sea into Denmark and the domain of German night-fighters.

Tail gunner Sgt Bob Thomas saw it first, a twin-engined, heavily-armed Junkers 88 closing in from astern like a hooded assassin, dagger raised. Bob's swift cry of alarm prompted skipper Flt Sgt Fred Brownings to throw the Lancaster over in a tight, diving turn to starboard. A flash of tracer cut empty sky and the night-fighter skimmed close overhead but lost his intended prey in the darkness. Thwarted, the Ju 88 vanished, undoubtedly seeking easier meat elsewhere. Navigator Plt Off Ron Walker's Canadian twang came calmly over the intercom with a heading for resuming their course. Jack now tuned in to Bomber Command's weather broadcast and passed the information to Ron, who soon realized the size of the discrepancy between the figures from HQ and his own calculations. Briefed to expect tail winds of 60mph, Ron was calculating double that – 120mph winds pushing the bombers into Germany. M-Mother was part of a sixty-strong force backing up pathfinder aircraft for the main bomber stream of over 900 aircraft, and that old adversary, the weather, was wreaking havoc with British plans. Jack's transmission of corrected wind speed met disbelief in Bomber Command HQ. Ignoring these warnings, it continued to issue signals advising the original 60mph and the outcome was chaos. Jack's crew, like many others, found themselves forced into 'dog-legging' (zigzagging) to maintain planned time over target. This process consumed petrol they could ill afford once they turned to contest the wind on their homeward journey.

Reaching the target, M-Mother had settled on its bomb run when the concealing darkness vanished in the blinding power of enemy searchlights. The Lancaster was caught in the lights, and Fred tilted it into a power dive, trying to outrace the lights exposing them to flak and fighters alike. For a 30-second eternity, the searchlights followed them down through a tumult of flak-savaged sky, then, mercifully, the night sky once more embraced them. Having outrun the searchlights and not wishing to prolong their presence, the crew released their contribution to the target statistics and gratefully turned M-Mother homewards.

Watching to starboard, Jack saw a German night-fighter coned by searchlights receiving the same violent reception. A single flare emerged from the ensnared enemy aircraft and burst as a double star, one red, one white; abruptly, the guns ceased, the searchlights were doused. Jack noted the colours for the intelligence officer. Their own antics over the target had detached them from the mainstream, and, clear of Berlin, Fred asked his crew for a consensus. Should they go round Berlin to rejoin the main force for safety in numbers or continue alone? Fuel calculations persuaded them to risk the night-fighters and continue independently. A fateful decision. A few minutes later, Bob again cried out an alert, 'Enemy aircraft dead astern, corkscrew port. Go!' The corkscrew was a violent but effective evasive action that, hopefully, twisted a bomber out of danger. This time it was too late. A burst of fire from a marauding Fw 190 blazed into the Lancaster. Jack was thrown from his seat just as cannon and machine-gun fire ripped through his compartment, smashing the radio to pieces. Outmanoeuvring the already stricken Lancaster, the agile Fw 190 made another two withering attacks. Not a religious man, Jack huddled on the floor through a storm of bullets. Frightened, he found himself singing 'O God Our Help in Ages Past'. It was as if he was heard by the Almighty, for the violence ceased – the Fw 190 had presumably exhausted its

ammunition. Amazingly, all four Merlins still pounded reassuringly. No fire. It seemed normal. But it was not. Clambering to his feet, Jack peered in disbelief from his tiny window at a gaping hole in the port wing. Some 6 feet of aluminium skinning had gone, exposing one of the main tanks. Fred had no idea how his crew had fared and the intercom was out, so a handwritten note passed from the navigator told Jack to check on those aft, and could he fix the intercom?

Calm now, Jack found the intercom set itself was undamaged, but he knew there could be a disconnection in the cabling further aft. He decided he would check as he accounted for the crew. They were still at 20,000 feet, so Jack took a torch and a portable oxygen bottle before setting off astern. In the Lancaster, this entailed clambering over the main spar, and Jack stared in disbelief at the damage beyond. A gale of slipstream howled in through a gaping hole in the fuselage. Where the mid-upper gunner's foot-bar should be was just space with a pair of legs simply dangling free. Fearing for the gunner, Sgt Ken Smart, Jack apprehensively tapped one of the legs and shone his torch, peering upwards into the turret. A reassuring thumbs up told him Ken was fine, although the hydraulics for his turret had been destroyed and restricted its defensive capabilities. Nearing the end of his single, 10-minute bottle, Jack returned to collect three more before resuming his journey down the fuselage. Struggling past Ken's turret, Jack headed towards the rear gunner's position some 20 feet away. Nearing Bob's isolated station, Jack swung the beam for a better view and almost vomited at the scene illuminated. Cannon shells had shredded the body of 19-year-old Bob Thomas, spattering his remains throughout the rear fuselage and shattered remnants of his turret. Jack had never seen a corpse and the sight of his bullet-riddled friend would for ever haunt him. Unable to remove Bob's body from the turret, Jack focused his thoughts on damage repair and, groping with plugs and cabling, was lucky enough to reconnect the intercom before his oxygen supply was exhausted. Communication restored, Jack conveyed the grim news of Bob's death. Only hours earlier they had posed proudly in front of their Lancaster for a series of crew photographs. Now, the badly damaged bomber was Bob's funeral bier and they were still far from home, facing 120mph headwinds and struggling to keep airborne. To avoid complete loss of control, the skipper had wedged his knees against the control column to compensate for trim controls that had been totally destroyed. With no tail gunner, and the mid-upper turret's hydraulics shot away, they were virtually defenceless in a bomber poised on the edge of total instability.

Then, once again, searchlights coned them. Unable to evade, they were like a rabbit in headlights. It took

Cannon shells had shredded the body of 19-year-old Bob Thomas. (*Jack Spark DFM*)

only seconds for anti-aircraft gunners to range. Any moment, M-Mother could be nothing but a flash of destruction, an incandescent omega of men and machine. Then Jack remembered the German night-fighter's predicament. Checking his flares, he found three red and three white and, without delay or orders, fired one of each into the night sky. It worked! Assuming the target to be friendly, the gunners ceased and darkness enveloped them. M-Mother droned unsteadily onwards.

Eventually able to take a positional fix, Ron found they were in mid-Channel but heading for the Atlantic, so rapidly calculated a new heading. Correcting their course, they turned for the south coast, searching for an airfield. Unfortunately, a German attack by over 140 aircraft on London had caused all airfield lighting to be switched off and the destruction of their transmitter had cut air-to-ground communication. Then, in the black desert below, an airfield beacon flashed its coded identity. Hastily checking his code book, Jack deciphered the call sign for Dunsfold in Surrey. Still unable to land without runway lights, Jack now fired red flares, hoping they would be correctly interpreted. After some anxious seconds, the runway lights came on and Fred offered his crew a final opportunity to bail out rather than risk a crash landing. Jack kept to himself the knowledge that his parachute had been destroyed, but all elected to stay with Fred and take Bob's body home, confident in their pilot's ability to land the crippled Lancaster.

Like their American counterparts but in nocturnal contrast, the crew of M-Mother braced themselves in crash positions with backs against the main spar. Slipping carefully a few feet beyond the threshold, Fred judged his moment and M-Mother delicately caressed terra firma. The transition from air to ground seemed fine until the bomber's weight settled. Only then did they realize that one of the main wheel tyres had been pierced and the drag of its shredded remains slewed the speeding aircraft left, off the runway, beyond the lights and into the darkness beyond. Bracing themselves, her crew tensed for the terror of impact, fire and explosion. Still travelling fast, the Lancaster suddenly crunched into something solid and stopped abruptly. For the briefest of moments, no one moved, then motivated by the stench of 100-octane fuel, her crew leapt for their lives.

Outside, they found themselves alone on the airfield enjoying, for a moment, the sweetness of early morning air. The ambulance and crash tender had lost sight of the bomber when it had drifted off the illuminated runway into the darkness and were now searching for their lost Lancaster. When they eventually found M-Mother, all involved gaped in disbelief at the scene illuminated by the ambulance headlights. The black-bellied British bomber had embedded itself in the starboard wing of an American Flying Fortress without either aircraft exploding. While the medical officer and ambulance personnel extricated Bob's body from his rear turret, Jack had time for a closer look at the B-17. It, too, had obviously taken a pasting and he wondered about the fate of her crew. Even though M-Mother was dear to him, Jack conceded that one Lancaster Mk III was much like any other. That the broken-backed B-17G had also meant something to her crew became evident not by its serial number or unit markings but in a name painted on her starboard cheek, Passionate Witch. Bomber Command lost seventy-three aircraft that night, which became infamous as the 'night of the big winds'. Jack survived

this and twenty-six further operations before being rested as an instructor. He was awarded the DFM and commissioned in December 1944. Amazingly, ND572 was repaired and flew on with 57 Squadron before being lost in a mid-air collision on 2 March 1945. Jack never forgot the Passionate Witch and wondered what had befallen her crew.

Dick Thayer was frustrated after a week in hospital. His wounds were healing and he was anxious to rejoin his crew before he missed too many missions with them. Unbeknown to Dick, he had been recommended for his nation's highest award, the Medal of Honor, for his courage and tenacity in manning both waist guns despite being badly wounded. Part of the award process required interviews, but Dick never attended them because destiny had not finished with the crew of Passionate Witch. Assigned a replacement B-17G, serial 42-32082, they immediately named it 'Passionate Witch 2'. George's desire for milk runs rather than the terrors of German airspace came with two consecutive missions that Dick missed, both against enemy airfields now being attacked more often because of their proximity to the area proposed for the invasion. D-Day was only ten weeks away and heavy bombers were increasingly being used against tactical targets. Finally, Dick wangled his way out of hospital and resumed his role as left waist gunner. Hubert Roughton, still hospitalized and destined to be invalided home, had been replaced by Staff Sgt Fremont H. Granade in the ball turret, while Carl Blichmann had moved into the right waist gun position. Dick now joined the crew for yet another theoretical 'milk run', an attack on the Luftwaffe, this time the airbase near Chateaudun, also favourably positioned to threaten the invasion beaches and currently home to German heavy-bomber and night-fighter units.

Passionate Witch 2 was in the Low Lead Squadron and the B-17 formation flew relatively unmolested in clear skies with bright sunshine hinting of spring to come. The target lay in a landscape of rich, arable land being earnestly tended by a rural population whose roles continued as wars and governments came and went. Only a few days earlier, Dick had seen them at work much closer to hand. From bombing altitude, agricultural detail was lost, but the rich pattern of green and brown, evidence of man's more peaceful preoccupation, contrasted sharply with the purpose of airbase gunners racing to their emplacements and bombardiers peering earthwards, each intent on target destruction. Conditions offered clarity both ways. Desultory fire trailing them over France grew more intense, and, as a countermeasure, George Silva and other radio operators were busily engaged thrusting bundles of chaff down chutes cut into the fuselage of each aircraft. Bursting into the slipstream, each shimmering strip of foil decoyed itself on enemy radar as an aircraft. It was not guaranteed and German anti-aircraft units could offset its effectiveness by varying the frequency settings on their Würzburg radar units. These gunners were efficient and several 452nd aircraft suffered damage as the flak further intensified, but the group was also good at its job and the Flying Fortresses remained resolutely steady on their bombing run despite shuddering through residual shockwaves from shells exploding nearby.

On board Passionate Witch 2, John Rowland was once more engaged in his craft as he worked at his bombing control panel, where instruments provided altitude, speed and additional key information, while he tracked the lead aircraft. The lead bomber initiated

Moments later a second round burst between the Nos 3 and 4 engines and the fuel tanks exploded. Passionate Witch 2 is pictured spinning down in flames. (*USAF Official*)

release by the formation at the mean point of impact. Calculations allowed for wind speed, drift and the bomb-type's trajectory to predict a release point and plot of fall. Far below, gun predictor personnel were rapidly making their own calculations in azimuth and elevation for aircraft speed and height to predict a position for the timed shells to explode. War was mathematics; men and lives were incidental and any magic surrounding Passionate Witch 2 was about to be destroyed in the sorcery of lightning bolts flung heavenwards. A detonating shell destroyed the nose compartment, perhaps killing John Rowland and navigator, John Osswalt. Cook's call on the intercom went unanswered and the devastated nose section meant the occupants were dead, or badly wounded, or, horrifically, had been blown out of the aircraft.

George heard his pilot say they had lost the bombardier and navigator but never discovered exactly what happened. Moments later, a second round burst between the Nos 3 and 4 engines and the fuel tanks exploded, ripping off the starboard outer engine and some 40 feet of wing. In microseconds of sheer terror, George had no time to don his chest pack. The world as viewed from his tiny radio room window rolled sickeningly over, sky became ground and a vision of an earth spiralling below swung across the larger window overhead as Passionate Witch 2 rotated into a vicious spin. Tumbling from his seat, George fell amid

bundles of chaff, and his parachute pack floated past, just out of reach. George felt himself lifted and pressed against the fuselage like 'going downhill in a barrel' as the B-17's rate of gyration increased. Struggling to move, he barely managed to catch his parachute. With leaden arms, he fought to clip it to his harness, as centrifugal reaction increasingly suppressed his freedom of movement, finally immobilizing him inside the doomed bomber. Pinned down, George knew he was going to die. Now or in an instant from now – he had no sense of time or how far he had fallen. His life would end in an evisceration of violence on some foreign field. Even his eyelids had been forced shut – death had blindfolded him as he spun round and round, ever falling in a real-life nightmare. Suddenly, something exploded. George heard the screech of metal being literally torn apart and, instantly, he was slapped by cold air. Now able to open his eyes, he found himself accelerating clear of surrounding debris and tugged his ripcord. Surely he would slam to earth before his parachute opened? A loud smack of silk and it seemed he was tugged backwards as the parachute deployed. Strangely, streams of dots were crossing his vision and, now in gentle descent, he realized these were dozens of bombs falling past him from the rear echelon of his formation.

Nearing the ground, he observed a gun emplacement, perhaps the very one that had put him in this predicament. He wanted to turn away, but the Army Air Force had not expected him to leave its aircraft and he was untrained in parachute-steering techniques. However, Hollywood had given him a few tips – something to do with pulling really hard on the shroud lines in the direction you wanted to go. Emulation of some forgotten celluloid hero now nearly killed him, as his efforts partially collapsed the canopy and sent him plummeting earthwards. He hastily let go of the lines, and the parachute luckily reopened, depositing him only 100 yards from the gun emplacement. He was swiftly captured, but, before being bundled away, George caught sight of tail gunner John C. McLaughlin lying nearby and being cared for by the Germans. He had a broken arm, a broken leg and was coughing up blood – indicative of an internal haemorrhage. In a small compassionate gesture, the Germans allowed George a few moments to comfort his comrade and pass him a cigarette. Mac was taken to Orleans hospital, where he died of his wounds on 29 March. George saw no other survivors.

On the bomb run, Dick Thayer was mentally counting down to release. Against fighters he could retaliate; against flak he felt helpless, with prayer seeming the only protection. Anxiously anticipating the familiar lift as Passionate Witch 2 disgorged her bomb load, then the relief of manœuvring clear, he saw instead the flak ranging in on them, stepping closer. The blast when they were hit threw Dick to the floor – which suddenly became the ceiling, as the B-17 rolled over into her death throes. Frozen in place, all Dick could see was a vision of his parents. Spurred by their love and the loss he wanted to spare them, his resolve strengthened and, somehow, he fought his way to an escape hatch and fell clear as the aircraft exploded. Falling now, he was surrounded by burning debris and opening his parachute risked setting it alight, so he deliberately delayed pulling his D-ring until the earth's rapid approach gave him no choice. He was descending onto the target and, when his canopy burgeoned, he was amid 'bombs . . . coming down by the hundreds'. Fortunately, a strong

wind swept him out of that danger and away from explosions below. He was now drifting over a gun battery, comprising, he noted, eighteen guns – just as he remembered being told at briefing. Landing unharmed, he had no chance of escape, and, seemingly alone, he wondered if there had been other survivors.

The pilot, Robert M. Cook, somehow survived his B-17 disintegrating violently around him and rapidly became another guest of the Third Reich. Six of his crew perished when Passionate Witch 2 exploded 2km south of Chateaudun. Poor Mac lived only hours and the three survivors were soon processed into captivity. Dick Thayer found himself at Stalag 17B near Krems in Austria when the award of a Silver Star was promulgated for his father to accept on his behalf. Only later did he learn of the Medal of Honor recommendation. Initially, conditions at Stalag 17B were tolerable, but the latter part of 1944 saw a marked deterioration in food supplies. He later recalled, 'About the only thing the Germans fed us was soup made of dehydrated cabbage and other dehydrated products . . . the only thing in that soup that hadn't been dehydrated was the worms.' Warmth also became a problem and the 'Kriegies' – the prisoners' own adaptation of the German word Kriegesgefangener (prisoners of war) – soon resorted to removing anything combustible from their surroundings. Buildings and bunks soon acquired the skeletal proportions of their occupants, but encouraging news circulated from secret radios told them the war's end must now be only weeks away. Other, more sinister news also circulated about Germany's treatment of subjugated peoples, particularly the Jews. Descriptions of Nazi atrocities were at first disbelieved by the Americans. For the majority of US prisoners, the treatment had been hard but not brutally dehumanizing, even after they had witnessed Allied aircraft bombing nearby targets. Soon, all were to be exposed to the true nature and horror of their oppressor's tyranny.

On Easter Sunday 1945, the POWs were ordered to march west, away from the advancing Russians. Dick, raised to accept American small-town standards of decency and mid-Western security, was appalled by events witnessed on the 180-mile forced march.

I saw a large group of Jews being driven along the road by the Germans. They were pitiful cases. When they stopped to eat, many of them got down on the ground and ate grass like a grazing heifer. When they were ordered to move on, I saw nine of them too weak to get up. The German guards killed all nine as we looked on. They shot 'em like rabbits with no more concern than you would step on an ant. They made believers [of the atrocities] out of us.

Marching west was at least the right direction, so Dick made no effort to escape, although maps, emergency provisions and other items to support an escape were kept hidden for immediate use if necessary. The war's denouement found Dick with hundreds of other prisoners, their guards and elements of the German army hiding in woodland so close to Allied lines that American forces were visible across a nearby river. Fears that the German army would embroil the POWs in a desperate, last-stand bloodbath and bring 'friendly fire' pouring in on them diminished as the hours passed. On 3 May 1945, following the

George Silva, now the only living survivor of the crew.

surrender of local German forces, the 13th Armored Division of the 3rd Army liberated the jubilant prisoners.

Decades later, an elderly ex-RAF radio operator was troubled by the memory of a B-17 called Passionate Witch and contacted the US Embassy. Following an investigative trail, Jack Spark eventually located George Silva, now the only living survivor of the crew, and the two veteran radio operators, exchanging stories, became firm friends. From this friendship came mutual respect and admiration. These two octogenarians themselves symbolize a generation of courageous young airmen, volunteers from democratic nations, who took war to the heart of a grotesque dictatorship and fought it relentlessly by day and by night.

CHAPTER FOUR

God Save Me! God Save Me!

One of the most fascinating, rewarding and downright dangerous digs I have experienced was during the autumn of 1972. In those distant, unregulated days, the only requirement for recovering aircraft wreckage was a landowner's blessing, finance and enthusiasm. Nowadays, one requires foreknowledge of the aircraft's identity to obtain a licence, so the excitement of excavation in a quest to identify is largely a thing of the past. All we knew about the bomber buried at Great Horkesley on the Essex–Suffolk border was its type – a B-24 Liberator.

To discover its full story, we simply intended to unearth what remains there were for a serial number to unlock relevant records. While other, slightly saner, enthusiasts were engrossed in observing then state-of-the-art technology at Farnborough, the weekend of 9–10 September 1972 saw the first soil being scraped off a steeply sloping field on Ridgnalls Farm with appreciation being expressed to landowner Peter Rix. The field's gradient would soon precipitate a drama for us diggers, but my late arrival on site started with its own degree of excitement when I unwittingly met a specimen of Britain's only potentially lethal snake. Hearing the stimulating sound of a busy JCB backhoe, I ran down the slope, to be called by Stewart Evans, gesticulating from the far side of a ragged hedge. He was pointing towards a gap leading to the site, but, not seeing it, I stopped to shout over for guidance. I then heard an angry, sibilant hiss and, not comprehending its direction, paused to figure it out. It came from my boots! Looking down, I saw my left foot was firmly planted behind the head of a large and very angry adder. Stewart later related how, one second I was there – the next I was several feet skywards in a take-off the envy of any Harrier pilot. Snakes may be fast but I beat this one and, landing beyond striking distance, watched it slither away, dignity restored. I presume the autumnal sunshine was ideal for a quiet snooze until the sudden arrival of a size-nine boot spoiled his day. I scurried off in the opposite direction for less zoological companionship, but this was only the first danger this site had in store for me.

Reaching the dig, I saw some exciting finds had already been unearthed, including the tail assembly with one of the fins clearly marked with a large, dark blue T in an off-white square. This immediately identified our aircraft as from the 490th BG based at Eye in Suffolk.

Further information was dramatically given by another section of the tail still bearing the bright yellow stencilling 294835, so there, beyond doubt, was the identification we sought. These discoveries delighted us and we were further pleased to welcome on site the renowned Eighth Air Force author and historian Roger Freeman, a guru in matters Eighth. As a youngster living nearby, Roger had a personal connection with this aircraft and later wrote, 'I personally witnessed the B-24 crash on 29th May 1944. It was one of the most frightening of my wartime experiences as this aircraft, with its wing afire, was in a wide spiral and I was convinced it was about to end up on top of me and another boyhood friend . . .' Fortunately for the future of Eighth Air Force history, it missed.

By now, our hillside excavations had released a plethora of B-24 parts dotted around a crater some 12-feet deep in light soil but waterlogged to a depth of some 2 feet at the bottom. There now occurred a potentially fatal mishap, caused, it has to be said, by the ineptitude of the machine operator we had hired. I had already observed how his positioning and movements

A dark blue T in an off-white square immediately established the aircraft as a 490th machine. Stewart Evans ponders the story behind our discovery.

lacked the deftness and dexterity of operators on other sites. We were now pulling out the port inboard wing section with the main undercarriage leg still folded in place, so there was considerable weight to be extracted, well beyond our machine's direct lift capabilities. The best approach for the task was on the highest rim of the crater, so we duly guided the machine in and its stabilizer legs were lowered. Gradually, the chain shackles tautened and the wing section was slowly extracted like a giant tooth from the opposite bank and hauled towards the edge nearest the machine. All seemed ready for the digger's legs to be retracted and the digger driven slowly away, pulling the wing over the rim to safety, but unfortunately the driver miscalculated or made a mistake. As soon as the legs had been retracted, the machine shot backwards over the edge of the crater. For a second, I simply froze in fear while my stomach leapt to my throat as the JCB fell – then stopped, its engine nose up and stalled. Somehow, it had dropped onto the wing section, which prevented it from tumbling upside down into the hole and trapping its driver upside down underwater. There would have been no time or equipment to reach his cab and free him. In the silence that followed, the entire edifice creaked, teetering dangerously from side to side, but, fortunately, it held. The broken wing had bought us time, but, precariously poised, the driver dared not move. Quickly assessing the situation, five of us rushed to the front bucket and held on, adding some counterweight. Others had raced to the crater's edge and were frantically shovelling earth to try and fill the void beneath the machine's overhanging wheels.

All four Pratt and Whitney Twin Wasp radial engines were retrieved. Ron Buxton checks for the still submerged propeller as an engine is dragged from the crater.

Swapping my bucket place with another digger, I slid over the edge to join them in assessing the predicament. It was very intimidating working beneath a machine that might topple onto us at any moment, but a plan was emerging. One of our group, Don Buxton, was a competent digger driver and agreed to swap places with the poor machine operator still in his cab. This exchange of places occurred with some delicacy and much anxiety as team members shovelled or hung on, counterbalancing as best we could. Once in the cab, Don gingerly extended the machine's arm rearwards until it touched the opposite bank. Then, skilfully, he slowly straightened it like a giant elbow. This pushed the digger wheels towards the bank and he gently engaged forward gear. A flurry of shovelling and heaving helped as the big black rotating tyres touched earth, first churning chunks of soil into the crater but then gouging some grip. Don's technique was a masterpiece – he allowed the wheels to bite as his 'elbow' straightened and the machine clambered from the pit like a walrus beaching itself. As it trundled clear, we all collapsed with relief.

After this drama, further cautious excavations revealed a myriad more finds, including the remains of the bomb load, which, thankfully, had already exploded. The size of the fragments and split casings were indicative of a low-order detonation. Other finds included engines, propellers, numerous oxygen bottles and many fittings still in superb condition despite the crash, fire and explosions. Items from this site were given to museums in honour of the crew and, in many respects, to pay tribute to those of the team no longer with us, especially Ron Buxton and John Fisher.

Having established the serial number, we were soon able to establish the particular misadventure resulting in the demise of 42-94835. Local enthusiast Mike Jones later enhanced my initial research, aided by Roger Freeman, and collectively we are indebted to former tail gunner Newman Sanders, who takes up the story.

I was inducted into the US Army A.F., Fort Jackson, late January or early February 1943 – Camp Jackson, Columbia, South Carolina. They gave us a two-piece field mess kit. For lunch, they piled up the vegetables, mashed potatoes and meat on to the mess kit, then smack in the middle, they dropped a scoop of ice cream. I was there a couple of weeks. During this time I had a terrible cold virus but that didn't stop them from compulsory attendance to a VD film. Already nauseated, the sight of VD patients with sores on their lips and penises were more than I could take. I began to throw up all over the floor in a GI

cinema. To say the least, I had very little knowledge of gonorrhoea and syphilis – to put it mildly, that was enough to gag a maggot or make a buzzard puke. February, some of us were instructed to dress for a cold climate – long handles (woollen underwear), wool socks and ODs (wool) and heavy wool overcoat. If you had guessed our destination after the warm-up, guess again! Our troop train's destination turned out to be, not a cold northern city but as far south as you could go, Miami Beach, to be billeted in one of the biggest hotels on Ocean Boulevard: the Winter Haven – 50 dollars per day before the war. I'll tell you it was some hot, especially with all those wool clothes on. Next day we received more shots, clothes suitable for the warm climate. Had our chow – army-style – in a cafeteria two blocks away – marches and orientation most of each day, ending up on the beach for PT and finally saluting the flag and dismissal. There were blackouts at night – German subs came in pretty close. By the way, a good many of the guys could not read and write. A buck sergeant from Massachusetts was our drill instructor. His first move was to summon the

Newman Sanders was inducted into the army early in 1943. Pictured later in his military career, he wears a typically decorated A-2. (*Newman Sanders*)

platoon to a back patio. Next, he asked if anyone had a pocket knife – almost without exception, every recruit pulled out pocket knives. 'Just keep holding 'em up and my corporal will relieve you of them. The reason you cannot have a weapon is because you hillbillies that come through here have tried to cut my guts out. When you go to ship out, you can pick up your knife.' I was then one month before shipping out for airplane mechanic's school – Sheppard Field, Texas (Wichita Falls) for six months. Eight hours school – three hours PT – one hour exercise; one hour obstacle course; one hour running – six days a week . . . At Sheppard Field we learned the mechanics of the B-25 and the B-26 – Mitchells and Marauders. The instructor pointed to a little, short metal tube outside the fuselage – 'Anyone know what this is for?' He tried to get someone to blow through and unstop it – turns out it was the relief tube.

September 1943, having made Private First Class . . . to gunnery school at Tyndall Field near Panama City, Florida, for six weeks gunnery training. This is where Clark Gable received his gunner's wings . . . we had lots and lots of trap/skeet [clay pigeon] shooting. We also had a few days air to air, actually shooting at a sleeve pulled by another plane. My my . . . it's about that time again! Another training film about VD which focused more on syphilis than on gonorrhoea. At least I didn't have any nauseating virus this time. No holds

barred in the film – WACs and GI Joes alike with their social diseases: venereal warts, blisters above and below the neck. It was awful! Never again touch a woman! However, it was probably short-lived for most, quickly forgotten.

Early November 1943 – to Salt Lake City, Utah, for assignment. I had been promoted to buck sergeant upon leaving Tyndall. My folks at home were real proud of my three stripes as well as my gunners wings . . . I had trained for six months for B-25s and B-26s and where do I end up? Here at Salt Lake City, I was assigned to a four-engine B-24 Liberator – Riley Cavin, pilot, as a tail gunner, together with nine other men. Not, as it would have made sense, as a B-25 Mitchell or B-26 Marauder mechanic and top turret gunner . . . But then, nothing the armed forces did made sense . . . Early January 1944 we wake up in Tucson, Arizona, at Davis-Monthan airbase. We thought we were in heaven when we had our first breakfast with genuine china to eat from. We thought the cooks were pulling our legs when they asked how we wanted our eggs cooked – ah! They weren't kidding – honest to goodness, they said, 'sunny side up, over lightly, scrambled?' – you name it. Wow! How can it get any better than this? Next we were issued Class A passes to come and go as we pleased as long as we weren't scheduled for a flight training mission. My wife and baby daughter visited me a couple of weeks or so where she learned to walk. That Class A pass was great as the rest of the crew let me know when we were scheduled to fly . . .

Next assignment late January 1944. 490th Bomb Group in Mountain Home, Idaho, for flight training. It was cold and raining with that red Idaho mud to trudge through in and out of the various buildings. We were skeet/trap shooting in the snow at times. Well do I remember our first pass into Mountain Home. The one-armed bandits. Personally speaking I never went in for gambling of any kind. George Marshall, our top turret gunner, swung from one handle to another like a chimp, quarter after quarter . . . On another occasion when we were on a training mission from Mountain Home, we flew over San Francisco Bay and got down quite low, like three or four thousand feet. One man was lying on the floor, feet towards the front of the Liberator, with the hatch open, taking pictures of the bay below. Just forward a bit from where his feet were, one of the guys had the urge to 'shake the dew off the lily' so, without thinking, he takes the little black hard rubber-type funnel off the side of the ship and let it go. The salty urine was force-blown up through the open hatch where the photographing was taking place. Suddenly the photographer jumped straight up and started spitting out what he thought was ocean water coming up through the hatch. By this time, the guy on the funnel surmised what was happening along with the other two of us. We were all laughing hysterically and the one doing the pissing couldn't stop the flow. What a riot! The 490th BG's B-24s were in terrible condition. Just about every mission the meat wagons and the fire trucks were waiting for us to crash land. Maybe a gas or oil cap was not secured with safety wire. Once, we had a gas cap come off the top of the wing behind the No. 3 or No. 4 engine with gasoline spraying out. We nearly froze to death at 20,000 feet even with long handles, wool clothes plus two pairs of socks, coveralls and sheepskin boots, pants, jacket, helmet – silk gloves under sheepskin gloves. Most of the time it was about 65 degrees below zero that high. A couple of weeks

before overseas departure we received electric suits, boots and gloves. Boy! What a godsend for us to keep warm . . .

Once, while out on the runway waiting for the officers from briefing, we saw another B-24 as he began to move down the runway with the No. 3 engine smoking. As it began to lift off, fire began to billow out and by the time they were 200–300 feet in the air, the whole 3 engine was raging with flames. The instructor pilot and the trainee pilot banked the plane into the burning wing. Stalling, it side-slipped to the ground exploding into thousands of pieces. Two men were thrown a hundred or two hundred feet but, somehow, their number was not up. They lived but spent a long time in hospital.

Early part of April 1944 we make several stops – via South America and Africa – before landing at our airbase near Eye and Diss. First stop was Lincoln, Nebraska. The group got into an awful storm – we could not get above the rain and overcast. Visibility was zero. Finally, the pilot tried to get under it. We were so near the ground we were almost on the water towers and electric lines around Lincoln – it was awful and scary. The group spread out for miles. As the planes landed, one by one, some ran out of gas as they hit the runway – one blew a tyre. Next, Morrison Field, West Palm Beach Florida, where everyone was restricted to the base but the navigator slipped out. The next day we were all up at the crack of dawn and off to the 'Devil's Step-Child' ready to board for our journey to England . . . All the crew were there, bright-eyed and bushy-tailed, except William Halliday, the navigator. Finally, he comes running, out of breath and about to be left behind. He had his dress uniform on as he climbs aboard. Within minutes we were rolling down the runway with four of us in the waist compartment. The pilot gives the engines full throttle. As we

Bringing the 'Devil's Step-Child' overseas had its share of adventures. (*Newman Sanders*)

lift off, I look out the waist window and see fire coming from No. 1 engine. We got very excited in the waist and probably all of us pressed our intercom buttons at the same time. Result, we couldn't get through to the pilot. Finally, in desperation I grabbed my parachute pack and snapped it on and ran through the bomb bay to alert the pilot. He immediately told everyone to get ready to bail out when we gained some altitude. All the fellows up front had piled all of their gear on the floor just behind the cockpit, with the parachutes at the bottom of the pile. The pilot and co-pilot had their backpack parachutes on but the other two officers and enlisted men did not have their chest packs attached. The navigator had stripped from his dress uniform to put on his flight coveralls. There he stood, shoes, socks and garters as well as his little 'cock sucker' overseas cap on, otherwise stark raving naked, panic on his face. They all frantically began to dig into the pile to find their parachute harnesses and packs. Halliday found his first and donned it over his 'birthday suit'. What a spectacle to behold standing there – can you imagine this guy jumping and landing right in the town square of West Palm Beach? I returned to the waist section ready to bail out. Suffice to say, the pilot, Riley Cavin, shut the turbo off and the fire extinguished itself. We landed and ground crews work on it. It caught on fire three days in succession. Finally we headed to several stops in South America without the use of that particular turbo. The first leg was Trinidad then Atkinson Field British Guiana then Brazil. Boy, was it hot. As we crawled into cots with mosquito netting, I was afraid of those mosquitoes as I had malaria when I was in 7th grade. Those insects were like dive bombers coming in popping it to anyone that had some part of his anatomy against the net. Next Fostelaza then an eleven-hour flight to Dakar, Africa, followed by Marrakech, Turkey, then St Mawgan, England, eleven days after leaving the USA. Briefing and money exchange and then from St Mawgan on to Eye, our home away from home.

Our plane arrived in late April 1944 and we began practice missions over England before the group would be declared combat operational. About the middle of May, five of the enlisted men were at the hardstand for our B-24, 'The Devil's Step-Child', when we heard this thunderous noise through the high clouds – a B-24 and a B-17 had collided. One or two lived through it. On May 28 1944 we had the scare of our entire military lives. There were hundreds of bombers returning from raids over Germany. Our plane somehow got into the prop wash of those planes and we fell 8–10,000 feet. In the tail turret I felt like I weighed a ton, unable to move except at moments when the centrifugal force would release me. I can imagine what it would be like caught up in a tornado. We must have been doing flips, twists and turns etc. Finally, at one of the moments of release, I was able to move my right hand to the release knob for the sliding doors. I was thrown through them about six feet to land on my back on the corrugated aluminium floor. I reached for my parachute pack to hook onto my harness. Two of the crew were bent over trying to pick up their parachute packs – they seemed unable to reach down or straighten up. Suddenly, the pilot pulled it out of the dive. We safely returned and landed – the plane was later condemned because of the stress. I went on sick call because of the back pain but the flight surgeon said, 'there's nothing wrong with your back'.

Next day, about 3 a.m., May 29th 1944, we were preparing for another practice mission with a borrowed plane [later identified by Roger Freeman as 'Mandy J III']. A few hours later it is a beautiful day, about 14,500 feet, I sat in my turret enjoying the balmy weather. Everything seemed just about perfect . . . the four engines purring like kittens. Suddenly the emergency bell starts ringing to abandon ship, bail out, hit the silk, jump! The plane was flying beautifully so why the bell? I had no inkling that anything was wrong, as the plane appeared to be flying perfectly smooth and normal. I open my turret doors and step inside the waist section, still puzzled as to why that bell was ringing. I wondered if it was accidental. Then I noticed the two men, Schmid and LaFitte, in the waist section had already snapped their chest packs in position. With a certain amount of scepticism, I picked up my parachute pack and snapped it on. One of the men had already opened the hatch in the bottom of the plane between the tail and the waist. They both began to holler and point indicating that I should jump. There was no way that I would be foolish enough to make that plunge into the atmosphere without knowing if anything was wrong with the plane. Finally, one of them closed the hatch and I stepped over into the waist section with them. The hatch was again opened and Schmid grabbed me and began pushing me towards the opening saying to go ahead and jump. What ensued can now be looked on as hilarious. Still unaware of what was happening as the plane was handling normally as far as I could tell, I proceeded to shove Schmid and say, 'No. *You* go ahead'. How long this grab, push and shove went on is beyond me until finally, LaFitte says get the 'so-and-so' out of here indicating through the window that the plane was on fire. One glance convinced me as I now saw the whole wing section of the No. 1 engine was a blazing inferno. Without further ado, I squatted over the open hatch and did the 'ole swimming hole, watermelon, roll-out. Both arms around and clutching my chest chute for fear of having difficulty locating the handle as I wanted to make sure I was out of the prop wash before yanking the handle. We never had any instructions about jumping except get out, count to ten before pulling the handle and, 'if it don't work, bring it back!' Seconds later, as I get ready to pull the ripcord I realize the plane has been completely abandoned and is in a close circular spin as though ready to grab its prey. The B-24 was no more than 200 feet above me and we were descending at about the same speed. All I could see was the belly of that monstrous machine of destruction. Only the Lord knows the reason it was falling in such a fashion . . . For some unexplainable reason, my back was always to the ground, while I stared up at the plane's belly. No matter how desperately I tried to manoeuvre myself, I always came 'right side up' looking at the underside of that plane. Death seemed ready to claim its prey. I fell about 14,000 feet, not daring to open my parachute – the plane still holding its speed; neither getting closer or any further away. I knew that, if I opened my chute, the burning plane would devour me. All this way down, I screamed to the top of my voice, 'God save me! God save me!' The only way I realized the ground was close and reaching up for me was by glimpsing the landscape from the corner of one eye . . . There was no choice as the B-24 seemed determined to stick with me to the bitter end, death reaching its clutches from above and below. Lord, this is it! And I pulled the ripcord handle and hit the soft

earth in an oat field almost instantly on my back. The plane crashed simultaneously about 300 feet away and was immediately engulfed in flames.

I was sure the parachute didn't even have time to open as I felt I had buried six feet into mother earth. Jumping up, frightened, dazed and breathless, I started to run away from the plane but the wind caught in my chute and jerked me down. As I rose again, I got my breath and wits back so I unbuckled the parachute and made a dash for a hedgerow. By this time the raging fires had heated up the hundreds of cal. 50 ammo on board as well as the ten × 500lb bombs. The exploding ammo sounded louder than firecrackers and the gas tanks were exploding. Behind the hedge now, an older Englishman ran up to me and started hugging me with tears streaming down his face. He just knew that there was no way I would make it – I looked to be 100 feet from the ground when my chute opened. He said he had counted eight other chutes coming down. Our encounter was very brief as the MPs arrived and escorted me to a waiting ambulance. No one was killed, although Eugene Schmid and I spent June and July in the 65th General Hospital. Schmid had a fractured shoulder and I with a fractured back.

What went wrong with Mandy J III will never be fully known, but the pilot, 1/Lt Riley F. Cavin, felt it was caused by a ruptured exhaust line. His co-pilot, 2/Lt Steven J. Buich, had the controls and Cavin had just completed a routine instrument check, noting nothing untoward. They were flying a training mission as lead position in the third element. Mandy was fully bombed up because the 490th was honing its formation skills for a combat debut the following day. Buich had lowered his seat to get a better view and was concentrating on holding his slot through some moderate turbulence, causing the B-24 to fishtail. Concerned by this motion, Buich checked his instruments and noted the rpm indicator for No. 1 engine was oscillating between 2,200 and 2,400rpm. Cavin's gaze to starboard had just noted Nos 3 and 4 running fine, but a check on their port side startled him into action. Their No. 1 engine was on fire! Flames were emerging from the cowl flaps. Already, a harsh finger of fire had melted the small inspection plate on top of the cowling and was stabbing outwards some 10 inches. Cavin immediately hit the feathering button and took control. Buich thought the No. 1 had cut out before Cavin feathered it, but neither had time for a polite discourse on the issue – they were dealing with a rapidly developing fire in a fully loaded bomber. Conscious of the threat they posed to other aircraft, Cavin broke formation in a left, skidding turn. This gave him a better view for avoiding other aircraft and, as they turned, he closed the cowl flaps to help contain the carbon dioxide in the afflicted area and told Buich to pull the CO_2 extinguisher. Cavin opened the throttles for his other engines, set the fuel mixture for No. 1 to shut off and turned off the booster pump. He then rang the alarm bell as a crew warning and told Buich to go aft and turn off the fuel supply to the No. 1 engine and prepare to bail out. Fuel management was usually assigned to LaFitte, but the engineer was at his battle station in the waist.

Peering out, Cavin could see the strengthening blaze was now melting through the cowling and wing surface, causing large sections to peel away in the heat. This clearly affected control, because the B-24 failed to respond when he attempted to correct his turn.

Riley F. Cavin's original crew pictured at Mountain Home. *Rear left to right*: Joe Vittum, bombardier; Riley F. Cavin, pilot; Steven J. Buich, co-pilot; William Halliday, navigator. *Front left to right*: John Wooden, radio operator; Leonard L. LaFitte Jr, waist gunner; Alfred Tolar, nose-turret gunner; George W. Marshall, top-turret gunner; Newman Sanders, tail-turret gunner; Eugene Schmid, ball-turret gunner. (*Newman Sanders*)

From the top turret, Sgt George W. Marshall reported the fire's increasing intensity, as molten metal streamed back in the slipstream. His report convinced Cavin their race to beat the conflagration had failed and he rang the alarm bell to abandon ship.

Hastening back to the cockpit, Buich clipped on his own parachute, attached Cavin's, then bailed out. Cavin continued struggling with the controls and throttled back the No. 4 engine to gain some degree of symmetry, but damage to the port wing made it impossible to recover from the left-hand downwards spiral. Looking at the source of his woes, he dispassionately observed that the fire had turned from a white-red flame to a devil-red banner some 10 feet long, with black smoke smearing the sky behind. This indicated that the oil supply had ignited and he could do no more. Unfastening his seat belt, he pulled the throttle leavers back, left his seat and leapt through the open bomb bay. A few seconds later his parachute deployed and he noticed his descent was accompanied by several pieces of aluminium sheeting fluttering earthwards around him. Below, he saw the B-24 continuing to twist round and round. He did not notice the tiny figure underneath, falling almost in unison.

The bomber was terrifying not only its tail gunner. Royal Observer Corps volunteers manning the Boxted ROC post also became increasingly alarmed as the abandoned bomber corkscrewed ever closer. Finally, whipping by low overhead, it crashed and exploded a few hundred yards away. Floating into a nearby tree, one airman was too near the burning bomber for his peace of mind, and soldiers billeted nearby answered his frantic cries for help. This hapless individual was Steven Buich, whose proximity to the wreckage was not his only discomfiture. His abrasive tree landing had painfully skinned that most tender and important part of a young man's attributes and it later took many reassurances from the flight surgeon to convince him all would heal well and full functionality would be unimpaired! Meanwhile, others were approaching the plane, thinking there were airmen trapped inside. J.A. Osborne of Greenfields Cottage, Boxted, was attracted, like any 15-year-old, by the excitement of seeing a crashed aeroplane and was running towards it when intercepted by a soldier and bowled into an adjacent ditch. Just then, the bombs exploded sending a giant column of smoke heavenwards, black and angry against the spring afternoon sky. Fortunately there were no civilian casualties, and, taking advantage of an enormous crater caused by the exploding 500lb bombs, a bulldozer simply shovelled in the engines and tail assembly, little thinking they would later be the focus of further excitement.

Other than the injuries sustained by Newman Sanders and Eugene Schmid, the remaining crew were unscathed, although the nose turret gunner, Staff Sgt Alfredo Tolar, always regretted the loss of his ring. 'When I pulled the ripcord on my chute, the pilot chute came out but I could not get the rest of the chute out. After what seemed a great deal of time, the main chute did open. The cords from the chute wrapped around my fingers and pulled off my High School ring. It lies somewhere in the Essex soil.' In fact, Tolar had been obliged to tear open the parachute flaps and tug the nylon canopy clear as he fell. He and the others were returned to Eye and eventually completed their combat tours. Newman's destiny lay elsewhere and he continues his account.

After two to three weeks into our recuperation and therapy, we discovered a lake down below the hospital. We came up with an idea, No. 8 sewing thread, straight pins and some flour to make some dough balls. It was real good therapy catching the 'shad', which happens to be one of the bonniest fish there is. The setting was beautiful for us to while away the hours and days. Also we met our beloved CO there, Col Lloyd H. Watnee, as he had cracked up on his second tour of duty. Col Frank P. Bostrom replaced him. The ward Schmid and I were in must have had thirty to forty beds and many of them were from bicycle accidents. One man in a private room near the nurses' station was bound up like a 'mummy' with feet and hands tied up in the air – he later died. I vividly remember the night of June 5th to the morning of June 6th as the big planes were being pre-flighted and running up. My bed was rolled out in the middle . . . It seemed like the very ground the hospital was on trembled and shook from the thousands of planes warming up and taking off with their deadly cargoes. As soon as I found out what was taking place, the invasion, Lord how I longed to be in on it instead of where I was. The Lord had saved me to serve

another day, another place. During that two months in the 65th GH [General Hospital], I started having boils on the back of my neck. They used black Ithamol drawing salve to bring them to a head although at times they still had to lance them. The boils started again after I was discharged and returned to the base. As a result, they sent me back to the 65th for a culture to see whether the new penicillin would destroy the 'bug' that was causing the problem – sure enough it did the trick. At the hospital I was put in a rather embarrassing situation. In order to get the penicillin shots every two or three hours for a 24-hour period, they sent me to the VD ward. Boils and VD had nothing in common except that penicillin would cure both. Instead of climbing into my assigned bunk, I came by every two hours during the daylight hours for the shots, and then I would visit other patients. On one occasion we lined up for shots at the nurses' station. She carefully instructed all of us to step right up in front of her, turn around, drop the pants or PJ bottoms and bend over . . . Finally about 9 p.m. I put on some PJs and hit the sack. All during the night, a nurse would tap us on the shoulder, 'It's that time again, turn over, backside up and pull down your PJs': Zap. Upon returning to the base our Group had changed over from B-24s to B-17s, eliminating one man from each crew. In November 1944 I found myself on my way to Italy via a British army troop ship along with 499 other displaced AF gunners headed for Naples. I was then assigned to the 340th BG on the island of Corsica – here I became an engineer gunner on a B-25 Mitchell . . .

Newman's experiences with the 340th are another story, but he survived and returned home thinking little of his 490th BG experiences until contacted by Joseph Millikan, himself a 490th veteran and then the unit contact for the recently formed Eighth Air Force Historical Society. This led to contact with Roger Freeman and Stephen Gleed, one of the dig organizers. Learning that his B-24 had been excavated spurred further interest and a return to England during 1978. The trip was a tremendous success. Newman visited the Freeman and Gleed homes, the latter still housing some artefacts from the site, including a superbly restored Twin Wasp engine. During their meeting, Stephen presented Newman with the gun control grips from his turret plus other items to join the parachute D-ring still held as a treasured trophy. Stephen's investigations had also identified the elderly man whose embrace had so warmly welcomed his survival thirty-five years earlier. Harold Grass, a retired gamekeeper, had always remembered the airman's miraculous survival and Newman himself was convinced that God had granted him extra years to fulfil other tasks.

Suffice to say, I made many promises to the Lord that had brought me through all those close calls and more that I did not mention. October 4 1945, home at last and once more a real live civilian! The Lord saved me from death so many times it was time to set things right with God concerning my eternal destiny . . .

From a fallen and falling airman whose prayer was answered, Newman Sanders has spent the rest of his life as a devout Christian.

CHAPTER FIVE

An Error of Judgement

In combat, decisions need to be made. Fast. Only with hindsight can an error of judgement be recognized and subjected to the later comment of historians who were not there and never confronted by such choices.

On 24 August 1944, the Mendlesham-based 34th BG flew its final B-24 mission. A command decision had been made to convert from the robustly featured four-engined Liberator to its more shapely sister, the B-17 Flying Fortress. Crews argued then about the

A command decision had been made to convert from the robustly featured Liberator to its shapelier sister, the B-17. 34th BG Liberators pictured over Suffolk nearing the end of their tenure at Mendlesham.

Leading the entire group was Maj Joseph Ora Garrett, Commanding Officer of the 4th Bombardment Squadron. (*Scott Mackey*)

merits and demerits of each type and the debate rolled on down the decades. However, one common denominator I acknowledge is the courage of the crews, irrespective of the type flown. For their finale in the Consolidated product, the 34th had a long haul from the east of England, over the North Sea, to the Walther armaments factory in the German port of Kiel, notorious for its many anti-aircraft guns.

Leading the entire group was Maj Joseph Ora Garrett, Commanding Officer of the 4th Bombardment Squadron. A professional Army Air Force man, Joe had wanted to fly since childhood and, after graduating from Canton High School, Georgia, he attended the North Georgia Military Academy. As well as embarking on a military career, Joe had earlier begun an entirely different type of life journey when he crashed a Marriett State High School Junior–Senior Prom in 1935. Amid the lights and fun, Joe discovered student Elizabeth Hodges and, with the future Mrs Garrett, the attraction was mutual. As the young couple's relationship developed, events that would affect their lives and those of millions of others were unfolding in Europe when lowering war clouds loomed on the world horizon. The year Joe enlisted in the US Army Air Corps (USAAC) was a tremendous one for world history – on 1 September 1939, Nazi Germany invaded Poland. Pleading for help from its allies, France and Britain, Poland fought valiantly, but, though its forces were evenly matched in courage, their *matériel* inferiority was swiftly exposed, as the Blitzkrieg struck deep into the Polish heartland. Hitler scorned Prime Minister Chamberlain's peaceful entreaties, so, on Sunday, 3 September, the British government declared war on his Third Reich.

Against Hitler's Messerschmitt, Dornier and Junkers aircraft, the Polish air force was almost totally outclassed. The PZL P.11 fighter, with its high-wing, open cockpit and fixed undercarriage, harked from an era now vanished. The PZL P.37 twin-engined bomber, while modern, was not available in sufficient numbers and was rapidly overwhelmed. Later, the same grim *matériel* inadequacies plus planning deficiencies would evince themselves in France and the Low Countries. Only when matched against radar and comparable Royal Air Force types such as the Hawker Hurricane and superlative Supermarine Spitfire did the wave of German air superiority break.

This was now August 1940, the month that Joe Garrett was commissioned into a USAAC that, had it too been embroiled in combat, would have fared little better than its European counterparts. American types later to wrest control of the skies were embryonic or still on the drawing board. Joe had been cavorting around in a diminutive primary trainer and recalled, 'We used to chase ducks. It was a close race, but the ducks usually won.' Duck dog-fighting apart, Joe's piloting skill was recognized and he progressed to instructor status at Gunter Field near Montgomery in Alabama. Overtly supportive of the Allied cause, America was drawn fully into combat by the infamous attack on Pearl Harbor, on 7 December 1941. Joe's early contribution to the war effort was to train the growing number of pilots required for combat overseas, including several groups of British flying cadets. Promoted to Squadron Commander in 1942, Joe flew many hours imparting his flying abilities to young men whose graduation took them to the harsh college of air combat in the Pacific or the European theatre of operations (ETO).

In 1943, Joe himself took a step towards the ETO when assigned to Blythe, California, as a squadron CO with the Liberator-equipped 4th Bombardment Squadron, 34th BG. In March 1944, the 34th BG headed for Mendlesham, Suffolk, and Joe entered combat. As a Command Pilot, Joe did not have his own crew but flew with Lead Crews in the co-pilot's seat. As a Squadron Commander, his role was to direct formations and make any on-the-spot judgements appertaining to the attack and monitor the Group's performance. The Kiel mission was his thirteenth and he would be displacing regular co-pilot 1/Lt Arthur Bortz to fly with 1/Lt William K. Mackey and crew in B-24 44-40443 'Jerks Berserk' while Bortz flew with another crew. This would be 21-year-old Bill Mackey's twenty-second sortie and his fifth with Major Joe Garrett, his senior by two years and a lot of rank. Unfortunately, illness deprived Bill of his regular engineer, Staff Sgt Louis Longinette, but the role would be covered by Staff Sgt Saul Spivak. For the 34th BG it was mission number 63 and all those at briefing knew just how formidable were the anti-aircraft defences facing them. Their operational swan song in the B-24 would commence at 0800 hr and thirty-nine of their Liberators would participate but split into three segments as part of the 93rd Combat Wing. Mackey, call sign Clambake Red Lead, would head the 34th BG 'A' Group of twelve aircraft with a further twelve comprising the 34th BG 'B' Group and another twelve flying with the 93rd CW 'B' Wing as a composite group with B-24s from the 493rd BG.

Bill taxied Jerks Berserk – itself an ex-493rd BG aircraft – to the end of the runway, ran a short distance to straighten the nose wheel, then held the bomber on her brakes as he

Crew number 8. *Rear left to right*: 1/Lt Arthur Bortz (co-pilot displaced by Joe Garrett); 1/Lt John C. Gallagher, navigator; 1/Lt Gordon T. Matson, bombardier; Staff Sgt Burton C. Holtzman, nose-turret gunner; 1/Lt William K. Mackey, pilot. *Front*: Staff Sgt Clifford H. Smith, tail gunner; Staff Sgt Louis Longinette, engineer; Technical Sgt Serrafine Corrales, radio operator; Staff Sgt Bernard Horbath, waist gunner. (*Scott Mackey*)

Staff Sgt Saul Spivak, engineer on the ill-fated flight. (*Scott Mackey*)

completed the final cockpit checks with Joe. Bill knew the foibles of Jerks Berserk, having flown the combat veteran for eight of the twenty-six missions it had accumulated with the 34th BG. Both men felt the Liberator shudder with contained power as the four Twin Wasp engines were each revved up to 1,000rpm and the instruments checked. Spivak had confirmed all exits and bomb-doors closed; a final check on the fuel load was carried out and the fuel-cock settings were correct with the hydraulic booster pump 'ON'. The weather briefing had promised good conditions and the summer early morning was already becoming slightly hazy. A pearlescent layer of altocumulus, mackerel patterned, drifted gently over Suffolk's harvest-ripened countryside. Bill's mind was now focused on less pastoral activities as they received clearance from the tower and released Jerks Berserk. As he steadily advanced the throttles, the howl from the engines increased as the B-24 began to roll. Laden with twelve 500lb bombs, ammunition and gasoline, the bomber was a dangerous amalgam for the ten men

it carried and these were always anxious moments. Any malfunction risked this combination becoming a horrific catalyst violently consuming the lives of all on board. As speed increased, Bill felt air embrace the big twin rudders and he used them to hold Jerks Berserk aligned on the runway. Nearing 80mph, Bill gained elevator control and gently eased the control wheel towards him, reducing stress on the bomber's nose wheel. At just over 130mph, Jerks Berserk eased away from Mendlesham for the last time. It was 0800 hr. 1/Lt Russell Lindstrom was 60 seconds behind – in 30 minutes, all thirty-nine ships would be airborne without mishap.

Bill signalled an affirmative to Joe, who unlocked and retracted the undercarriage. Firm pressure on the brakes stopped the wheels rotating as the gear came up, and, climbing steadily, Jerks Berserk was joined by increasing numbers of her sisters. The long rhythmic waltz of assembling aircraft ensued in an orchestration of engine power. At this time, the USAAF had gained much experience and employed very sophisticated methods, including radio beacons, to assemble its aerial armadas over East Anglia. Buncher 19 was a low-power radio transmitter located near Manningtree and was the 34th BG's normal formation assembly point. On board Jerks Berserk, the radio operator, Technical Sgt Serrafine Corrales, tuned into the Morse signal emitted by Buncher 19 as his B-24 began to follow a rectangular pattern to and from the signal. Other aircraft, likewise homing on Buncher 19, gradually assumed their formation slots behind Jerks Berserk. The choreography went almost precisely as planned and the bomber formation conducted itself to Splasher 6, a stronger signalling beacon located near the rural community of Scole, on the Suffolk–Norfolk border. Th

morning, the summer air shuddered and the skies of eastern England echoed from the reverberations of over 1,300 heavy bombers launched by the Eighth Air Force to pound aviation, oil and other industrial targets in Germany.

In his role as Command Pilot, Joe conducted the 34th BG formation through these busy airways. Encountering the layer of altocumulus at 6,500 feet, the group became slightly scattered as they climbed into clearer skies at 8,000 feet. Observing a B-17 formation assembling nearby, Joe steered the 34th BG away and ordered Bill to gently weave Jerks Berserk, allowing stragglers to catch up as they 'essed' away from the English coast north of Great Yarmouth at 0934 hr. The cloud line mirrored the curvature of East Anglia's shoreline but did not trespass over the North Sea and the formation now climbed over waters almost hidden in summer haze. If it continued, it would handicap bombing accuracy, but it thinned as they neared the enemy coast at 1106 hr, 5 minutes later than planned. Visibility would be 'clear and unlimited' over the target. Clear for bombing; clear for anti-aircraft gunners defending the port and for units of the German navy at anchor. The Americans were assured of an unwelcoming reception. Two 34th BG aircraft had aborted over the North Sea: one had a runaway propeller governor; a second ship blew an engine cylinder. 1/Lt Noble Wright had double trouble. His No. 3 engine failed en route and his No. 4 turbo supercharger simultaneously became unserviceable only 30 minutes from the target. They attempted to attack a Luftwaffe base on Spiekeroog Island but were driven off by flak and salvoed their bombs.

The main formation continued without serious challenge. A flotilla of minesweepers observed at 1100 hr lacked the firepower and an anchored convoy of some twenty-four ships only observed the diamonds glinting high above. Sometimes the passing American bombers would stream long white contrails, but today they offered only the flash of late morning sun on silvered wings. Two hours after departing the English coast and dog-legging over northern Germany to avoid known flak concentrations, the Liberators reached their Initial Point at 1117 hr. Seven minutes earlier, the formation had released its first bundles of chaff and two types of tiny tinsel strips were fluttering earthwards, contorting like silvered bait to deceive the enemy gun-laying radar. In counter-deception, German defences included smokescreens, and the target area was being hidden from view as the bombers braced themselves in a barrage of intense flak. At briefing, the intention had been for the Lead to be taken by the high squadron Lead aircraft flown by Lindstrom with Capt Young as Command Pilot. However, Lindstrom's formation was now too far behind to pull ahead, so Joe decided that Jerks Berserk would retain its position and lead them through the storm of flak besmirching the heavens. Hundreds of shells were exploding directly ahead of the advancing Liberators. They were at 22,900 feet and, poised over his bombsight, 1/Lt Gordon T. Matson had Jerks Berserk under his command. Amazingly, either smoke pots intended to conceal the target had deployed too late or the wind speed and direction had been miscalculated. The primary objective was clear. Jerks Berserk was leading them resolutely through a maelstrom of flak, the ferocity of which surpassed anything Joe had ever seen. At 1135 hr, aircraft 42-94780, 'Smitty', took a direct hit. Fate had been particularly unkind to this B-24 flown by 1/Lt Gerald Howard and crew. They had been the last to take off at 0830, their original purpose to

fly as an airborne spare. Another aircraft aborting had drawn them into a vacant slot. Now, hit in its No. 1 engine, Smitty fell out of formation, its left wing blazing fiercely. In seconds, the entire aircraft was engulfed and spiralled downwards, out of control. Moments later, the port wing disintegrated and an enormous explosion ripped the Liberator into countless pieces of debris. Somehow, Howard escaped – he was the only survivor. With true valour, the 34th BG bore down on its objective.

Gordon Matson could clearly see the harbour; the crosshair in his bombsight was sliding steadily towards the release point. There were only seconds left. Five. Four . . . Then an enormous fist punched Jerks Berserk. Instinctively, Gordon released the bombs. They were two seconds too soon and the timing was disastrous for bombing accuracy. 1/Lt Stephen R. Nelson, the Deputy Lead bombardier, should have taken over, but there was insufficient time and the release point had passed. Compounding the problem, standard operational procedure was for the formation to release on its leader, so six aircraft, assuming Matson had released intentionally, also salvoed. Bombing results at the primary target would later be regarded as 'poor'. Only three aircraft from the 'A' Group had retained their bombs and they achieved slight recompense with more accurate bombing on the secondary target, Hemingstadt, which they attacked from 23,000 feet at 1147 hr after using the Rally Point as their Initial Point.

Dropping out of formation, Bill Mackey and Joe Garrett fought to control Jerks Berserk. Part of her port wing had been blown off and the left aileron and flap were damaged so badly they were useless. The No. 1 engine had been smashed from its mounting and now drooped incongruously from its nacelle, the weight and drag slewing the B-24 into a downwards spiral. Gasoline streamed from leaking fuel cells and shrapnel had torn holes in both wings. Miraculously, the fuel vapour did not ignite and the skill of her crew kept her airborne. Attempts to feather the No. 1 engine achieved only partial success and the damaged blades failed to rotate and so remained almost face on, imparting further drag. The undercarriage had been knocked from its up locks but, luckily, remained retracted. Damage to the bomb bay prevented the doors from closing more than a quarter and their instruments registered zero hydraulic pressure. Simply staying aloft required full left rudder and maximum exertion on the port aileron. As senior officer, Joe had some decisions to make and their lives could depend on his judgement.

Denmark was only a short flight but still occupied by the Germans. Neutral Sweden was a better option and, unknown to Joe, another 34th BG B-24 was already heading that way. Flown by 1/Lt Giles Avriett and crew, 'Near Sighted Robin', serial 41-28851, had also been hit by flak and left formation with No. 4 engine feathered. They landed successfully in Sweden to face internment for the duration but were at least alive. Joe discussed the options with Bill Mackey. Jerks Berserk was holding 142–5mph but losing height at 500–800 feet per minute and still streaming fuel, even though Saul Spivak was busily manipulating the transfer pumps. Responding to Joe's orders, the remaining crew quickly set about jettisoning unnecessary weight and began tossing overboard flak jackets, ammunition, guns and anything else not vital that might reduce the rate of descent. Luckily, the Luftwaffe was absent and US fighter protection for the mission had been excellent. Reaching the German coast, they had reduced

the loss of altitude to between 100 and 300 feet per minute and were keeping their disabled aircraft on the heading required by the navigators on board. Regular navigator 1/Lt John C. Gallagher was supported by the Group's lead navigator, 1/Lt Thomas J. Hogan. Both men were busily calculating distances and rate of descent, and working with Spivak to assess fuel consumption and distances.

As they left the enemy coast, Saul reported 700 gallons of gasoline, which, in theory, was enough for the crossing; but the fuel cells were leaking at an unknown rate. They could definitely reach Sweden – could they reach England? As Command Pilot, it was Joe's judgement. He decided upon England. He felt they had a good chance. The Liberator was still limping gamely along, shedding discarded equipment, her crew fighting the odds for every inch of altitude. Gingerly, Bill Mackey and Joe assessed the B-24's flying characteristics, noting with anxiety that it was on the verge of stalling at 130mph. This precluded any chance of ditching, because, unlike the B-17, the B-24 was notoriously poor for ditching

1/Lt Thomas J. Hogan, the group's lead navigator.

because of its high wing and roller-type bomb-bay doors. Major ETO modifications introduced in January included an additional hatch to speed egress, but this and other features that had been introduced had barely alleviated the problem. A B-24 hitting the sea at 130mph with bomb-doors already open would give no time for those fortunate enough to survive the impact uninjured to evacuate. Joe abandoned this option – it was certain death. Sitting purposefully in his radio room, Serrafine was anxiously transmitting distress calls. At 1243 hr, the listening station at Cockthorpe on the north Norfolk coast picked up his signal, but it was too weak to obtain a good fix. For Air–Sea Rescue (ASR) to be effective, an aircraft's position had to be fixed by more than one Radio Direction Finding (RDF) station. There were several RDF stations dotting the English coast, with Cockthorpe being the closest to the hapless Jerks Berserk. On receipt of the transmission from Serrafine, Cockthorpe RDF revolved its antenna to align with the strongest receipt strength. Two other stations doing likewise allowed the triangulation room to plot the coordinates in a triangle. The smaller the triangle on the map, the better the fix. The call letter for Jerks Berserk was Daisy D-Dog and Cockthorpe caught three signals from Corrales within a minute. It was 1243 hr and the signals were swiftly passed to ASR control, where a large, perspex-covered operations map divided the North Sea into grids. Those receiving the signals could sense the desperation on board a damaged bomber descending remorselessly towards the wave tops. This would be the war's busiest month for emergency homings, but Daisy D-Dog's weak signals hindered

receipt of a strong, positional fix. Somewhere, far back along that single line of transmission, the crew of the ailing bomber now faced further problems.

Loss of the No. 1 engine was described in the Pilot's Training Manual as the worst possible configuration, even without the engine sagging half-off the mainplane. Bill and Joe had adjusted the other engine and propeller settings to maximize endurance and were carefully monitoring head temperatures to avoid their three good engines overheating. Saul had been transferring fuel and busily computing some worrying and unpleasant statistics. On four engines, a B-24 could cruise comfortably at 181 gallons per hour. With one engine out, fuel consumption for the others increased to over 200 gallons per hour as they pulled more power to maintain air speed. Seven hundred gallons reported to Joe as available on leaving the enemy coast gave them sufficient for a landfall over the UK; but damage to the fuel tanks must have been more serious than first recognized, because he now reported only 200 gallons remaining. The loss was disastrous – 500 gallons had vanished in only 20 minutes – the bomber's lifeblood had been haemorrhaging into the heavens! Within minutes Saul further reported a detailed but demoralizing fuel tank status. No. 4 held only 25 gallons; likewise No. 3, and there were 90 in No. 2. All but 15 gallons in No. 1 had drained away before any chance of completing a transfer to No. 2. They now had only 140 gallons remaining, with more gasoline still bleeding away as their hopes of reaching home also evaporated into the stark reality of ditching or a parachute descent into the North Sea's inhospitable embrace. In reality, their only option was to jump and hope ASR reached them before they drowned or succumbed to hypothermia.

Dragging homewards like a wounded stag, the B-24 crawled a few miles further and Corrales continued his pleas into the ether. Nineteen signals were picked up between 1244 and 1357 hr. Only one, at 1347, allowed a clear, class-one fix to be taken, but Corrales was unaware of this. The crew now estimated that they had only 3 minutes of fuel remaining and Joe ordered them to attach their dinghies. Recognizing an inadequacy in its equipment, the USAAF had adopted the British one-man C-type dinghy pack for both fighter and bomber use. Containing paddles, a telescopic mast, sail, CO_2 bottle plus bellows for inflation, a neatly designed canvas bucket for baling out, leak plugs, six distress flares and sea markers, it saved many lives. Checking each others' parachute and dinghy attachments, they faced the dilemma of bailing out immediately or running on until the engines cut. The difficulty with leaving it until the very last minute was that the sudden loss of power might make the aircraft immediately uncontrollable, allowing no time to escape in a coordinated manner. Joe ordered the crew to line up on the bomb-bay catwalk and Bill held the aircraft while Joe attached his own dinghy before sliding back into the right-hand seat. Joe controlled Jerks Berserk as Bill clipped his dinghy on, then clambered aft to join his men poised over the bleak expanse of empty, grey sea sliding uninvitingly by some 3,000 feet below. The plan was to jump in unison, so they would land close together for mutual support. Joe lifted his left arm then dropped it in signal. Glancing back, he saw they had started to jump and, moments later, a second glance revealed an empty bomb bay. Joe needed to move swiftly to stand a chance of landing nearby for the comfort of mutual reassurance. At 6 feet 2 inches tall plus

the encumbrances of parachute and dinghy, Joe's bulk hindered his speed of departure. Levelling the Liberator, he knew it would be only seconds before it keeled over out of control and he had to be clear. Lifting himself from his seat, he released the control column and turned aft, intending to leap from the bomb bay. Thrusting clear, he suddenly found himself snagged and was tugged backwards just as the B-24 began winging over, spiralling seawards. Joe's dinghy pack had caught between the seat and the starboard control yoke. Joe felt the unbalancing motion as Jerks Berserk entered a steep, sliding dive seawards and he struggled to disentangle himself. Precious moments were lost. Too late. He could not escape before impact and now had only one chance. Get the bomber back under control. Reversing his actions, he dropped into his seat and forced a response from both control wheel and rudder pedals. At first, his vision held nothing but an expanse of rapidly approaching water; then, reluctantly, the horizon appeared, still at a crazy angle but levelling off as the nose came up. Checking the altimeter, he was at 1,200ft and, taking stock as he tried to calm himself, he felt it was too risky to chance another departure, even though he thought the engines were about to stop. He was sure more than 3 minutes had elapsed but, incredibly, the three Twin Wasps were still pounding rhythmically. For how long? The engineer's panel was behind him, out of view on the far side of the bulkhead, and Joe did not dare to risk letting go of the controls to check on the fuel available – there was now not supposed to be any. He decided to risk flying until the engines quit, then take his chances ditching. No longer strapped in, he realized the impact would assuredly kill him, but both his hands were required on the control wheel. More positively, he managed reconnection to the radio and felt a boost of hope when a friendly American voice crackled over the receiver. 'Sailor 62', a Mustang from their 55th Fighter Squadron, 20th Fighter Group (FG) escort, was some miles back circling his crew. All nine had clambered into their dinghies. Although scattered, they were thankfully alive, if damp, and the sight of a P-51 clipping low overhead, its pilot waving encouragingly, boosted morale. Decades later, that fighter pilot was identified as l/Lt Dale Larrabee in his P-51, 'Claudine I', and he recalled the incident.

The 20 FG were assigned to escort B-24s to Kiel. We did and when the last box finished their run, we escorted them back out over the North Sea and started letting down on our run back to base. I spotted some rafts in the water and asked our leader if I could go down and check it out to see if it was what it appeared to be. After determining there were nine rafts, each with a person aboard, I went back up to altitude that would allow me to contact home base. I relayed the information to group, asked them to call ASR so they could get a fix and that I would orbit until they called back saying they had gotten a fix. After getting a return call, and I don't remember if it was Group or ASR that returned the call, I went back down to fly top cover on the rafts. I stayed until I was running low on gas and then headed for base. I could see it was a very desperate situation for the guys in their dinghies but there was not much I could do for them.

The airwaves over the sea waves were busy that afternoon. Joe needed guidance to steer his way home, and additional reassurance was gratefully received from his own 34th BG.

Dale Larrabee circled the downed airmen in his P-51 Claudine I for as long as his fuel situation permitted. (*Dale Larrabee*)

Overhead but some miles astern and also homeward bound, Capt John W. Notman and crew on Daisy B-Baker picked up ASR signals and relayed them to Joe. Minutes went sluggishly while the sea waited patiently beneath the unsteady wings of Jerks Berserk. Joe sat, his arms and feet cramped, holding the controls, all the time expecting the engines simply to quit – maybe he would have time to jump, maybe not. His mind was attuned to every beat of the engines, but they kept on unfalteringly. It was unbelievable – had the fuel system been damaged so the fuel gauges had provided erroneous information and deceived Saul Spivak?

As Joe continued his solo flight towards England, his crew anxiously awaited rescue, and their hopes lowered when, with a final sweep of farewell and good luck, Dale Larrabee and Claudine I were obliged to leave. Elsewhere, strenuous efforts were under way involving the RAF's 16 Group, the American 479th FG and the specialist 5th Emergency Rescue Squadron, all of which had alerted or launched aircraft. That afternoon, nine survivors were picked up by an RAF High Speed Launch (HSL) at 5225 N – 0207 E – they were from a B-17 of the 96 BG. As the day wore on, rescue plans for the 34th BG crew were handicapped by information from returning bombers, which conflicted with one another because the dead-

There were loved ones far across the ocean who, if providence did not stoop to assist, would soon be receiving those dreaded 'Missing In Action' telegrams. Friend, Evelyn Michael, and pilot's wife, Ann Mackey. (*Scott Mackey*)

Bill Mackey thought of his childhood sweetheart, Ann, now his wife after their exuberant dash into marriage. (*Scott Mackey*)

reckoning positions offered varied substantially in latitude and longitude. They had bailed out at approximately 5340 N – 0405 E. Lonely and anxious, sitting in their tiny dinghies on the sea's interminable swell, Bill Mackey and his crew saw no further signs of support as dusk revealed the first stars. Even in August, it would be a long, cold night unless a surface vessel appeared, and they had no way of knowing how near or far was the rescue service. For Bill, at least, the water held no fears. He was an excellent swimmer and had even been offered a swimming scholarship but had chosen the military instead – not even the Navy at that. His rubber dinghy boasted an anti-spray cover sweeping up into a hood for improved water-proofing, but Bill knew they had all been soaked and frozen before clambering into the tiny yellow craft. Once more, night followed day and the myriad stars again mocked man's insignificance; yet, in fact, every young man of that lost crew had consequence and value. There were loved ones far across another ocean who, if providence did not stoop to assist, would soon be receiving those dreaded 'Missing In Action' telegrams. Bill Mackey thought of his childhood sweetheart, Ann, now a proud pilot's wife following their exuberant dash into marriage just before his graduation as a pilot. He remembered his Mom's concern, yet

pleasure, and his young brother Eric's complete surprise when they had arrived for the graduation last July. That day, his proud Mom realized she now had a son, grown up, married and bound overseas as a bomber pilot. Years earlier, she had been petrified when his uncle had taken her boy for a flip at Trenton/Mercer airport, New Jersey, then turned the biplane upside down in front of her very eyes. New Jersey seemed a lifetime ago – the others undoubtedly thought likewise about Vermont; California; Wisconsin; Maryland; Pennsylvania and New York – each state had a son or sons now adrift, drenched and shivering with cold, nine American lives on a sea they had never heard of until those early days at Mendlesham – now they cursed its grey tracts.

Joe nurtured Jerks Berserk for a further 1 hour, 45 minutes towards a horizon only of sea. Then, thankfully, the distance firmed from seascape to a welcome golden-edged green as the beaches and fields of north Norfolk greeted the weary aviator. Joe had maintained some 1,000 feet of altitude but now had to decide whether to crash-land or jump. Crash-landing a B-24 was a dangerous prospect and would take longer. Once it was below some 600ft, the option of parachuting was removed – there was no time to deploy. If the engines then quit . . . parachute it was. Holding Jerks Berserk stable, Joe carefully detached his dinghy. Now it was not needed, he did not want a repeat performance of it hooking up as he tried to escape. A beach below gave way to sparsely populated farmland, but there was a small town ahead, so he had no choice but to risk turning Jerks Berserk through 180 degrees to go seawards on its last journey. Nursing the B-24 into a gentle curve, Joe judged his moment. Now! Avoiding the control console, he was off the flight deck in three strides and threw himself forwards, out of the bomb bay. Narrowly avoiding the aircraft's tail, Joe immediately tugged his ripcord and the parachute snapped open. He had no time to allow for deceleration and the force of it opening tore a 3ft rent along one of the panel seams. The resulting contact with the landscape severely winded him and he lay amid the wheat, his head cushioned in his hands, simply savouring the sweetness of life. He then became aware of a farmworker approaching warily, pitchfork poised in readiness. Alarmed by the prongs, Jim managed a brief exchange that soon established his non-Germanic credentials. A second worker soon appeared with Britain's cure for every ailment, the inevitable cup of tea. Joe appreciated the gesture if not the brew and, once rested, borrowed a bicycle and was guided to the nearest police station to contact Mendlesham and await collection.

Nearby, another policeman, Thomas Payne, found himself involved in the story. A large American bomber, seemingly empty, had literally swooped to earth in his parish with unfortunate consequences for one local resident. Jerks Berserk, far from continuing seawards, had swung back inland. Descending in a shallow dive towards the town that Joe had tried to avoid, it skimmed over the cemetery then crunched into a field between the graveyard and the outskirts. Shedding pieces, it slithered onwards at over 100mph, then smashed into Pereer's Farm on the eastern edge of Holt. Luckily, the farm's occupant, Mrs Kate Edwards, had been visiting her sister in Norwich, some 30 miles distant, but returned to find her home had been literally lifted from its foundations by 25 tons of errant aircraft. A torn-off propeller rested in her piggery, the vast silver fuselage lay broken in the garden and the bomber's nose

Shedding pieces, the B-24 slithered onwards at over 100mph. Note the propeller deposited in the pig-pen. (*Ray Zorn*)

The aircraft smashed into Pereer's Farm on the eastern edge of Holt. (*Ray Zorn*)

and gun turret were embedded in the ground floor. Two exterior walls had been demolished and Mrs Edwards was undoubtedly embarrassed to see her porcelain 'po' on public view beneath a bed itself exposed to the elements. PC Payne had kindly retrieved some jewellery, her late husband's watch and some precious items of china that had amazingly survived the impact. He had also found her dog trapped in one of the sheds. A minor miracle occurred when an engine torn from the bomber bounced clean through a cowshed, much to the consternation of its occupants and the attending farmhand. Other engines had bounded away into the orchard, scattering unripened apples and ensuring a poor harvest later on.

Among early arrivals at the scene that summer afternoon was Russell Pointer, who raced home from work on hearing that a bomber had crashed near his home. Fortunately, his family were not involved and, decades later, Russell would still be perplexed by accounts from the Air Raid Patrol wardens revealing how they had found a large briefcase in the wreckage, 'full of' foreign banknotes. Local knowledge also related how the crew had bailed out and survived.

On 25 August, an RAF HSL scooped nine Americans from the clutches of the North Sea – these fortunate survivors were not from the 34th BG and their comrades at Mendlesham continued the long wait. Two days later, a further nine Americans were rescued but still not

The airman was aged about 20 and, in life, had obviously been a tall, broad-chested, handsome figure. The body of Bernard Sabbath was washed ashore on the Danish coast. Bullet wounds indicate an unsolved war crime. (*Scott Mackey*)

Mendlesham's missing airmen. Efforts to locate them had so far failed. Captivity was better than death so, in desperation, the Allies had earlier transmitted an international distress call on the recognized waveband of 121.5 megawatts. Giving an approximate position for the lost 34th BG aircrew, this transmission was acknowledged by a German radio station at Elbe Weser. American and British aircraft continued to search but found nothing. Had the Germans both rescued and captured them?

A month later, on 25 September 1944, Jens Martin Jensen, a Danish wreck master, was inspecting the south beach at Stenbjerg when he discovered the corpse of an 'English airman' at the water's edge. The body was naked with the exception of some boots and the tattered remnants of a flying suit. Even though it had evidently been in the water for some time, Jens could see the airman was aged about 20 and, in life, had obviously been a tall, broad-chested, handsome figure with thick, dark hair. Circumstances would suggest he had drowned, but the body had an obviously fatal bullet wound in the right chest with another through the thigh. Around his neck were dog tags bearing the number 16129636 and the name Bernard Sabbath. Jens dragged the body further

A crude wooden cross was erected, but callous treatment of the young airman's body prompted determined action by local Danes. (*Scott Mackey*)

ashore into nearby sand dunes to prevent the sea reclaiming it and then sought advice from his superior, Chief Beach Inspector Axel Rasmussen. With German forces occupying their country, the Danish authorities were initially overruled regarding a proper burial and, on 27 September, German soldiers simply interred the corpse where Jens had left it. A crude wooden cross was erected but the callous treatment of the young airman's remains greatly upset Axel Rasmussen and the people of Stenbjerg, so Axel bravely sought consent from the Germans to allow a proper funeral. Approaching Capt Hansted Knippenberg, Axel overcame initial indifference by citing how maltreatment of enemy dead reflected badly on the German military image. With further guile, he then explained how the local seafaring populace were very superstitious and believed that the soul of a drowned person reclaimed by the waves would emerge restlessly to seek peace on land by haunting the coastline. To allay such fears, proper burial in consecrated soil was essential. Rather than incur local displeasure, Knippenberg acquiesced and arrangements proceeded to inter Sabbath in the churchyard at Stenbjerg on 2 January 1945. Axel was charged with keeping it low key, and, in a nation still subjugated, any overt support for the Allied cause prompted by the funeral risked his

deportation to a concentration camp. However, word travelled fast in the close-knit, quietly defiant community, and, on the bus back to Stenbjerg, Axel found himself accompanied by a very large wreath in red and white signifying a free Denmark. This had been paid for by donations from local people, but, knowing it would provoke the Germans and provide an excuse for preventing the funeral, Axel asked for it to be kept hidden.

As the cortège passed the home of fisherman Jens Christian Mikkelsen, this brave Dane and his wife stepped forward with a small posy of flowers. Fortunately there were no Germans present, so Axel quickly hid the tribute in the coffin and Sabbath was laid to rest in a dignified service. Unfortunately, there were some repercussions for Axel. To show respect, the local lifeboat station and some houses had flown flags at half mast and Axel soon found himself in front of the Germans. Demonstrating Teutonic churlishness, an officer objected to the presence of flowers and Axel was alarmed in case the large wreath had appeared. Talking hard to avoid serious punishment, Axel was lucky to find a more sympathetic senior officer. It transpired that, following the service, local women had placed a small home-made floral tribute on the grave and the officer accepted that this was beyond Axel's control and allowed him to leave. Should the large wreath be discovered, there would be serious consequences, so it was destroyed and the smaller adornment removed only for another to appear next day. That the Germans behaved so reprehensibly might be just typical, but it might also indicate that Sabbath's remains were sensitive and bore silent witness to an atrocity. Had the broadcast on an international frequency resulted not in rescue but in cold-blooded murder? In January 1948, the now identified remains were repatriated at his family's behest for final interment at home. In later years, the fate of the crew attracted the rumour among 34th BG veterans of a merciless U-boat machine-gunning helpless survivors. Research to date has not resolved the mystery of bullet wounds seen in Sabbath's body when he is known to have been unharmed when he abandoned his aircraft.

Post-war, families sought to establish the fate of their loved ones. Allegedly, one even hired a private investigator to uncover evidence of a war crime. Following the publication of the first volume of *Eighth Air Force Bomber Stories*, Bill Mackey's nephew, E. Scott Mackey, contacted me, having seen my brief account. Scott had been doing 'a lot of research' and shared his results for this story. He had spoken to Joe Garrett and learned something of later events in Joe's life.

Joe had a successful post-war flying career, initially ferrying de-mothballed B-29s back into service then graduating into test flying the B-47 and later demonstrating the ubiquitous C-130 Hercules worldwide. In retirement, Joe served the local community of Cherokee County, near Canton, where he had grown up. In 2001, Scott contacted Joe and they conversed on the phone about the uncle Scott had never known. Joe revealed how he had been so broken up by the sense of loss and responsibility that he had suffered a mental breakdown. Scott sensed that the decision Joe had made over the North Sea nearly 60 years earlier still haunted him, and the veteran was understandably very sensitive. He had come back, lived a full and rewarding life but always bearing that sense of guilt. Scott Mackey spoke quietly to the man who had made an error of judgement that still echoed down the generations of his

own and other families. Scott sensed the sadness shielded by defensive anxiety about his telephone call, but there was one thing Scott quickly realized. We of later generations cannot judge. We were not there – we have no right. Scott's research was closing a chapter for his family, which had been opened by his Aunt Ann, Bill Mackey's widow, when she wrote in July 1945 to Army Air Force Headquarters, Washington, requesting information on the fate of her husband. After bouncing down official corridors, Ann received a brief account of events attached to which was a map of the North Sea. The distance flown scaled to only 4 inches coast to coast. There was a tiny cross 1¼ inches from England. Bill Mackey has no other cross – his name and six others are carved with pride on the Wall of the Missing in the US military cemetery near Cambridge. There are over 5,000 names and they gently face over 3,800 white marble crosses. By some quirk, Saul Spivak's name is not listed with his comrades but appears with 1,270 others on a similar wall at Margraten in the Netherlands, where there are also 8,300 similar headstones. If the North Sea took such ranks of white marble, they would be in serried ranks over waves concealing countless lost hopes and incalculable misjudgements. Not least of these would be man's gross inhumanity to man that prompted young men from the New World to aid the Old. Many did not return to resume life as did Joe Garrett, but his life, too, was broken by the nature of a war demanding more of a man than he had available to give. Only the unceasing North Sea knows the true fate of the men whose lives and hopes slid for ever into its cold embrace.

Joe Garrett never forgave his own error of judgement – with hindsight, he should have flown to Sweden. He finally rendezvoused with the crew only a month after speaking to Scott Mackey.

A new home arose on the site of Pereer's Farm and, in a small gesture for the Mackey family, the present owners, Mr and Mrs Cooper, allowed me to search their garden with a metal detector in August 2002. Ammunition from the lost bomber still occasionally surfaced and, true enough, under the grass track just beyond the garden fence, one round of .5 ammunition emerged. From beneath nearby turf came a few fragments of Jerks Berserk and, probably from Kate Edwards's bedroom, the broken remains of a 1940s-style scent bottle. It was fitting for the fragments of bomber to journey to Scott Mackey in remembrance of a young man with a place of honour in the history of his family.

CHAPTER SIX

Adopted Bomber

Many schoolboys in East Anglia during the Second World War took an avid interest in aircraft and their local airfields. The skies were laden with machines, then commonplace, now legendary. In those machines were men, themselves barely parted from boyhood and, all too often, robbed by fate of a future.

Whether the lives of three such young men crossed is lost in time's uncertainty, but the likelihood exists that 12-year-olds John Symonds and Tom Brittan saw 19-year-old Dewey D. Steele take off for his first mission. All were bonded by Old Buckenham aerodrome, then home to the 453rd Bombardment Group and its Liberators. One of these machines would play a part in all their lives, albeit, for Dewey, a very brief part. To both John and Tom, the B-24H-10-CF would become more than simply serial number 42-64469, upgraded to an 11-series by the modification centre. 'El Flako' was to be one of 'their' aircraft – each having

For two English schoolboys, B-24H-10-CF would become more than serial number 42-64469. El Flako undergoing maintenance on her hardstand. (*Frans Ammerlaam*)

independently 'adopted' the bomber as his favourite. During the last few months, they had tracked its comings and goings from its hardstand close to the road. The enthusiastic schoolboys had supported their machine on many missions and her markings were as familiar to each as the footpath home. Initially the B-24's factory finish of olive drab upper surfaces and neutral grey beneath with dulled-down national insignia made her indistinguishable from her many sisters dotted around the Norfolk airbase. Her pedigree was from the Consolidated Fort Worth plant, where she had been assembled from a knockdown kit of parts shipped from the Ford factory in Willow Run. She had begun the journey to Old Buckenham under shipment number 5142-GZ as one of the Group's original aircraft and was flown overseas by Crew #15 commanded by 2/Lt Roger G. Counselman. They took the new bomber across America from Hamilton Field, California, to Morrison Field in Florida, then flew the southern route across the Atlantic, saying farewell to sunshine as they slipped into England's wintry reception early in 1944. Upon arrival at Old Buckenham, the B-24 was assigned to the 732nd Squadron and coded E3-I. At that time the 453rd were denoted by a large blue 'J' in a white circle on the twin fins of each B-24, but, in May, this was replaced by painting the outer part of the vertical tail black with a diagonal white stripe to ease recognition during assembly. Taken on charge by Master Sgt Martin Drellick, the bomber soon acquired the name and nose-art that caught the attention of the schoolboys. Featuring the navigator's rectangular perspex windows as eyes, an unknown nose-artist assimilated these into some fearsome features by adding a shark's mouth arrayed on the aircraft's nose with an aggressively exposed set of teeth. Just aft of these was a cartooned burst of flak with the taunting nomenclature of 'El Flako', which soon drew attention from Tom and John.

Such posturing was unsupported by the aircraft's operational debut on 3 March, when the intended target was Oranienburg. Richard C. Holman's crew became concerned about the aircraft's fuel consumption and aborted the mission. Two days later they abandoned a sortie to Cazaux because of a problem with the bomb doors. On 6 March, El Flako dropped its first bomb load – on *British* soil! Marshall L. Johnson and crew had taken off for Berlin but accidentally released their payload only 3 miles from the airfield over the village of Carlton Rode. Luckily the ordnance fell on fenland and, other than pride, there were no casualties caused by this mishap. The crew made amends on 8 March by delivering their explosives to the correct address at the VKF ball-bearing plant in Erkner on the outskirts of Berlin. Thereafter, El Flako overcame her stage fright and accumulated an ever-increasing array of bomb symbols adorning the sheet of heavy steel armour-plating mounted on the cockpit's exterior. Notable among these missions was that of 22 April 1944, the infamous 'Night of the Intruders' (*see my book of the same title describing events*) when Me 410s of Kampfgeschwader 51 created havoc among Liberators returning in darkness to their airfields. Several bases were attacked and fourteen B-24s lost, including 'Cee Gee II' from Old Buckenham. The intruders had infiltrated American formations, and, in the ensuing chaos, many Liberator groups scattered, seeking safety elsewhere; but Marshall Johnson settled El Flako safely into Station 144 at 2240 hr. This adventure had been his crew's seventh mission in El Flako and the bomber's nineteenth successful operation. During the next six weeks, she tallied another

A splendid study by Dutch aviation artist, Lam van 't Hof, showing El Flako with sister ships and a 'little friend' 4FG Mustang. (*Frans Ammerlaam*)

sixteen targets and was one of the aircraft making history on 6 June – D-Day – when the Johnson crew took her to attack targets in support of the landings. This was his crew's last operation in El Flako. During July, a further eleven bomb symbols appeared on the scoreboard, all representing missions flown by the Albert T. Warfield crew. Their return from France on 28 July saw El Flako make an emergency landing at RAF Pershore in Worcestershire with flak damage necessitating repairs to the No. 4 engine. It was 9 August before El Flako returned to combat and her list of targets reflects the Eighth Air Force's reversion from predominantly tactical targets to more strategic objectives within the Reich. The Warfield crew had flown El Flako twenty-four times, including one 'Truckin'' operation to France when the fast-moving US Army had overstretched its fuel supply lines and B-24s found themselves ferrying gasoline to airfields near the front line.

By 2 November 1944, a weary, battle-scarred El Flako was adorned with seventy-seven mission symbols and, from the far side of the hedge, her honours were proudly supported by Tom Brittan and John Symonds. To the tiros of 2/Lt Carl Isaksen's crew, the tattered paintwork and mission scoreboard might have been comforting, because they offered evidence

of the many times she had taunted German anti-aircraft fire and returned. This morning, the defiant old bird had not been their originally assigned ship, and a hasty shuffle had seen them shifted from 42-94990 'Ken O Kay III' to El Flako for their combat debut.

As Sgt Dewey D. Steele checked his right waist gun, he undoubtedly had those pre-mission fears felt by every one of his predecessors in the veteran bomber, but his Irish descent was unlikely to have seen him overawed. At 19, the youngest of four children, Dewey was the 'darling' of his parents, Ernest and Ruth. Popular, handsome and intelligent, he had been born in Freeville, upper New York state, on 25 March 1925. The family later moved to Cortland, where Fall Creek, weaving through the surrounding hills and woodlands, provided ample opportunity for adventurous youngsters to play. When the opportunity arose, Dewey's patriotism quickly drew him from rural pursuits into the Army Air Corps, where his life moved rapidly through training. In early October 1944, he bid farewell to his wife and family when the Army ordered him to Idaho to complete his training and thence travel overseas. When the young air gunner departed, the couple were expecting their first child, but Dewey Steele was not the first of his family to reach the ETO. His elder brother, Ray, was already serving as a sergeant with the 369th FS, 359th FG at East Wretham in Norfolk. The brothers were an energetic cycle ride apart but enjoyed a great reunion, and Ray pedalled over several times as Dewey settled in and prepared for his first combat mission.

Realization that the Reich was increasingly dependent on dwindling resources of fossil fuels had elevated oil-related objectives on the target list for Allied air chiefs. On 2 November over 1,100 bombers were operational, with 146 Liberators attacking an oil refinery at Castrop-Rauxel in the heavily defended area of the Ruhr around Dortmund. Assembling at 22,000 feet, the 453rd faced little opposition on the route in, but that situation would change. Elsewhere, the German defences reacted in depth and the B-17 forces suffered grievously from fighter attacks taking advantage of lapses in American fighter cover. The B-24's main adversary that day was flak – short for *Fliegerabwehrkannonen* (anti-aircraft guns). From the autumn of 1944, Germany relied increasingly on anti-aircraft protection because fuel and pilot shortages forced it to husband its fighters, and nearly half of the Luftwaffe's manpower was employed in its flak units. Technological development enabled engagement of enemy aircraft by radar prediction, just as similar apparatus enabled the bombers to drop on targets unseen. Today, a dense undercast at 10,000 feet forced the attacking aircraft to use radar for release, just as radar operators in the flak units guided retaliation without visual contact. Both sides recognized the increased vulnerability of bombers forced to fly straight and level to the release point and the Liberators disgorged bundles of 'chaff' to confuse their opponents. Equally, the Luftwaffe fire control officers had information from Würzburg-D radar units fed to predictors, and development of the radar into a wider range of operational frequencies attempted to offset chaff and other Allied electronic countermeasures. Once the target became clear, flak could concentrate its barrage for greater intensity, because the bomber's focal point was known. Pilot Allen Bryson noted in his diary, 'Target today oil refinery in Ruhr Valley . . . No flak until bombs away then

all hell broke loose. One plane in Lead Squadron got a direct hit in the tail and went into a dive. Two men bailed out before they hit the clouds. The plane went on down . . .'

That unfortunate aircraft was El Flako. Others observed that the aircraft received a direct hit behind the bomb bay. The explosion ripped away one wing and the bomber fell in grotesque gyrations with the tail and waist section still barely attached to the fuselage from which spewed a trail of lighter debris including oxygen bottles and chaff. A moment later these sections separated and crews watched with fascinated horror as the remains of El Flako, twisting over and over, tumbled into the overcast sky and vanished. 1/Lt J.K. Crockett noted for the Missing Aircrew Combat Report, 'Direct hit behind the bomb bays after bombs away – broke in half . . . Approx 1224 hours'.

Initial German records show 672 bombs dropped, of which 152 did not explode – presumably some of these were delayed action. They recorded casualties of nine dead and four missing with eleven wounded, mostly in domestic dwellings close to the target – 'collateral damage' in today's terminology. The nitrogen plant at Castrop-Rauxel was badly damaged, so output would be seriously disrupted. Further German files detail the fate of El Flako and her crew. The Report on Captured Aircraft KU3283 recorded the date of 2 November at 1224 and the location as 'Luenen – South, near south shore of the canal port'. The type was given as a Liberator, but markings, serial number and equipment details could not be ascertained because the aircraft had been completely destroyed. The forward section had fallen into the drained Datteln-Hamm canal bed – presumably empty because of previous air attacks. The bodies of Carl Isaksen and his co-pilot, 2/Lt Earl L. Johnson, were found still strapped in their seats. A further six bodies were also noted: 2/Lt Vanig Vartanian, navigator; with Sergeants Robert L. Perrin Jr, top-turret gunner; Robert L. Pekouske, nose turret; Dewey D. Steele, right waist; James A. Dietrich, tail gunner; and Staff Sgt James K. Phillips, left waist gunner. This was at first thought to be the entire crew, but a follow-up report from a Captain Maasz dated 10 November confirmed that the aircraft had contained ten men, not eight, and advised the additional dead as 2/Lt Malcolm B. Rubin, bombardier, and Sgt Edwin W. Bringardner Jr, radio operator. Whether these two were the parachutists noted by other aircrews is unknown, but, despite the hope proffered by such sightings, all ten airmen had perished.

At Old Buckenham John Symonds and Tom Brittan watched in vain for the reappearance of El Flako. To the disheartened schoolboys, her fate was guessed at but unknown, and the memory of that combat veteran lingered during their ensuing years. More than fifty years elapsed before chance closed the pages on these memories and, for John Symonds, provided the opportunity of a special pilgrimage to honour 'his' old aircraft and her crew. Once they were the warriors he worshipped from the far side of a hedge. Now they were part of a youth lost in the savagery of war while his own lost youth had ebbed naturally in the peaceful years bestowed on him by their sacrifice.

In 1997, John's stepdaughter Ginny and her husband, Ian Barrat, moved to Arnhem in Holland, where their children attended school. The Dutch, as always, were most hospitable in making the family welcome and school friendships soon created bonds between parents. This connection introduced John to Dutch historian Frans Ammerlaam, who was very involved in

work commemorating wartime events surrounding Operation 'Market Garden', which had immortalized Arnhem in the history books and established the legend of 'a bridge too far'. Frans had not been born until 1953, but he and John were soon immersed in conversation, including John's boyhood days watching his heroes fly from Old Buckenham. This led naturally into the story of his adopted aircraft and his recently reawoken curiosity over its fate. John had read an account stating the aircraft was lost over Turnhout in Belgium, but did not know much else. This kindled the historian's curiosity in Frans and he embarked on research to learn more about El Flako. Use of the Internet soon established where it had fallen and that Carl Isaksen, Robert Perrin, Robert Pekouska and Dewey Steele were buried with 5,324 of their comrades in the Ardennes American Cemetery and Memorial near Neuville-en-Condroz in Belgium. Soon, Frans had arranged for him and John Symonds to visit the cemetery and pay their respects, while additional activities on the Internet triggered a response from Tom Brittan, now living in France. Further research in Germany established contact with retired teacher and amateur historian Horst Munter, whose interest focused on aircraft losses around Dortmund. Included in his files were German documents describing the destruction of El Flako and where debris from the bomber had fallen. Horst had been only 6 years old at the time and grew up in a Germany he viewed as having been liberated from a tyrannical dictatorship at an appalling cost in human lives. Even within his locality, he had identified some 150 aircraft crash sites and his work contributed to the history of his region, helped other historians and assisted relatives to understand more fully the fate of family members killed in action. Horst kindly shared his file on El Flako with Frans, who was now in touch with the Steele family. Between them, the two historians planned to recover some items from El Flako for Dewey's nephew, who was himself serving as a communications officer in the USAF. Col Robert Steele supported and encouraged their endeavours, which had further developed to include a memorial service on the crash site during German Armistice Day commemorations on 18 November 2001.

Horst knew that the forward fuselage had fallen into the canal, but investigations indicated that other parts had dropped in woodland close to the Gahemer outdoor swimming pool. Further sizeable sections came to earth west of what was now a Shell refinery and storage depot. Patient fieldwork finally pinpointed these sites and one, set close to a tranquil woodland footpath, still had trees with trunks scarred by the crash. Using his metal detector, Horst established a cluster of readings and some easy spadework soon found numerous fragments beneath the woodland's soft soil. His skill as an art teacher is evident in sketches he made of his finds and some of the part numbers were confirmed as coming from the bomber's No. 2 and No. 3 engine nacelles. These bore the manufacturer's prefix 32, denoting the Consolidated model number, with occasional parts prefixed 28 indicating they were designed for the company's earlier Catalina flying boat but then utilized on the model 32. Either way, his findings tied in with local accounts and the crash report, so a wreath of poppies could now be placed on the exact spot where a significant piece of the wreckage had fallen. Enthused by the efforts of Frans and Horst, John Symonds also determined to attend the commemoration, so the gathering was truly international.

The carpet of golden leaves rustling beneath their feet as they approached the crash site symbolized life's circle and caused reflection on young lives ending here so violently countless leaves ago. John Symonds was moved when further pieces of his adopted bomber emerged from a layer of leaf mould reaching over fifty-five autumns into the past, when his life, like Dewey Steele's, had been in its spring. John was overwhelmed with memories and sorrow, silently saying a prayer for the families and crew. While Frans fought with a larger piece still gripped firmly within the roots of a tree, the older Englishman contemplated life from the perspective of its autumn. He remembered the night El Flako failed to return and how a distraught crew chief, a frequent visitor to John's home, scoured the skies. Every time an aircraft flew over, Martin Drellick and his English friends raced outside, hopeful hearts pounding, then, once more, that quiet despondency. These fragments from a shattered bomber represented smashed lives denied the richness of future opportunity and fulfilment. Dewey never enjoyed the freedom he died to protect, but his spirit continued in the Steele family, with Bob as a serving USAF officer. Duty had prevented Bob from attending this small woodland service of remembrance, but he had entrusted Frans to read some words on behalf of the family to German press covering the event:

Thanks to the people of this town who remember not only their own countrymen who died in war, but also those of other nations who died, like my uncle Dewey. As a young 19-year-old, he was really no different from any 19-year-old from Germany, Russia, or China. I hope

Some easy spadework soon found numerous fragments beneath the woodland's soft soil. (*Frans Ammerlaan*)

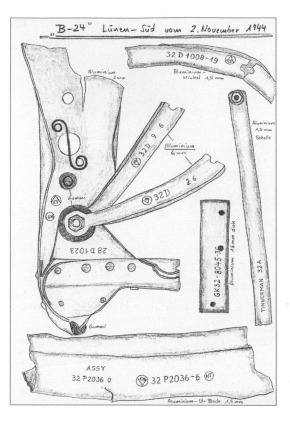

Sketches by Horst Munter of finds made at the crash site. Part 28D1023 nose cowl support bracket was originally designed for the Catalina but incorporated into the Model 32 Liberator. Part 32 P2036-6 is part of the No. 2 engine supercharger support and Part 32D 1008-19 is from the No. 3 engine cowling. (*Horst Munter*)

and pray that all our nations today will similarly remember the military troops who are fighting for the cause of justice and freedom. Please pray for their courage, safety and success.

Following the ceremony, Frans collected some soil to accompany parts of El Flako being returned to the family as a gesture of goodwill and friendship. John took a piece to return to Old Buckenham and later presented it to the Flying Club, where it enjoys a place of honour in their control tower situated close to where her hardstand had been. The group then adjourned to a nearby hostelry, where local inhabitants recalled the bomber's final moments as it tumbled from the sky. They remembered how, as the sound of aero-engines receded, the anti-aircraft guns fell silent until the next time. Nearly six decades later, those guns had been stilled for ever and were now only troubled memories to some of those present. People from nations once at war reflected on an assortment of pieces from a bomber that, like the guns, was now only an echo in the heavens and in the minds of the boys who had adopted it. In death El Flako and her crew had bonded former adversaries and helped give the freedom of speech now being enjoyed over some superb German beer.

CHAPTER SEVEN

Skipper 'an' the Kids

Although I was born in bonnie Scotland, I have to confess my aviation archaeology has generally been confined to East Anglia's rich and relatively flat topography; an agriculturally quilted landscape of fields, marsh and woodland. Comparatively speaking, such terrain is 'soft' and has enveloped numerous crashed aircraft, whereas this island's northern climes are hard centred, featuring clouds frequently stuffed with mountains. Many a lost aeroplane, descending with fearful crew, failed to materialize in clear skies beyond. Such victims of bad weather, mechanical malfunction or human error would often leave only a scar of surface wreckage with brutally mutilated bodies to be retrieved from remote surroundings. Strenuous efforts ensured airmen were recovered for proper burial, but the aircraft wreckage was often understandably left to the ravages of time. Only later did history add value to such discarded debris, either as a source of fabricated parts to assist in the restoration of types now rare, or for museum display in mute testimony, honouring fallen heroes whose stories were lifted from oblivion by the evidence of tragic sacrifice. So, in 1988, this less-than-intrepid aviation archaeologist — already the wrong side of 40 — found himself reluctantly heading for Highland landscapes and the land of his birth.

Not one distillery doorstep would be crossed for the fondly thought-of malt whisky. I was to join members of the East Anglian Aviation Research Group (EAARG) — all younger — intent on reaching the wreck of a Norfolk-based, 388th BG Flying Fortress named 'Skipper "an" the Kids'. It was strange to note that, over four decades earlier, the purpose of its final flight had been, according to some veterans, a navigational exercise with a sub-plot to collect whisky for Knettishall's forthcoming Christmas festivities. Disaster had overtaken it, and, as we journeyed north that December, the sombre scenes of a modern air disaster confronted us as we drove past the lowland township now for ever linked with an aviation tragedy — Lockerbie. Debris from the Pan-Am Boeing 747 clipper 'Maid of the Seas', downed by a terrorist bomb, still littered the landscape, and chunks of structure dotted the A74 hard shoulder. A Chinook beat overhead with an underslung load of wreckage or possibly the remains of innocent people lost in this horrific terrorist outrage. The unspeakable malevolence of those perpetrating such mass murder came close to home, considering that, only a week or so earlier, I had flown on that very aircraft on the same route during an

Skipper 'an' the Kids in flight. Note externally hung bombs. (*H. Baxter*)

American business trip. My thoughts were with the families of those who had perished, and recovering the wreckage of the 747 would make an invaluable contribution to bringing the killers to justice. My hope was that retrieving parts from the grandfather of that aircraft would also make a valuable contribution by honouring the young airmen involved and ensuring the family grief experienced forty-four years earlier would also not be forgotten.

Sunday, 10 December 1944, saw the 388th BG airborne on the Group's 233rd mission to attack German transportation targets near Koblenz. This successful operation was uneventful and merits little mention in the Group's history. What lingers still in the memories of surviving veterans was the fate of their B-17, Skipper 'an' the Kids. A champion with many sorties to her credit, she had survived over sixty missions and was perceived with airmen's superstition as a 'lucky' ship. Her credits included leading the 388th to Brux, Czechoslovakia, when they were awarded a Distinguished Unit Citation and her gunners claimed two Me 109s destroyed. She had emerged from the June 1944 debacle at Poltava in Ukraine when an intrepid Luftwaffe assault destroyed forty-four Fortresses and scarred a further twenty-six. Skipper had also ensured her crew's safe return on 28 September 1944 from one of the most heavily defended Luftwaffe targets of them all – the IG Farbenindustrie

Surviving many sorties unscathed, Skipper was perceived as a 'lucky ship', but she became increasingly combat-weary. (*H. Baxter*)

oil refinery at Merseburg. Her record of repairs grew, as did the number of aluminium battle-damage patches peppering her wings and torso, but Crew Chief, Master Sgt Paul Irela, deserved credit for her 'lucky' reputation. He and his men laboured to ensure Skipper was always in trim and combat ready whenever humanly possible. By December, they were endeavouring to maintain what was clearly a borderline case for being declared 'war weary', as the previous month had been arduous for her ageing airframe. Respect was now tinged with adverse comments – a 'war-weary old clunker', according to one pilot, and 'a dog' to another. Following further maintenance, she required a long-range test flight and assessment by experienced engineering and flight personnel. Advantage could be taken of this exercise to break in a recently arrived 'rookie' crew, provide some air-time for those requiring it to substantiate the additional pay allotment and, of course, replenish Knettishall's whisky stocks. The airbase, like many others, had numerous bars, and a whisky shot was also used, if wanted, to help combat crews unwind when they were being interrogated following a mission. Whisky runs were common practice in the USAAF and in the 388th BG in particular. Lt August Bolino, a former navigator, recalls:

> One mission turned out to be comical. We were told one day we were going to make a secret mission to Scotland. And we got into our Fortress and started flying towards Prestwick. We were, of course, very fascinated by this. What could be our secret mission? When the Fortress landed, there on the flying field was a supply of Scotch whisky, which we loaded in the waist and brought back to the field. It seems that every few months somebody was assigned to go up to Scotland to get Scotch for the weekend parties.

Understandably, no official records stipulate this as one of the flight's purposes, but the 388th BG's former Weather Officer, Lt Edison Jeffus, also remembers.

> The 388th had great parties at the officers' club and, no matter how much we and our guests drank, we never ran out of Scotch, Irish whiskey or gin – but American-made Bourbon was always in short supply. (One may not fully realize just how much alcohol is required to maintain high morale among a bombardment group's wartime flight crews and their supporting ground personnel, but it is not inconsequential.)

This particular flight would serve both formal and informal requirements, and, fulfilling these, eleven men boarded Skipper. Some excellent research by Ayrshire aviation buff Graham Herbertson gives us an insight into their lives. Graham has spent years 'researching every facet of this aircraft and her crews'. His sole aim was to present his findings to the next of kin, because some were still seeking closure despite the passage of many years.

Commanding the aircraft was Capt John N. Littlejohn Jr from Savannah, Georgia, whose experience belied the fact that he was still only 22 years old. John had already completed one full combat tour and had just returned to Knettishall for a second. He would be an ideal mentor to 2/Lts Jack Dean Merkley and Robert Nelson Stoaks, pilot and co-pilot of a recently

Commanding the aircraft was the experienced Capt John N. Littlejohn Jr, who had just returned to Knettishall for a second tour. (*Graham Herbertson*)

arrived replacement aircrew. Merkley, from Blackfoot, Idaho, a former university pharmacy student, was two years older than his tutor and was anxious to accumulate additional flying hours for both financial and promotional reasons. Bobby Stoaks, a Hollywood Californian, was still only 18 years of age and must have been in awe of the sapient Littlejohn. Merkley's crew had arrived in October, having trained on Liberators, so now needed conversion to the Fortress, particularly because, if the flight endorsed Skipper as combat-ready, she was likely to be their assigned aircraft. This trip would be ideal for learning her idiosyncrasies and

Merkley's crew had arrived in October 1944 having trained on Liberators. Several of those pictured would perish on board Skipper. Albert Thomas is fourth from left in rear row. *Front left to right*: 2/Lts William V. Frey, Jack D. Merkley, Robert N. Stoaks, Leonard W. Bond. (*Graham Herbertson*)

provide an excellent navigational exercise. Three navigators were on board, with tutorage provided by 23-year-old 1/Lt Richard William Rosebasky, who came from the small town of Stockett, Montana, and was navigator with Capt Rye's Lead Crew. A 'quiet and likeable guy', 'Rosy' had nine missions accredited and could use this flight to enhance the skills required of a Lead Navigator. His juniors – both also 23 – were 2/Lts William Victor Frey, Merkley's navigator, a first-generation American from German parents in Oak Hill, Illinois, and Leonard Wilbur Bond from St Johns, Michigan. Bond was of English descent and had enlisted in the cavalry on his twenty-first birthday but then transferred to the Air Corps and entered gunnery school in Fort Myers, Florida. After he had completed his gunnery training, his further potential was recognized and he entered training as a navigator and bombardier. He was commissioned in July 1944 and embarked for the ETO during October. His last letter home, four days prior to the fateful flight, touched on the travails of wartime travel,

Dear Folks, Just received your letter of 17th November. It is the first mail that we have received since we came to England. How is everyone at home? I am feeling fine. Just a

little tiring though . . . Was glad to hear all my stuff got home O.K. Gordon [his brother] can wear the watch if he wants to. Tell him to take good care of it. I have another one just like it with me but I busted the crystal on the way over here. It was pretty rough one night and our boat was really hitting the waves. I hit my watch against the bed and it didn't do it any good . . . Was glad to hear that Dad is feeling better – has he got his stone teeth yet? . . . You asked about Xmas. I don't think there is anything you can send me. I don't have room for anything. It's a good thing I sent a lot of my clothes home because I have lost just about everything I brought over. About all I have left is just what I had on – nice mess – they are getting kinda dirty now. Let me know if you get my checks O.K. Love, Leonard.

Bond's usual function was bombardier on the Merkley crew, but he would undertake a navigational role for the flight to Prestwick. Radio communications were to be tutored and managed by Staff Sgt Wade Dalton Kriner, aged 20, who was a Pennsylvanian from Du Bois and an experienced gunner on Lt Meagher's crew. Kriner had already received the Distinguished Flying Cross Air Medal with four oak-leaf clusters, the Purple Heart, and had trained from waist gunner to radio operator as the requirement for gunners diminished. Supporting him was Cpl Albert Edward Thomas from Findlay, Ohio. Albert had trained on Liberators with the Merkley crew and refers to it in his last letter home, dated 1 December 1944.

Dear Folks, No letter from you for some time now. I am permanently stationed somewhere in England. Quarters aren't too bad and food is good and plenty of it. I just can't get used to this weather. I like to see the sun shine once in a while . . . There is lots I could talk about but very little I can write about. I am on a Fortress now instead of the one I trained in the states; this Army does funny things some times, for the best I hope. Forget about my Xmas for the present time, I may request something later. Tell them all I said hello and will write them as soon as I can. Take care, God bless you all, and write when you can. Your Son, Albert.

The individual assigned as engineer for this flight was Mississippian Cpl Joseph A. Payne, who, although he had entered the military a year previously, had arrived at Knettishall only two weeks earlier, following a furlough in America. This flight would undoubtedly provide him with valuable experience in simulated combat conditions.

It can be seen that some aircrew on Skipper were not performing their primary roles, but such cross-functionality would also be part of aircrew training. There were two men listed as pure passengers. First, 39-year-old Major James Russell 'Doc' Bell, who was the 388th HQ Flight Surgeon and had recently been given special orders by the 388th CO, Lt-Col Chester Cox. These necessitated five days' temporary duty in Prestwick, and Doc Bell was originally ordered to fly in an Air Transport command aircraft but took advantage of Skipper leaving directly from Knettishall. This also enabled him to log flying hours to earn an airborne staff officer's salary, a welcome addition, especially with a wife and two young children to support in Cannonsberg, Pennsylvania. The second passenger, Master Sgt

Maj James Russell 'Doc' Bell, the 388th HQ Flight Surgeon, took advantage of a lift on Skipper. (*Graham Herbertson*)

Master Sgt 'Jimmy' Brown in Highland regalia. (*Graham Herbertson*)

'Pat', Brown's Scottish sweetheart. (*Graham Herbertson*)

Charles Spencer 'Jimmy' Brown, had a romantic motivation. This 24-year-old hailing from Rhinelander, Wisconsin, had experienced Scottish hospitality before and was looking forward to meeting his Scottish sweetheart, Pat, during his five-day pass prior to the seasonal festivities. Jimmy may have had some gifts to deliver, so utilizing 'Skipper' was an ideal opportunity to play Santa.

Whatever other reasons existed, official records simply say the 560th Squadron B-17G, serial 42-97286, departed AAF Station 136 for a cross-country navigational training flight. Prior to take-off, the flight crew were briefed on expected weather conditions by 2/Lt Norman J. Putnam, Assistant Station Weather Officer. Delayed an hour for reasons unknown, Skipper 'an' the Kids took off at 1058 hr, heading north towards its first turning point at Sleaford. Plans still allowed 3 hours in Scotland, with a return to Knettishall envisaged at *c.* 1700 hr, well after the base had received its operational aircraft back from Koblenz. Flying up the east coast, Skipper reached Selby, still following the general route of the A1 to Masham then continuing on her north-westerly heading to cross the Scottish border. Weather forecasts in Norfolk had given a high cloud base, but, as predicted, this lowered and thickened the further north they droned. Prestwick itself was suffering light rain and dense, low cloud, multi-layered from 900 to 18,000 feet with light rime ice in cloud above 3,000 feet. The bomber's estimated time of arrival was 1230 hr and the tower at Prestwick was listening on the B-17's radio frequency of 6,440 kilocycles, but no transmissions indicating any problems were picked up. Ninety minutes later, concern increased – there was no sign of the silver Fortress. Capt John N. Littlejohn Jr had 877

hours' pilot time, 381 on the B-17, and it is feasible he took the controls from Stoaks in the co-pilot's seat to support Merkley when, or if, concern increased regarding their exact position. Later Rosebasky joined Littlejohn and Merkley in the cockpit – possibly to utilize the large collection of maps stored in the carrier on the pilot's seat. Despite the experience of those on board, deteriorating weather conditions with frequent blustery snow showers made navigation very difficult and they had no radar. A major factor in the unfolding tragedy was the variation in actual wind strength from that forecast. Wind strength at Prestwick had been predicted as approximately 25mph from 345 degrees (north-westerly), whereas actual conditions encountered were an easterly wind of some 18mph. On the assumption that they were close to Prestwick's eastern approaches, a gradual descent would have commenced, with an expectation of emerging from the murk close to their destination. In fact, Skipper was off course and approaching the mountainous Isle of Arran. It is puzzling that no positional fix was sought, but Graham Herbertson later offers a hypothesis explaining why.

At Prestwick, the radar set detected an aircraft on its approach, but, at this crucial moment, the set failed and the aircraft could not be tracked, nor could they establish radio contact. During briefing the crew had been advised to keep watch on Prestwick's frequency of 6,440 kilocycles and had been given its r/t call sign of 'Burton', but no signals from 'Practice Bomb' – the bomber's own wireless transmission code – were ever received.

As darkness fell, anxiety for the missing B-17 increased and contact with alternative airfields produced no news. Skipper had taken on board over 8 hours of fuel, but this would now be exhausted – the aircraft must have gone down, but where? The USAAF officer put in charge of the search was 1/Lt Louis Appleton, an Operations Officer with Headquarters, ETO Division of the Air Transport Command located at Army Post 741 in London. Early evidence came from a Royal Observer Corps post at Corriegills on the east coast of Arran, which plotted an unidentified aircraft flying in a westerly direction about the time Skipper was due to land. Arran, off the south-west coast of Scotland, is some 20 miles west of Prestwick and rests like a sleeping giant in the Firth of Clyde; its topography and climate a 'Scotland in miniature'. When sunlit, the rugged mountainous beauty of the island attracts hillwalkers with its breathtaking scenery but also conceals its deceptively treacherous environment for the unwary airman, and its granite peaks had already claimed other victims. A further eleven names looked certain to be added to the list unless the aircraft had overflown and fallen into the sea. Poor weather and nightfall had made an immediate search impossible, but, next morning, police and home guard scoured accessible parts of the island. Despite poor flying conditions, one machine was airborne, surveying more remote mountains, but it was forced by worsening conditions to abandon its search that afternoon and remained grounded by weather throughout Tuesday, 12 December. Further testimony pointing to the B-17's fate was provided by an Arran farmer who reported first hearing then seeing an aircraft pass overhead heading for a glen in mountainous terrain where shrouded peaks sat sinisterly in its path. A break in the weather allowed another aerial search on 13 December, but neither of the machines involved saw any evidence of the missing Fortress. Appleton recognized that

snowstorms hampering the search on foot could also now have hidden the lost B-17. Further participation by air was impossible because of low cloud and snow, so it was two days before aircraft again swept over the more remote regions. Criss-crossing low over isolated mountain peaks still streaming wind-whispered snow from their ice caps, the airmen saw no evidence of their lost compatriots.

Christmas celebrations at Knettishall must have been muted, not only by a lack of Scotch but also by the mystery surrounding the loss of Skipper 'an' the Kids. The tragedy also affected others off-base. Percy Prentice, then a 14-year-old lad whose mother was a laundry lady for Littlejohn and the other crew, recalls that his family were heartbroken – all the airmen's laundry was ready for collection but no one came.

The winter was one of the worst for some half a century and provided the Germans with an opportunity for their last major Western offensive, the 'Battle of the Bulge', when continuing adverse weather, reducing the effectiveness of Allied air superiority, facilitated a German breakthrough. Inclement weather also contributed to the loss of the legendary bandleader Maj Glenn Miller, whose C-64 Norseman disappeared over the English Channel five days after Skipper vanished. A Missing Aircrew Report for the lost B-17 was prepared on 16 December by Station 136's Statistical Officer, 1/Lt Earl W. Sweeney, and attached to it was a tracking chart annotated with an arrow to Arran: 'A/c is believed to have been lost somewhere in the vicinity of Isle of Arran'. However, it was not until 7 January that the dreaded telegrams were transmitted from Washington, DC. That received by the Thomas family was typical and, in less than fifty words, lives were laid waste:

THE SECRETARY OF WAR DESIRES ME TO EXPRESS HIS DEEP REGRET THAT YOUR SON CORPORAL ALBERT E THOMAS HAS BEEN REPORTED MISSING IN FLIGHT. TEN DECEMBER IN EUROPEAN AREA. IF FURTHER DETAILS OR OTHER INFORMATION ARE RECEIVED YOU WILL BE PROMPTLY NOTIFIED = DUNLOP ACTING THE ADJUTANT GENERAL.

For Leonard Bond's mother, Irma, those words may have confirmed a dreadful premonition, for she broke into tears during a family gathering sobbing that she could not stand the fact that Leonard 'lay dead somewhere in the snow'.

On Friday, 2 March, the families of the missing airmen received a further communication from Headquarters Army Air Forces Washington. That received by the Bond family was a sad, if necessary, template:

Dear Mr Bond,

I am writing with reference to your son, Second Lieutenant Len. W Bond, who was reported by the Adj. Genl. as missing over Prestwick, Scotland since Dec 10, 1944. Additional information has been received indicating that Lt. Bond was the navigator on a B-17 (Flying Fortress) bomber nicknamed 'Skipper and the Kids' [sic] which departed from England on a training mission to Prestwick, Scotland, on Dec 10, 1944. The report reveals that your son's bomber was neither seen or contacted after it left its base but that a farmer

on the Isle of Aaron [sic] reported hearing a plane, believed to be Lt Bond's and seeing one fly directly overhead. It is further indicated that adverse weather conditions existed in this area. No other information is obtained in this headquarters relative to the whereabouts of your son. Believing you may wish to communicate with the families of the others who were in the plane with your son, I am enclosing a list of these men and addresses of the next of kin.

Please be assured that a continuing search by land, sea and air is being made to discover the whereabouts of the missing personnel. Any additional information rec'd will be sent immediately to you by the Adj. Gen'l of this Headquarters.

Very sincerely,

E.A. Bradmore, Major Air Corps Chief Notification Branch, Personal Affairs Div., Assistant Chief of Air Staff Personnel.

It seems doubtful that, by that time, any 'land, sea and air search' was being undertaken to the extent implied, but, the day following this letter, 'additional information' was about to be forthcoming.

On Saturday, 3 March 1945, a 21-year-old Brodick man, Verner Small, had a day off from his duties at the island's power station in Brodick and was hillwalking over Beinn Nuis. Heavy snow had fallen that winter, but that day's thawing conditions were full of the promise of spring, ideal for enjoying the island's splendid views. Verner, reinvigorated, was briskly homeward bound over Beinn Nuis. The view was breathtaking, the clean air exhilarating, and he paused, soaking in the scenery. Then the glint of metal near the base of a cliff nearby caught his eye. Peering over the edge, he saw what looked like the wing of a small plane and he descended carefully to investigate. He was a keen diarist, and his entry for that day reads:

> Went for a climb in the afternoon up Beinn Nuis. It was a lovely day, warm and sunny (my nose is quite sunburned!) but it was might [sic] cold on top. On way down I looked over the edge of the precipice and beheld a plane where there wasn't no plane before, so scrambled down to investigate. It was a new crash all right as there was at least one body. I didn't examine him too closely, but he was humming quite a bit, poor devil. It was mighty eerie, as the icicles were falling from the cliff and rattling on to the fuselage; it sounded like someone raking around. The number was H297829 [sic] and the map reference of the place (foot of Beinn Nuis Chimney) 451629. I think it is an Auster.

The body he found was lying face down in full flying kit including a leather helmet. One leg was drawn up and the arms stretched out in front and it looked to Verner as if the poor soul had been alive following the crash and was attempting to crawl away from the wreck. Verner hastened to report the find and telephoned Police Constable Archie Galbraith, who called back later asking Verner to lead a squad of police and Royal Navy personnel to the site the following day. His diary reads:

Sun. March 4th. Very wet, with low clouds in morning cleared about 1300 hours and bright sun thereafter. Set off with Naval party at 9.45 hours. Top of String [the road bisecting Arran] 1015 hours. Pouring like blazes and fairly strong wind. Headed for top of Gleann Easbuig, crossed it and hit Beinn Nuis on S.E. shoulder. Clouds very thick and had a terrible job to find plane. Eventually reached it about 1300 hours. Turned out to be one of the Flying Forts missing since November [sic] so no wonder the body was stinking. Found another 6 so there will probably be 3 more underneath. I have to go up again with the Yanks. Arrived home about 16.30 (16.00 at String where we got a cup of tea from the WVS [Women's Voluntary Service].

What Verner had taken to be the wing was the bomber's fin lying on its side, so he assumed the machine was smaller with fewer crew. Still proud on the wreck was the 388th's black-squared H with the tail number 297286 and the call letter L in black below. This was the only recognizable piece of Skipper 'an' the Kids. At some 200mph, the B-17 had smacked into a narrow gorge, known to climbers as The Chimney, on the granite face of Beinn Nuis, exploding a cascade of debris and crew onto the rocks and heather below. Such was the force of impact that some parts were scattered over a quarter of a mile. Verner was not called to lead the Americans to the site and was somewhat disgruntled to find this task allotted to a Naval Petty Officer. He was, however, contacted by the local press and noted, tongue in cheek, in his diary for 6 March:

Had an exciting evening. *Daily Record* phoned to get my story, expect to see headlines in tomorrow's paper – 'Lone climber discovers plane crash; unnerving experience for intrepid youth.'

Several papers covered the story with varying degrees of accuracy and one somewhat embellished its account headlined,

US Airmen Collapse on Rescue Bid. American airmen sent to Arran to recover the bodies of 10 of their comrades killed in a Flying Fortress crash on 2,597 ft Ben Nuis, collapsed from exposure during the search. The men, unused to mountain climbing, had to skirt precipices under difficult weather conditions in making their way to the gulley where the wreckage lay . . .

None of the other papers reported this 'fact' and gave relatively straightforward accounts, though erroneously citing the loss of ten, not eleven, aircrew.

Sombrely, the dead were extricated. Verner recalls that ten caskets were loaded onto the RAF launch at Brodick Pier, which might account for the misleading press reports. This supports local legend that there were insufficient body parts to fill eleven caskets, such was the force of the impact. Even for the ten they had, rocks were placed in one of the caskets to give the impression that there were complete remains inside. Capt Littlejohn's remains were

found in the cockpit debris with those of Merkley and Rosebasky – these three are now interred in a group burial in Fort McPherson National Cemetery, Lincoln County, Nebraska. All the victims had first been buried in Cambridge with their comrades, then later taken home at the request of their families. The true cause of the tragedy was never established, but the onus rested on Littlejohn, as will be seen. To avoid the wreck being reported again, the tail section and other large pieces were chopped up and buried where soft soil allowed. Having researched this incident more thoroughly than anyone else, Graham Herbertson feels the original investigation treated Littlejohn rather harshly and offers the following contribution in mitigation:

The manner in which the USAAF reported the loss of 'Skipper "an" the Kids' to the crewmembers' next of kin did nothing to suggest there was any wrongdoing on the crew's behalf. Reporting restrictions meant that they received only the briefest of information. Following declassification of the Accident Report in the 1970s, it is apparent the USAAF actually blamed the aircrew, particularly Capt Littlejohn. The findings recorded were: 'The cause of the accident is unknown but it is attributed to the pilot trying to approach Prestwick contact and becoming confused while in low cloud or poor visibility and striking high ground while in full flight.' The report then adds: 'It is strongly recommended that pilots clearing for Prestwick from airdromes in England and particularly from combat bases not only be thoroughly briefed as to the radio aids and weather conditions here but are also checked to see that they have maps, radio range-cards and radio aid facility charts for this field. If pilots will avail themselves of its complete services, accidents of this type can be prevented.'

To me, these statements imply that the pilot was lost ('confused'); the crew was not thoroughly briefed regarding radio aids available at Prestwick or weather conditions in the Prestwick area. The pilots did not 'avail themselves of its [Prestwick's] complete services'. There had been a lack of 'maps, radio range-cards and radio aid facility charts' on board. In my opinion, this implies Capt Littlejohn was guilty of gross negligence and the manslaughter ('the crime of killing a person without intention to do so') of his eight fellow crew members and two passengers. The three navigators were also implicated in their apparent failure to take on board the appropriate navigation aids. It appears that the aircrew was blamed for the crash without conclusive evidence. This is despite common law dictating that deceased aircrew could be found grossly negligent only in cases where there was absolutely no doubt whatsoever. To me, such a statement unduly blackens the well-respected name of Capt Littlejohn. Without evidence suggesting technical malfunction caused the crash, then the investigators seem to have automatically taken the decision to blame the crew. It appears that Capt Littlejohn was held responsible simply because he was the senior aircrew officer and the officer who signed for responsibility for the aircraft. However, I believe there is evidence indicating other factors, not considered at the time, which I feel caused the crash. The USAAF documents must be reassessed combining this additional evidence with that gleaned from 388th BG veterans to provide a more accurate picture.

It is important to remember that there were no survivors who could provide first-hand accounts of the incident and give an insight as to what went wrong. There were also no voice or flight data recorders ('black boxes') on board to record the vital moments of the aircraft prior to its demise. The families of those killed on board Skipper 'an' the Kids were not given the opportunity to view and question the findings. Anyone reading the official documentation will not realise what I suggest was the true cause. It is for these reasons that I aim to put the record straight; to ensure no blame is attributed to the crew members and, hopefully, to provide their families with the necessary, if belated, peace of mind and closure.

One must first consider those facts and the evidence pointing to crew negligence being highly unlikely. I believe the following argument refutes, although it does not unequivocally exclude, the report's claim of crew negligence. The experienced members of the crew *were* familiar with Prestwick's facilities. The vast majority of Eighth AF aircrew flew into Prestwick during their transatlantic crossings. In fact Capt Littlejohn, having just returned from the States for a second tour of duty, might well have just reacquainted himself with Prestwick's facilities. As many 388th BG 'whisky runs' were made to Prestwick, there would have been plenty of opportunity for Knettishall's operations staff to be aware of these and to notify crews who did not know. The Skipper crew were briefed about the facilities and the weather forecast prior to their departure. Eighth Air Force 1E Aircraft Clearance Non-Operational Cross Country Flight Form was signed by Capt Littlejohn and confirmed by V. A. Memmolo (Duty Flight Clearance Officer), thus confirming acceptance of the weather forecast made by the 388th BG Weather Detachment's 2/Lt Putnam. Maps, radio range-cards and radio aid facility charts would have been on board. All three navigators undertook intensive and comprehensive training to ensure in-flight navigation efforts were of an extremely high standard. One of these navigators, First Lieutenant Rosebasky, was also an experienced Lead Navigator. I suggest the presence of these navigators would have resulted in much cross checking to avoid the basic error of forgetting 'maps, radio range-cards and radio aid facility charts'. So why were the crew blamed? Although I do not prescribe to a conspiracy theory, I feel this concept must be acknowledged as contributing to an incorrect conclusion being reached regarding the cause of the crash. The advantages and disadvantages for the USAAF taking this line should be considered: blaming the aircrew had some 'advantages'. There is no concrete evidence that the aircrew were *not* to blame for the crash. Indeed, the investigators' report found no evidence in the wreckage of any technical malfunction capable of causing the crash. The report can therefore be used to justify an unequivocal conclusion that the aircrew was to blame. The apparent lack of concrete evidence concerning what happened during the flight means that the decision to blame the aircrew cannot be established beyond doubt to be manifestly false. As long as there is no unequivocal evidence in favour or against aircrew error, the conclusion to prove pilot guilt cannot be changed. The mere fact that an aircraft has flown into a mountainside and not over or around it is prima facie (accept as so until proved otherwise) evidence of incompetence. However, allocation of responsibility to the crew has some 'disadvantages'. Although some of the available

evidence – for example, non-use of navigation radio aids – indicates an element of aircrew error, there is insufficient evidence to prove it. Blaming the pilots requires a subjective interpretation of the few facts that exist. An equally valid, but different, subjective interpretation of the same facts could conclude that equipment or some external influence was to blame. Without the certainty of evidence from a cockpit voice or flight data recorder, the weight accorded to certain facts over others gives rise to the accusation that the pilots can be blamed only if those who judge them use speculation. In the RAF, the 'Queen's Rules' dictate that deceased aircrew could be found grossly negligent only in cases where there was absolutely no doubt whatsoever. Finding the pilots grossly negligent without evidence of ineptitude raises the question about whether the USAAF adopted this answer as a simple expedient. If the families had known this conclusion at the time, it might have incited their anger, believing that blaming their kin provided too convenient an answer for a series of awkward questions.

There are 'benefits' in this case if other reasons could be found for the tragedy. If the military authorities were able to blame conclusively the weather forecasting capability, this would have provided a definite cause of the disaster. It would also show that they were willing to defend the reputation of an aircrew that could not defend themselves. However, wartime exigencies might support resorting to the easiest conclusion. The consequences of a fuller investigation might disrupt operations, affect morale by undermining confidence, prove expensive or embarrassing if exposed. Apportioning responsibility elsewhere lessened the duration of the investigation and its possibly widespread retributions. Conversely, these 'benefits' supporting other reasons can be counterbalanced. The USAAF may have had to concede deficiencies in their weather forecasting capabilities. Finding these at fault would raise questions about whether those who had provided the information and predictions for the forecast should bear some responsibility for the deaths of eleven people. This might have adversely impacted aircrew morale given the importance of their need to have confidence in the tools and techniques given to them to carry out their tasks. In no court of law would a judge, without hard evidence, and without the families of the dead being able to plead the case for the defence, find deceased defendants guilty of manslaughter unless proved otherwise. Yet the USAAF seemed to have had this power. If an allegation of a conspiracy theory is discounted, then one must consider that there must have been some degree of negligence within the investigation team or the procedures they adhered to. Was there negligence within the investigation process? The investigation team were probably limited by time and resource constraints to undertake a thorough investigation. Accidents such as this were also commonplace in 1944, thus requiring time and effort for their investigation. Notwithstanding this, the evidence cited in the Accident Report points towards there being an element of negligence, or at least a lack of thoroughness, in the investigation, because some unambiguous evidence has clearly not been considered. There are also discrepancies in the recording of facts, which indicates the potential unreliability of such records. For example, the 1E Aircraft Clearance Non-Operational Cross Country Flight Form shows only nine on board, another 388th historian stated eight. What was the true reason for the

flight? What were the roles they played? How many were recovered from the crash site? However, just as the deceased aircrew cannot defend themselves, neither can those who undertook the investigation. It is therefore unfair to blame them for negligence.

Although the passing of time limits the availability of documented evidence and reduces the credibility of verbally relayed accounts, I am certain it is still possible to identify an alternative and probable cause. Furthermore, I feel the available evidence could have led the investigation team to this same conclusion and I offer the following hypothesis.

The primary purpose of the flight was a navigation exercise to train Lt Merkley's rookie crew in navigation techniques used in combat within the environment of their 'new' aircraft. Thus, the techniques of dead reckoning (DR) and pilotage would have been the adopted navigational methods. A crew's maintenance of radio silence during a combat mission was key, so a training flight, simulating combat conditions, would result in the exclusion of radio aids until they were within range of Prestwick as if returning from combat. The briefed weather forecast in the Prestwick area was: Cloud cover 9/10ths. Light rain. Dense, low cloud, multi-layered from 900 to 18,000ft. Wind – 25mph from 345°. The prevailing weather conditions seen in the latter stages of the flight were: Cloud cover – 9/10ths at 2,000ft to 10/10ths at 1,500ft. Light rain and snow. Some low cloud present. Visibility 4–6 miles. Ceiling variable. Wind–13–18mph from 090°. The prevailing winds were therefore at extreme odds – some 105° – from those briefed. Because of the prevailing 'blind conditions', this change in wind direction was unbeknown to the crew. Skipper 'an' the Kids was known by the Prestwick tower radar to be in their vicinity yet flew straight by, directly towards the Isle of Arran via Corriegills and Glen Rosa. The crew was clearly within range to contact the Prestwick tower when it appeared necessary to do so by the tower's staff. The crew also had the equipment, knowledge and experience to do so when required. I suggest the crew unwittingly reached a location where they did not believe they were and crashed, oblivious to their plight. To understand why this could have happened, one must consider the fundamentals of air navigation, the roles of the three navigators, available navigation procedures, techniques, instrumentation used plus other influencing factors, such as the weather forecast and prevailing weather conditions. Few things are simpler than getting lost in the air. True, there are many aids to air navigation, but equally there are many impediments. The navigator must have the knowledge and skill to prevent himself from getting lost and staying lost, or he will become a danger to himself and a menace to others. The weather is the navigator's greatest and most persistent enemy, seldom his friend. Air navigation calls for a high standard of intelligence, quick wits and a well-founded education.

The 'full-time' B-17 navigator had his own station situated in the port side of the nose armed with a bagful of maps, charts and calculating instruments including his sextant, to help him to keep track of the position as he flew, or to find it if he got lost. Most bombardiers, similarly stationed in B-17's nose, on the starboard side, were also trained in the art of navigation. The air navigator's training course in the USAAF was a full and varied one, involving many hundreds of hours of classroom study and air experience.

It taught him to use all the varied maps and charts of his profession, to understand and allow for the various anomalies in navigational instruments, to use the stars, sun and moon plus such subjects as radio, radar, meteorology, mathematics and physics. The course also taught a good deal about aerodynamics, airframes and engines, and explained the different kinds of operational flying as well as purely navigational subjects. In this assessment, one can touch only upon one or two topics and then only lightly. I begin with standard navigational techniques normally used in US heavy bomber operations, which would have been those used on board Skipper 'an' the Kids. *Dead reckoning* (DR) – keeping account of heading and air speed and assessing departure from the last known position. *Pilotage* – keeping account of position through constant visual reference to the ground. *Radio aids* – keeping account of position through the inference of information received by on-board radio devices interrogating ground-based radio transmitters. To consider the techniques during their final flight, there are those simulating combat conditions followed by those normally used during final approach. It is assumed that use of radio aids during this navigational exercise was restricted to use during the final approach, emulating a combat mission. Radio silence would have prevailed during the flight's main phase so DR and pilotage were the techniques used. During an actual combat mission they would normally follow a lead or Pathfinder Force (PFF) ship equipped with 'Gee' or 'H2X' radar. Skipper 'an' the Kids did not have radar and, irrespective of the lead ship, crews in combat were still required to navigate using DR, which was still the cornerstone of combat navigation although aids such as 'buncher' or 'splasher' radio beacons helped during take-off, assembly or returning from missions. The phrase 'dead reckoning' is a corrupted derivation of the first syllable of the word 'deduced', a word which more or less explains that there is an element of uncertainty about it. All B-17 navigators had to be competent dead reckoners. DR made them independent of aids such as radio and radar, which might be unreliable or unavailable. Normally, the pilot and navigator are able to identify their whereabouts by means of a map when they near their destination and have visual contact with the ground. DR is the art of calculating the course, track, ground speed and position during flight from knowledge of the probable wind velocity and true air speed. Unless the wind is dead ahead or dead astern, it will always blow the aeroplane off its course, and the track over the ground will deviate. Consequently, DR navigation requires the navigator to calculate the extent and direction he has to 'aim off' in order to arrive at his intended destination. He consults his maps to find the bearing of his destination from his point of departure plus the weather forecast to indicate the speed and direction – that is, the velocity – of the wind. He establishes how much compass error he must allow for, and finally arrives at the magnetic course to steer. Normally, he has methods of finding out if the wind changes direction or speed when airborne and instruments which simplify calculations necessary in applying corrections to the original course. DR is not a precise form of navigation, but those skilled in its use can rely upon being no more than 20 miles out at the end of a 200-mile flight, even though the ground has been out of sight the whole way. Pilotage is undertaken, as the name implies, by the pilot maintaining visual contact with the ground

and plotting his course with reference to known features seen during the flight. It is limited and ineffective over a featureless landscape or when weather conditions preclude visual contact with the ground.

In the absence of on-board radar or following a radar-equipped formation, the normal procedure for navigating a B-17 over enemy territory during combat was DR while maintaining radio silence. I therefore believe that the navigational exercise aspect of this flight would have been focused on preparing the rookie crew for navigating during combat. In northern Europe flights were mostly undertaken during 'blind' or heavily overcast conditions so training would have concentrated on using DR. The B-17's communication radio could be utilized as a navigational back-up by calling ground-based facilities in the vicinity which might also be tracking them using radar. Further support came from transmitters at known locations emitting radio signals at predetermined frequencies. By tuning in the radio compass to the frequency of these radio beacons, they could check position and enter it in the log on the navigator's table. The number of ground-based navigation aids supporting this crew were limited but they were available during the final stages of the flight, particularly when the aircraft was positioned to approach and let down into Prestwick. Additionally, SBA (Standard Beam Approach) was available at this busy hub. Prestwick had seen some 12,357 Eighth AF aircraft movements and during August 1944 alone had witnessed some 7,847 aircraft movements. For these reasons, Prestwick was one of the few UK airfields with a radio range facility for letting down through cloud, the descent being to the south-west over the Firth of Clyde, clear of Arran's perilous peaks. This facility, combined with Prestwick's comprehensive range of navigational aids, was something that should have been a great aid to the crew during their approach.

I would now like to consider the navigational instruments – gyroscopic compass and magnetic compass plus the maps used supporting DR to infer heading, air speed and altitude. These, in turn, were used to deduce heading, ground speed, distance and time. The magnetic compass is often supplemented by a gyroscopic compass which, installed where the aircraft's local magnetic forces are weakest, transmits its reading to 'repeater' compasses in the cockpit and at both the navigator's and bombardier's locations. This type is known as the distance-reading (DR) compass. It is a combination of a magnetic compass and a gyroscope, each exerting a measure of influence over the other, and to some extent correcting or modifying each other's more serious defects. For instance, the magnetic compass is too uncertain for accurate turns because it is, among other things, affected by acceleration and deceleration, and the needle takes too long to settle after a change of direction. The gyroscope suffers from a process known as 'drift' and, although it accurately measures a turn, it has to be adjusted every few minutes or it will 'lie abominably'. With the DR compass, the gyroscope gives the magnetic compass's needle a measure of stability and the needle curbs the gyroscope's tendency to wander. Thus, the good qualities of both are established and the effects of their shortcomings moderated. However, the simple magnetic compass remains indispensable because the gyroscope is electrically driven and the source of power may fail. On most flights the magnetic compass is simply a passenger but is there if required. In aerial

navigation, compass directions are measured to the nearest degree, clockwise from the north – that is, from 000° to 360° – and are always expressed as three-figure groups. Thus, east, which is 90° from north, is written '090°'; south is '180°', and west '270°'.

Frequent use is made of the term 'bearing' in navigation. Any two objects separated by a distance have a 'bearing' one to another. The bearing is measured clockwise from north and may be expressed as a true (or geographical), magnetic, or compass bearing. By taking a bearing on an object whose position is known, a navigator can make a 'position line' on his map. He knows only that he is somewhere along that line, but if he can take another bearing on another object whose position he knows and make another position line (which will intersect the first) he has a more precise indication of his whereabouts. If he can find a third object and make a third position line he will have enough information to tell him his position with still greater accuracy.

Unfortunately, even the magnetic compass is not immune from error. It has a finely balanced, freely suspended needle, which responds to the influence of the earth's magnetic flow and, unless disturbed, this needle always lies in a north–south direction. The navigator flies by maps based on geographical representations, but the North Magnetic Pole, which attracts the compass needle, does not coincide with the Geographic North Pole. They are, in fact, many miles apart. The angle between the bearings on or above the surface of the earth is called 'variation' (VAR). It differs all over the world and is constantly changing, so that the variation one year at one spot is different from that the year before and will be different the years after. Finally, there was a veritable library of maps held in the map holder on the back of the pilot's seat for use by the pilot and co-pilot while the navigators had their own supply of maps.

As Skipper neared Prestwick, the bombardier and acting navigator, Lt Bond, would have sat next to the 'regular' navigator, Lt Frey, in the B-17's nose section. Sitting at his normal bombardier's station, Lt Bond had a repeater air speed indicator (ASI) and altimeter close at hand to assist navigation. The ASI and altimeter suffer from fundamental limitations compensated for by the navigator. The ASI, for instance, rarely shows the aeroplane's true air speed (TAS). It is a pressure instrument that, as the air grows thinner, loses pressure with height so the pressure registered by the ASI falls – with the result that the instrument grows more and more pessimistic until, at 40,000ft, it indicates only about half the aeroplane's true air speed. Navigators knew how much error to allow for at any given height to avoid being misled by the ASI but the error caused by the drop in pressure with height is not the only ASI issue. There are also position error and altitude errors, the first arising from the position of the pitot head through which the pressure is transmitted to the instrument in the cockpit, and the second from the increase and decrease in angle of attack. Although both these errors can normally be ascertained, weather sometimes precludes this with potentially disastrous consequences! Dealing next with the standard altimeter – this is also a pressure instrument. On the B-17 its dial indicates a scale of measurement in thousands of feet. Pressure is not always the same at any given height. For convenience, and by international agreement, a standard measure has been adopted. This

assumes (*a*) a sea-level pressure of 1,013.2 millibars, (*b*) a sea-level temperature of plus 15°C, and (*c*) a decrease of temperature with height of about 2° (1.98°, to be exact) for every 1,000 feet of height. But pressure varies with weather, and a fine spell might read 1,047 millibars at sea level while stormy weather might indicate only 911 millibars – a difference of 136 millibars. Therefore, if Skipper 'an' the Kids left Knettishall, which was enjoying better weather than Prestwick, and flew to Prestwick, which was in the throes of a 'deep depression', the aeroplane might have found itself at sea level with 3,780 feet still showing on the altimeter. In the given bad weather that might mean an unpremeditated and violent contact with the ground – in other words, a crash! Hence, it would have been customary for the pilot or navigator to make a check towards the end of any journey. During Skipper's flight to Prestwick, Capt Littlejohn would have known he needed to call the Prestwick tower to ascertain local barometric pressure. By means of an adjusting knob he could then set his altimeter to agree with the information received and he would have reduced the risk of error on landing. This practice would have been second nature to the crew. For this reason, despite their position being known to the Prestwick Tower and being perceived to be 'on approach', I firmly believe the crew did not believe they were on their approach.

Supporting why I believe they did not know they had passed Prestwick, I now consider the DR navigation process undertaken using the briefed weather forecast and how this would have been affected by the prevailing weather conditions. This is a conjectural reason for their 'failure' to contact Prestwick but has strong merits. Firstly, I have considered the weather forecast briefed to the crew and applied the same principles and calculations utilising a modern-day CR-5 flight computer to simplify the calculations undertaken in 1944 using navigation tables. The Skipper crew would think themselves subject to the following conditions. (Although this considers the final leg of the flight, from Masham to Prestwick, the same principles apply to the previous legs.)

- True air speed   206mph (180 knots cruising speed)
- Forecast wind direction /velocity   345°/25mph
- Estimated tracking   311°
- Estimated drift   +4°
- Estimated heading   315°
- Known variation   −5°
- Estimated heading   310°
- Estimated ground speed   185mph
- Known distance   128 miles
- Estimated flight time   42 minutes

This indicates that the crew believed the aircraft would fly:

- with a ground speed of 185mph,
- on a heading of 310° from Masham.

If they assumed the actual weather conditions aligned with the forecast weather, this would result in a flight time of 42 minutes to cover the 128 miles. However, given that the south-west of Scotland is now known to have been subjected to vastly different wind conditions from those forecast, then the crew would have been totally unaware of this because they were flying completely 'blind' (8/10th to 10/10th cloud cover). They were unable to check their progress through visual contact with the ground and were actually subject to the following conditions:

- True air speed   206mph (80 knots cruising speed)
- Actual wind direction/velocity   090°/18mph
- Actual tracking   310°
- Actual drift   −3°
- Actual heading   307°
- Actual ground speed   221mph
- Actual distance   155 miles after 42 minutes, assuming an unobstructed flight path
- Actual distance   128 miles after 35 minutes, assuming a flight path in direction of Arran's mountains.

This indicates that the aircraft would have actually flown:

- with a ground speed of 221mph (some 36mph faster than they believed),
- on a heading of 307° from Masham (some 3° to the left from where they believed).

The implications of this were such that Capt Littlejohn would have opened the engines' throttles to maintain their cruising speed (the true air speed shown on the air speed indicator) of 180 knots (206mph). As the crew would have believed they did not need to let down for an easterly approach to Prestwick until they were some 5 minutes away, that is, 37 minutes flight time, they would, in fact, have flown straight past Prestwick at this stage. They were also now some 3° to the left of their intended course and heading straight towards the Isle of Arran's mountains. Tragically, flying at the known altitude of 2,400ft – corresponding to the altitude of impact on Beinn Nuis – they would have hit the mountain only 35 minutes after leaving Masham, at around 1225 hr. This would have been some 2 minutes prior to their intended contact with Prestwick and explains why they did not contact Prestwick despite the tower expecting them to do so.

This hypothesized flight path is confirmed by the Royal Observer Corps plot at Corriegills at a time corresponding with Skipper 'an' the Kids' ETA (approximately 1230 hr) at Prestwick. In addition, the farmer's sighting of the aircraft directly over Glen Rosa heading for the Beinn Nuis area and the wreckage being found on Beinn Nuis indicates the crew thought they were still east of Prestwick. They did not think they were lost because they were on a straight path and did not believe they yet needed to

make contact with Prestwick. They would have been 2 minutes or so away from preparing themselves for letting down and would be just about to contact Prestwick for the normal procedure of requesting a barometric check for their altimeter, followed by clearance to land. Instead, they crashed into Beinn Nuis without knowing anything about their fate.

I am convinced that the crew did everything properly given the nature and 'operational' constraints of their navigational exercise plus the weather forecast they were given and the instruments they had available to them. The cause of the accident was simply the weather forecast being so dreadfully wrong with the crew completely unaware and prevailing cloud cover preventing any visual checks. This explains why Lt Putnam believed that 'his' weather forecast was the crux of the whole incident and why Edison Jeffus felt 'Lieutenant Putnam never forgave himself for missing that forecast and shouldered more of the blame for his tangential involvement in the crash than was proper'. I wholly agree with this statement. Indeed, it was only when Lt Putnam's forecast coincided with the adverse weather conditions plus the proximity of Arran's treacherous mountains that the tragedy occurred. The south-west of Scotland is a notoriously fickle region for predicting weather. The presence of cloud and precipitation is frequent, as one Atlantic low follows another in the prevailing westerly and south-westerly winds. It is therefore relatively infrequent that weather fronts come in from other directions. In the winter of 1944, however, the whole of northern Europe was immersed in the worst winter weather for fifty years. With hindsight, I feel it is unfair to blame Lt Putnam because this weather was unusually bad and the associated weather front came from eastern Europe, which was still in enemy control. Arguably, it would have been well-nigh impossible for the Allies to gather the necessary weather information from these areas to enable the weather detachments to forecast with any degree of accuracy. The information Putnam and the Station 136 Weather Detachment used was sourced from Weather Central, the British meteorological office at Dunstable. This office coordinated and issued forecasts to all Eighth AF weather detachments ensuring the same information aided consistency of forecasts. Such information was, in part, derived from each station in the UK including Station 136. Interestingly, Prestwick, as the main transatlantic terminal airfield, had the largest complement of Eighth AF weather personnel at any one airfield and was better positioned to provide information pertaining to the Prestwick area. For the above reasons, it is felt that no one could have predicted the forecast any more accurately than Lt Putnam with his given resources.

Climbing to the site on Boxing Day 1988, I was grateful for the weather giving us an unusually mild winter, in contrast to that in 1944. Even so, I could understand how the B-17 had been overlooked. We had no snow to contend with but soon found ourselves breathing cloud, and figures only feet away became grey shadows. Recent rain meant soggy moorland and slippery rocks. First evidence of the tragedy appeared lower down the mountainside when we found water-tumbled fragments wedged between rocks in numerous rivulets rushing to

'An eerily quiet battlefield shrouded in mist' – the crash site, Boxing Day 1988.

the brook below. Strangely, parts of the B-17 had merged with pieces of Liberator washed from another nearby wreck. Wheezing the last few hundred feet, I felt the EAARG should have left me to mince pies in East Anglia's easy, flat landscape. Such feelings vanished in a mixture of poignancy and excitement as large sections of the lost Boeing became apparent. Chunks of structure, a smashed Cyclone engine and a machine gun still clutched in a rock-face crevice; parts of the ball turret strewn on grass below – an eerily quiet battlefield, shrouded in mist. Digging in one of the trenches, EAARG members were jubilant to discover remains of the tail fin spotted by Verner Small. Numerous flak patches testified to Skipper's battle days, but the shiny aluminium skin was as bright as the day Alcan made it. The short December day limited time but, by 2 p.m., the group had several trophies light enough to transport and they began their journey to Norfolk being manhandled down the hillside. Pleased though we were, we realized the return of these items would have been happier forty-four years earlier if Skipper 'an' the Kids had slipped into Knettishall, its navigational training sortie successful and with cases of Scotch on board.

I wrote a feature on my festive season antics for the renowned aviation magazine *Flypast*, and this helped trigger a more determined recovery operation undertaken by enthusiast Peter Stanley. His service in the RAF provided advantages and Pete was able to organize a Royal Navy Sea King helicopter from 819 Naval Air Squadron to airlift some heavier items of wreckage off site. After obtaining a licence and all necessary permissions, Pete made his first

reconnaissance visit in 1989, with support from the Sea King obtained in May 1990. That month, Pete's excavations unearthed parachutes, a waist-mounted machine gun, the star and bar insignia from the fuselage and wing, even a fully inflated tail wheel. Things were proceeding well but circumstances altered, as Pete later recalled.

It was during this time that some unpleasant occurrences happened. We had spent many hours recovering two blades and a boss which had been located on a previous expedition. It was positioned ready for it to be airlifted off the mountain by a Sea King when the helicopter unfortunately had to cancel the lift following an SAR [search and rescue] callout. In addition to the blades, we had also recovered two horizontal stabilizers, which were also positioned for lifting off the mountain. As the helicopter lift had been cancelled, we set about re-burying the blades to prevent them being removed/damaged by souvenir hunters. During this time a lone walker approached, which was unusual, as the majority of walkers tend to keep to the high ridges and consequently never see the wreckage. This chap stopped and watched what was going on. Eventually, once the hole was filled in and the turf replaced, he wandered off. Not thinking any more of it, we set off down the hill carrying what we could. At this time the tail wheel had been recovered and was also accompanying us on our journey back. Unfortunately, due to impending darkness I decided to hide the many other artefacts we had recovered, in the valley below the crash site. It was at this time, I noticed a figure sitting on the ridge watching.

The following day we returned to the place where all the items had been hidden – unfortunately everything had been taken! With the help of the Head Ranger (Derrick Warner) and the local police, the culprit was identified as the lone walker we had seen the previous day . . . Bearing in mind I was the only MOD licence holder to recover items, the local police arranged for the Glasgow police to visit the suspect. This they did and fortunately recovered all our items. Time had run out on this trip, so the intention was to return to the mountain as soon as a helicopter could be made available to recover the blades and horizontal stabilizers.

A few months later, Derrick Warner . . . informed me that somebody had been unlawfully digging huge holes and scattering wreckage everywhere. I immediately arranged a visit, worried that our blades and stabilizers had been interfered with. My fears were justified, the blades had been re-dug out of the hole and were missing. Also missing was the more complete of the two stabilizers. A rusty, vandalized propeller boss was found a little way down the hill, scattered around it were broken hacksaw blades . . . the propellers had been removed by hacksawing through the prop ring. Unfortunately, we never managed to get the blades back or the stabilizer. The rest of this expedition was spent ferrying grass seed up the mountain and reinstating the land . . .

It is sad to think of unscrupulous individuals robbing the site for the selfish purposes of private collecting. Pete had intended these items for display in the Pathfinder Museum at RAF Station Wyton in Huntingdonshire.

It is sad to think of unscrupulous individuals robbing this site. Pete had intended to display this propeller in the Pathfinder Museum, but it was vandalized and the blades stolen. (*Pete Stanley*)

My *Flypast* story was not the first on Skipper and an earlier piece by aviation historian Graham Smith initiated Graham Herbertson's investigations. It is disappointing when efforts to ensure that airmen are remembered result in sites being raided, and such activities are to be condemned. More positively, my account furthered Graham's inspiration, and his contribution to this story and to honouring the crew has been significant. His principal purpose was to aid families still seeking knowledge of events, but his work also benefited the 388th collection at Market Weston in Norfolk. Housed in an original 388th BG Nissen hut close to the now derelict airbase, this collection pays tribute to the 388th's achievements.

Other recovery efforts were also undertaken by the Arran Junior Mountain Rescue Team, which retrieved a propeller and boss now housed in the Isle of Arran Heritage Museum as a monument to all airmen whose lives have been snatched by its merciless mountains. Such energy shown by these individuals and organizations is why I have dedicated this book to those who, behaving honourably, give of their time ensuring that others who selflessly sacrificed so much more are not forgotten.

CHAPTER EIGHT

What's in a Name?

Portsch Close, Seavert Close, Fortress Road – three names on a tidy, recently built housing estate in Carlton Colville near Lowestoft in Suffolk, the most easterly town in England. Young children play, teenagers in cars with sound systems worth more than the vehicle hurry away to avoid helping in the garden. Parents shrug, trowel in hand, then bend to the herbaceous border. Here, tending the garden just might reveal evidence of a wartime drama with roots that ran tragically deep in a family far away in time and distance.

2/Lt Robert Harsen Portsch knew it was time to get out. The Fortress was doomed, her port wing now a mass of flames but, glancing down, he could see they were still over the town . . .

Lowestoft. A name on a navigator's map – a place most Americans had never heard of until the US Army Air Force frequently used its prominent position as a departure point or weary airmen returning from combat welcomed the sight of its two piers, the harbour and distinctively shaped patch of water west of the town. The British quaintly called it a 'Broad' – a name conjuring up entirely different connotations for US airmen!

Bob Portsch had ordered his crew to parachute and was now alone in the blazing B-17. An only son, he was all his mother had, but Lillian Portsch had known her son could not stand by and simply witness the destruction of democracy. She loved him, realized the risks, but had the courage to let him enter combat. He was 21 years old when he enlisted on 6 July 1942

The Fortress was doomed, her port wing now a mass of flames but, glancing down, he could see they were still over the town. Pilot, 2/Lt Robert Harsen Portsch – left – with co-pilot, Flight Off Clifford N. Britton. (*Bob Collis*)

Lillian Portsch was a widow and Bob was her only son, but she accepted the risks when he enlisted. (*Bob Collis*)

and had later taken to the skies with youthful exuberance, shouldering a seriousness of purpose and dedication to duty.

This duty would now not let him abandon a fully laden, burning bomber over the innocent inhabitants of the town below. If he reached the outskirts, they would be safe and the sea lay only seconds away. Smoke and fumes filled the cockpit but there was a chance – set the autopilot and get out. The C1 autopilot was an early electro-mechanical computer and very effective for controlling the aircraft in normal flight and during the bomb run when the bombardier had control for fine-tuning the approach. In an emergency, it allowed time to evacuate the aircraft providing it could be set up to hold steady an empty machine and, in this case, one on fire with a feathered No. 2 engine. To engage the C1, Bob had set the master switch on a control panel in the pilot's console while a Pilot Directional Indicator enabled the direction to be fixed and a series of switches, lights and control potentiometers allowed sensitivity to be established for the ailerons, elevators and rudder. Once trimmed, the aircraft would hopefully hold its predetermined course and altitude, enabling him to escape. Almost blinded in the smoke-filled cockpit, Bob had to set the C1 to compensate for the drag induced by the dead engine. Slowly, the B-17 turned, its anguish evident in an ugly black banner trailing like a wraith in its wake. An agony of time elapsed – in reality, only seconds – before the bomber's nose pointed safely seawards. Bob had to get out and stop his beloved Ma facing a lifetime of loss and regrets . . .

Lillian Portsch was proud of her son and, sharing the same sense of patriotism, had given up her activities in the Newark Museum, New Jersey, to support the war effort directly, working for the Westinghouse Lamp Division. Her husband, Emile, had died when Robert was still only 10, and raising the boy during the difficult days of the Depression had been a challenge rewarded by the devotion she received. When he went to Bloomfield High School, she learned to share her fun-loving son with many friends, including his sweetheart, Susan Hunt, with whom he went steady until they both lost him to Uncle Sam. Susan would later remember, 'We thought that it was going to be for ever but our lives took different paths when Bob went into the Air Force.' Bob, the boy from the Bronx, later became engaged to Jane Chadwell in Nashville, Tennessee, but his life's focus was to fly in the service of his nation, and deep personal relationships were set aside. Bob also relinquished good career prospects in Sales with the Cynamid and Chemical Corp. of New York. His qualifications in chemistry from Brooklyn Polytechnic Institute plus his mother's parental status offered

protection from Army service, but Bob would have none of it. The letters and pictures sent to Lillian from Army Air Forces Pilots' School at Ellington Field showed a boisterous, confident young man in flying apparel with a deep Texas suntan, clearly enjoying life and the camaraderie among the cadets.

Bob's pilot training began in February 1943 in Class 43 J. The airbase straddled acres of former grazing land close to Houston and was proud of its training traditions dating back to 1917. Indeed, the first aeroplane entrusted to Aviation Cadet Portsch would not have been out of place in that era. Writing to his Ma, Bob described the Fairchild PT-19A: 'This ship is our training plane here at Primary. Top speed about 150 MPH – cruises about 100 and lands about 80. 175 HP.' Before clambering eagerly into the cockpit, class 43 J had endured a series of mental, physical and psychological tests to achieve their coveted Aviation Cadet insignia of a propeller and wings worn on the left shoulder. Now the fledglings were coached in navigation, radio, engines and airframes plus the theory of flight before being allowed to join their civilian instructors in the air. Robert progressed well, while the inevitable 'washouts' saw others depart from the programme before it moved on from primary to basic training camps scattered across Texas and Kansas. Bob found himself at Majors Army Air Field with an increase in horsepower flying the Vultee BT13 Valiant or 'Vibrator' – so-called because of the traits induced by its 450-horsepower Pratt and Whitney Wasp Junior radial. As part of Training Squadron VII, Bob mastered the idiosyncrasies of the Vibrator and then transitioned to the twin-engined Beechcraft AT-10 'Wichita', a machine manufactured

Officially the BT13 was the Valiant but acquired the nickname 'Vibrator' because of traits induced by its 450HP Pratt and Whitney Wasp Junior radial engine. Bob noted on this picture, 'August 1943 – an excellent shot of the BT13A we fly here at Basic. In the right lower background notice the B-17 Fortress.' (*Bob Collis*)

Bob found himself at Majors Army Air Field with an increase in horsepower flying the Vultee BT13 Vibrator. (*Bob Collis*)

ELLINGTON FIELD
CLASS 43-J

Tomorrow's Heroes

Bob transitioned to the Beechcraft AT-10 Wichita. This was his Class Book. 'Tomorrow's Heroes' would prove apt. (*Bob Collis*)

mainly from wood to conserve supplies of aluminium. Now wearing his silver wings, Bob progressed to his final weeks in training, which involved some seriously heavy metal as he learnt to handle the Consolidated B-24 and spent hours over Colorado, New Mexico and Texas acquiring the skills required not only as a pilot but as the captain of his own crew. After honing these talents from July to October 1944, Bob and his crew then received movement orders for the ETO.

Lillian Portsch said farewell to her boy in November 1944; as he gave Susan a farewell hug, he quietly urged her to 'Take care of Ma'. Not that Lillian needed mollycoddling, because, ever an indefatigable spirit, she had already taken the war to the enemy in her own way and qualified as a Civil Defense Corps nursing aide. However, her most significant contribution to the war effort would be undertaken by proxy. Like so many mothers with sons at war, she waited, worried and loved, suppressing the heart-stopping fear triggered whenever the telegram boy appeared. This anxiety was understood only by other mothers with boys battling the enemy far from home.

The Portsch crew found themselves at Station 137, named after the ancient and picturesque wool town of Lavenham in Suffolk. Joining the 837th Squadron, 487th BG, they

Bob's final weeks in training involved some seriously heavy metal as he learned to handle the Consolidated B-24. Bob pictured in his 'office', September 1944, Pueblo, Colorado. (*Bob Collis*)

A view from the 'office'. (*Bob Collis*)

The Portsch crew before heading overseas. *Rear left to right*: 2/Lt Richard R. Michael, bombardier; Flight Off Clifford N. Britton, co-pilot; 2/Lt William V. Ward, navigator; 2/Lt Robert H. Portsch, pilot. *Front*: Sgt Clarence V. Baker, nose turret; Staff Sgt James D. Bain, top turret; Sgt A.E. Lindemann, engineer; Technical Sgt Frank W. Powell, tail turret; Cpl Douglas E. Seavert, radio operator; Pte Epinenio Montoya, ball turret. (*Bob Collis*)

had to re-educate to fly the B-17G because, although the 487th had entered combat with Liberators in May 1944, subsequent Army Air Force policy standardized the First and Third Air Divisions on B-17s. As a component of the Third Air Division, the 487th relinquished its Liberators and converted to the Fortress while Bob's crew were still in training on the B-24. The transition was not difficult and they began accumulating missions from December during appalling winter weather conditions. On 6 February 1945 they participated in the now controversial assault on Dresden. Back then, the USAAF had a job to do, as Bob's engineer, Technical Sgt James D. 'JD' Bain, later recalled:

I remember it very well. We had been on a bombing run to Dresden, Germany, which took 10 hours and 15 minutes. It was the longest mission I flew. When we returned there was no

ground control approach and the fog was very bad. We made one pass and there were men with green flares at the end of the runway and we were too far to the right and missed the runway. We went around again and we were low on gas so we had to come on in and we bounced about 25 feet and the plane wouldn't stall and the runway ran out and we were too fast to be on the ground and not fast enough to fly. We continued on about a half of a mile more, went through a sheep pen, a ditch and all this pulled the landing gear out from under the right wing and we hit back onto a highway. The right wing caught a concrete mixer that stopped us. The co-pilot got a little cut on his head. He was going out through the fuselage and he wasn't moving fast enough and I gave him a push with my foot. The plane was completely demolished. It was a brand new B-17 airplane and that was the only mission it ever flew.

Historians continue to debate the necessity of bombing Dresden with its appalling casualty figures, but the crumbling remnants of Hitler's vaunted Reich were not succumbing easily despite the overwhelming weight of Allied air power. The numbers of aircraft involved were now enormous and the Portsch crew was simply one among an armada of some 1,262 bombers launched on 14 March to pound a range of targets. That morning, thirty-nine Fortresses reverberated over the medieval rafters of Lavenham intending to attack the Gerbrader Korting AG tank factory on the eastern outskirts of Hanover. Bob Portsch and crew were assigned an 836th Squadron B-17G-55-DL, not built by Boeing but, as denoted by the DL, a sub-series 55 made by the Douglas Aircraft Corp. in its Long Beach, California, plant. Serial number 44-6570, coded 2G-P, predated the crew's posting and had arrived in the UK on 27 September 1944 and flown in the Group's 100th mission. By now, Bob had flown seventeen sorties and been awarded the Air Medal on 23 February for his achievements. This had already been parcelled up and was en route to his adored 'Ma', who would undoubtedly take quiet pride in the honour earned by her son. Quite apart from the war experiences, he would have some other tales to tell when he got home, having recently returned from a furlough to London. There he had chummed up with Roland F. Doran, a former Cynamid colleague now navigating the 467BG B-24, 'Heaven Can Wait'. Most of Bob's crew were at a similar mission status under a style of leadership bonding them into an effective team, each confident in and dependent upon the other.

Their bomb load was eight 500lb high-explosive bombs plus two 500lb M17 aimable containers each holding 110-type M50A1 incendiary bombs. Fully laden, they took off uneventfully and began climbing to join formation at 6,000 feet. The coastline of Suffolk slid astern as the formation continued climbing towards the Continent. At 12,000 feet, Bob noticed their No. 2 engine was losing power. Suspecting an electrical fault, Bob ordered JD aft to change the fuse but to no avail. Instead of the required manifold pressure of 35in, their faltering No. 2 indicated only 16in and, after labouring to 20,000 feet, it failed completely. Unable to maintain position, Bob aborted the mission over Holland and turned for home. Descending to 10,000 feet and flying without the turbo supercharger apparently restored the No. 2 Cyclone to normality. However, anxious eyes monitored its instrument readings and maintained a constant visual check.

2/Lt William V. Ward plotted a direct course that took them the shortest distance to England's most easterly point at Lowestoft, with its nearby aerodrome at Ellough a frequent haven for returning cripples. Tension eased when the distinctive coastal curve came into view and the prospect of ditching diminished. The relief was short-lived as heightened senses detected the acrid tang of burning oil and sent shivers of alarm throughout the crew. Peering out at the reluctant power unit, JD saw nothing untoward, but, still suspicious, he asked Bob to open the cowl flaps. This would immediately cool the engine and might blow out any small fire hidden from view. At the very least, it allowed a better visual inspection. As the gills surrounding the radial opened, JD could clearly see smoke emerging from the motor and immediately alerted Bob to feather the propeller. Moving swiftly, Portsch and co-pilot Flight Off Clifford N. Britton cut power, pressed the feathering button and that for the fuel shut-off valve while moving the mixture control to 'idle shut off' and cutting the ignition. The next action was to operate the engine's integral fire extinguisher and, given that the fire was in their No. 2 engine, lower the undercarriage to prevent the tyre and brakes from igniting. Events then rapidly overtook their actions. JD saw the Cyclone suddenly burst into flames behind the firewall, so any protection this might have offered was already lost. Now over land, Bob immediately gave the order to bail out. Hardly had the crew reacted when the fuselage filled up with dense smoke. Ducting for the bomber's heating system ran from the No. 2 engine, and smoke must have surged along this into the fuselage, where men now groped blindly for parachutes and escape exits. JD was first to find the hatch aft and tugged hard on the emergency release mechanism. They were at about 4,000 feet when the door tumbled away followed immediately by the first of the crew. Soon there were only two pilots left on board. One was an only son whose sense of duty would not relinquish control to his computerized companion until the bomber was clear of the community below and set on course to explode harmlessly in the sea.

In that township beneath the burning bomber, attention had been drawn to its difficulties. Schoolboy Mike Farman later recalled:

[we were] in the school playing field at Gorleston Road School that afternoon, we heard the sound of a plane in trouble and, looking up into the cloudless sky, spotted this plane trailing smoke very high up. As we watched a silver object fell from the plane turning over and over and glinting in the sun. The parachutes appeared above us and drifted away in the distance . . .

The aircraft door released by JD would trouble Mike many years later, but, for now, he had intentions typical of so many wartime youngsters – souvenir hunting.

I was eight or nine years old at the time and us lads used to go to a crash site to nick pieces of the perspex windows if we could find any. We used to burn a hole with a red-hot poker in it and cut around the hole with a fretsaw in order to make rings for the fingers. After much filing and sand papering to round off the edges it was then polished with wire

wool and metal polish [Brasso]. My mother used to complain about the stink when the hole was burnt in the material and the waste of Brasso re the wartime shortages . . . By the time we came out of school we knew where that plane had come down. We went to the crash site and found the area roped off and police there and we were not allowed to go anywhere near the plane . . . It was a small paddock with a hawthorn hedge and mature elm trees here and there around the boundary . . . In 1950 I left school and started an apprenticeship as a carpenter and joiner at J.A. Gaze and Sons Limited, Kimberly Road. I had been there only a few weeks when the foreman took me across the yard to the lean-to sheds to move some old second-hand doors. When we shifted a few of the doors a large oval aluminium shape was exposed studded with rivets and part of the US Air Force [*sic*] star painted on . . . I asked Joe my foreman whose it was, 'Oh that's a door that fell off a Yankee plane during the war and landed out there in the yard . . . Some Yanks and the police came and looked at it and said they would come back and collect it and it's been here since, bloody years ago!' I could not believe it. Immediately I said, 'Not the Liberator that crashed at Elm Tree Road Crossroads?' To which a surprised Joe said, 'How the fxxxing hell did you know that?'

In response, Mike related his schoolboy recollections. In his mind, the aircraft had been a Liberator and this misapprehension also existed elsewhere, as the Police Report illustrates.

The plane burnt out and is a total wreck. Cause of crash unknown. Home Station Lavenham [Post Number 137 Group Number 487 Squadron Number 836]. The Liberator was carrying bombs and up to the present 8 × 500 G. P. bombs and 4 containers holding M17 incendiaries have been found. This is understood to be the complete load. A large number of incendiary bombs and cannon shells are scattered over a wide area. Although it is understood that the safety pins were in and the HE bombs were consequently safe, the occupants [3] of one dwelling house, approximately 50 yards from a bomb have been evacuated. Damage was caused to overhead electricity wires as a result of which the parishes of Kessingland and Carlton Colville will probably be without electricity for about two days. A straw stack was destroyed by fire and 2 bullocks were injured, one of which was slaughtered. A bomb penetrated the roof of a cowshed and is now lying in the cow yard. The above are the property of Mr. H.S. Hadenham of Grove Farm . . .

The discrepancy between the ordnance listed in USAAF records and the Police Report is believed to have arisen because the incendiary containers had split on impact. Not noted in the Police Report was the extraordinary escape from injury by Herbert 'Rufus' Hadenham. He was actually in the brick cowshed when *two* bombs hit the building. One came through a wall and hit one of the bullocks, injuring it, so that it later had to be put down, while the second bomb penetrated the roof, missed Rufus, and exited via an end wall into the cow yard.

Others who witnessed the aircraft come down would also find its final moments for ever imprinted in their memories. One of these was then a 9-year-old schoolboy, Leon Harvey:

It was during the afternoon playtime at Carlton School that I first saw a huge aircraft that appeared to be flying from left to right across my field of vision. I was standing beside the playing field shelter looking eastwards. Smoke was coming from the plane and suddenly black specks appeared dropping from the aircraft and their parachutes opened, except one who continued earthward without his parachute opening. There appeared no reason for this as his appearance and departure from the plane was similar to the other crew. Suddenly the plane dived earthwards and I ducked behind the brick air raid shelter. There was a loud explosion and when I next looked there were clouds of smoke rising. Returning home after school sometime later along Hollow Lane there were several pieces of debris still burning in the sides of the fields and live ammo still going off at intervals.

'Their parachutes opened, except one who continued earthward without his parachute opening.' The broken body of Doug Seavert was found near Dell Road School. (*Bob Collis*)

The unfortunate airman whose descent Leon witnessed was Staff Sgt Douglas E. Seavert, the radio operator. JD Bain thought Doug had pulled his ripcord too soon and struck the aircraft's tail. A note in the USAAF Report of Aircraft Accident supports this, stating: 'Crews should be instructed to make sure they have cleared the aircraft before popping their chute.' Shortly before that fatal mission, Doug had V-mailed his brother-in-law, George E. Moore, who was hospitalized in Memphis recovering from wounds received during the Normandy landings. Doug commiserated, then jotted down his own news: 'I had a forty hour pass last week and went to London. I had a pretty good time and probably will go back a couple times before I get through over here. I met a pretty nice gal that I'm chumming around with – no – nothing serious, just a little fun and good times.' The good times ended when Doug's broken body was found near the school in Dell Road, Lowestoft.

Bob Portsch kept the B-17 airborne and steady for his crew to escape as he swung the bomb-laden machine clear of the town so that it was heading seawards. Now it was his turn to get out – just a few seconds to set the C1 and ensure the safety of the civilians below. With the C1 locked, he moved swiftly to escape. He needed to move fast, the port wing was blazing fiercely. Then the port-wing fuel tanks exploded, tearing the bomber's structure apart. Half-rolling, the B-17 was seen for an instant in plan form by eyewitness Dick Wickham before it plummeted in a steep dive behind the tree line. Now too low to parachute, Bob's only hope was a crash landing, but there were dwellings ahead. Some accounts described the aircraft skimming over the roofs before it smashed to earth and slithered into an anti-tank ditch and a row of concrete

anti-tank blocks. Once part of the area's defences against the threatened German invasion of 1940, they now ensured the total destruction of the crashing aircraft. It disintegrated in a huge fireball, an eruption of burning fuel and debris showering the landscape, so close to houses that laundry was scorched on the washing lines. Bob Portsch had jumped. He was found in a tree close to the Elm Tree Road crossroads. Too low, too late; the young pilot's neck was broken, the D-ring on his parachute untouched. From the time the No. 2 engine became an inferno to the moment of impact had taken little more than a minute. That minute of serving others had seen 2/Lt Robert Harsen Portsch sacrifice his own life for his crew and the British population imperilled by the bombs still on board his aircraft. A danger now existed from the high explosives and incendiaries scattered across the countryside, but, other than the damage described in the Police Report, no further harm came to the community.

That there were no civilian casualties was incredible. Maurice A. Peters, a 14-year-old GPO telegram messenger boy, had a narrow escape. Cycling along Elm Tree Road, he heard an unusual sound and, looking back over his shoulder, was startled to see a Flying Fortress diving towards him. Terrified, the youngster cycled straight into the nearest ditch and flattened himself as the bomber skimmed over the field in front of him and exploded two fields further on. Other eyewitnesses recall parachutes descending into the town. One airman landed unharmed on telephone wires in Victoria Road only to fall from the wires and break his leg, apparently demolishing a Mrs Powell's garden wall in the process. Another dropped on farmland close to where Mr M.J. Cook was ploughing in a field adjoining the Lowestoft Road. Moving forward to calm the horses, Mr Cook and the animals were startled when the parachutist landed close by. Seemingly unperturbed, the airman calmly gathered up the folds of his parachute and strolled away. Another eyewitness was Terry Moore, then a pupil at Notley Road School, who remembered:

The aircraft was passing overhead flying inland with one of its port engines on fire and what we took to be either a door or a hatch floated away followed by several crew bailing out. The aircraft then began to bank to the left, but while doing so the fire spread along the wing towards the fuselage. It continued banking but was losing height and eventually disappeared behind some trees and rooftops followed by, after a short interval, a column of dark smoke. I don't remember any noise. At this time some of the parachutes were still descending. The remainder of the school afternoon was never ending but as soon as we were able to we were on our bikes and away . . . The end of Stradbroke Road at that time was no more than a fairly wide lane with hedges on either side running down to the Four-Cross-Roads. Hadenham's Farm was set back on the south side on a bend in the road and surrounded by tall elm trees. The plane had crashed just to the west of the house but not much could be seen owing to the hedge but there was smoke and a smell of burning in the air. Debris was strewn about the road with belts of fairly large calibre ammunition going up over the tops of the trees and down the other side. We were actually walking amongst all this. A few U.S. Air Force [sic] vehicles were parked along the road, two of which were refreshment wagons around which forces personnel were eating and drinking and, although

dressed in flying gear, there was no way of telling if they were the crew who had bailed out
. . . Other than a British Special Constable, there was no one else about. What I do
distinctly remember was the casual and somewhat jovial manner of those present . . . at
that age, death at a distance didn't amount to much. That awareness comes with age.
Schoolboy rumours were rife, some that I recall were: the plane had been hit by a German
armed trawler off Holland and had immediately turned back to drop the crew over land,
then turn to ditch in the sea. Perhaps this came about due to the full ammunition belts
and bombs which the plane had brought back. These were detonated the following
Thursday afternoon. Another rumour: the aircraft didn't go straight in but first hit the
ground in the field bordered by Elm Tree Road and Long Road and from there bounced
over the houses and fish shop to where it finally crashed. I have no idea if this is true.

As the years have passed since this incident my mind is often taken back to it when
some major and perhaps tragic event occurs today when people rush to watch and almost
queue up to have their few moments of fame on television or there is a press conference
plus endless speculation. How times have changed! . . . Another thing that was so different
from today's attitudes was that we weren't told to move away from the bullets and debris
lying in the road. We were stepping over them and the bombs were not too far away. The
plane itself passed over the school in its crippled state – can you imagine the outcry today
speculating on the potential disaster which could have occurred.

That the disaster did not occur was due to the heroism of an only son doing his duty no
matter what the cost. The injured crewmen were quickly collected and taken to hospital,
while those unscathed were taken to Dell House in Dell Road to await US military transport.
The bodies of Doug Seavert and Bob Portsch were first taken to Lowestoft mortuary and then
collected by the USAAF for interment at Cambridge, where Doug still rests.

Several days elapsed before the dreaded telegrams were transmitted to devastate the lives of
both families. For Lillian Portsch, the loss of her only son was particularly heartbreaking, as
Susan Hunt recalls: 'When the news of Bob's death came, I was with her and she was
unbelievably brave. I will never forget her strength and courage.' The day after the telegram,
Lillian received her son's Air Medal, too late to give any joy and, while a reminder of his
bravery, it offered no solace. Bob Portsch was taken home in 1947 at Lillian's request under a
policy for the 'Disposition of World War II Armed Forces Dead' and is buried in the family
plot at East Ridge Lawn cemetery, Delawana, New Jersey. Lillian, unstintingly selfless,
realized other mothers were grieving as she did, but she actively channelled this concern to
help and care by becoming a charter member of the Bloomfield Chapter of American Gold
Star Mothers. This organization was born from American custom during the First World War
of displaying a blue star in the window of any home with a family member in military
service. Should tragedy strike and that loved one perish, a gold star was superimposed over
the original to reflect the honour, glory and pride in the sacrifice made by the family. In the
true spirit of a Gold Star Mother, Lillian suppressed her own loss to support other mothers
and would do so for further casualties in the Second World War, Korea and Vietnam.

During those years, the sacrifice made by her son was not completely forgotten in England but, inevitably, faded from memory with no reminding marker. The numerous souvenirs scavenged by schoolboys such as John Holmes soon disappeared, as did the bulk of wreckage. John remembered a low loader transporting large sections of broken aircraft from the scene and he picked up his fair share of perspex for fashioning into rings or crosses, but these, like others collected at the time, were eventually discarded or simply vanished as the boys' lives moved on. Thirty years after the crash, Barry Lain and Neville Kent, members of the Norfolk and Suffolk Aviation Museum, conducted a metal-detecting survey. The museum was eager to acquire a Wright Cyclone engine for display, but their efforts yielded only fragments and they concluded that nothing of substance remained.

Lillian Portsch lived with the loss of her son but inwardly felt the pain as other young men came home and continued lives interrupted by the war. Bob's friend Roland remained in touch and it was at a birthday party she gave for him in her home that he met his future wife, Norma, and they named their first son Robert in honour of Robert Portsch. When ill health eventually forced Lillian into a nursing home, Roland made the arrangements and likewise helped take care of her affairs when Lillian died in 1984. The last in her family, she had been a fine, cultured and artistically talented woman, discerning in choice. Items from her home were bequeathed to the Newark, New Jersey, Museum where, when younger, she had been a voluntary worker. Some items were also left to the reconstruction of historic Williamsburg and, to perpetuate her work for the Gold Star Mothers, she left funds to establish a scholarship for deserving graduates from Bloomfield High School. When her home in Forrendale Avenue, Bloomfield, was cleared, Bob's documents and photographs were discarded and would have been lost but for the presence of her neighbours, Mr and Mrs John Testa, who literally rescued them from the garbage because they deserved, and were destined for, a more honourable repose.

Fate now commenced one of those confluences that would draw the story from comparative obscurity and mark it in those communities far, far from Bloomsfield. Lowestoft and its neighbouring village of Carlton Colville were expanding and new homes strode across former farmland in the Saxon Fields Development on Bloodmoor Hill. All building works in this historically rich nation have policies and procedures for the discovery of archaeological relics, but those remnants of conflict that emerged during land clearance in 1986 were not of Saxon origin: they related to a much later warrior. The jumble of metal pieces uncovered in a long-hidden, wartime anti-tank ditch were clearly from a crashed aeroplane, but workers lacked the certainty of identity and even safety – could there be bombs still extant in the debris? News of the discovery soon reached the Norfolk and Suffolk Aviation Museum and historian Bob Collis was swiftly on the scene. Bob also harboured some anxiety about missing ordnance and the existence of unexploded bombs. Later investigation revealed that three of the wartime bombs had been detonated in a field south of Grove Farm on 16 March 1945. The blast had broken windows in ten houses and caused other minor damage in four nearby roads, but fortunately there had been no injuries. Another report dated 12 April 1945 revealed that a 500lb UXB had been located in a tank-trap ditch. A Clearance Certificate with respect to

The 1986 discovery of an almost complete Cyclone engine delighted the Norfolk and Suffolk Aviation Museum. (*Bob Collis*)

'9×500lb' bombs dealt with by the USAAF had already been forwarded to Police Headquarters on 29 March 1945. The 12 April report noted that water in the ditch had 'subsided considerably' since the crash and that the bomb was now '1 foot below the surface, 2 feet into the side of the bank' and commented that the tail end was plainly visible, concluding that 'there appears to be easy access to removal'. Concerned, Bob had been unable to find the final report for clearance of the bomb, but, thankfully, no bombs appeared during the building work. He was later relieved to obtain local accounts indicating that someone fishing in the ditch in 1947 had again reported the bomb, leading to its being steamed out on-site by a British bomb disposal team. The 1986 discovery in the ditch of an almost complete Cyclone engine delighted the museum, and this find was accompanied by propeller blades and a cluster of other artefacts evidently disposed of in this convenient repository decades earlier. The ditch had later been filled in and their existence forgotten. Bob made his files available to media reporting the story and this, plus the professionalism of his approach, helped persuade the authorities to allow the Norfolk and Suffolk Aviation Museum to retain the wreckage for restoration and display. Bob felt strongly that the museum's exhibits should not only relate to the aircraft but also honour the two young airmen known to have died in

the incident. He now embarked on further dedicated and meticulous research, which was of great benefit to the museum, but he also magnanimously shared the results of his investigations with others. I have been indebted to Bob on countless occasions and the material in this chapter derives predominantly from his archives.

His research soon extended to contact with friends of Lillian and Bob Portsch plus contact with the Seavert family. The poignant account of a Gold Star Mother's courage moved Bob to determine that the community under construction also ought to recognize those that had fallen in the fight for freedom that the bright new homes now represented. Bob's idea was to name roads on the new estate in recognition of the men and their aircraft, and to form an association with townships in America whose soldiers had died in Suffolk on that distant spring day when men like Bob Portsch and Doug Seavert had overflown East Anglia. Those airmen, on sunlit-silvered wings, high above, had accepted the challenge of defeating a dark and dishonourable enemy whose politics would have destroyed a democracy that had endured for centuries and fathered their own nationhood. Bob found his concept quickly adopted by the developers and supported by local politicians in Carlton Colville Parish Council and Waveney District Council. Five roads were named with links to the story: Portsch Close, Seavert Close, Bloomfield Way, Fortress Road and Ohio Close.

Jeffrey L. McLaughlin was enthralled to discover pieces of his great-uncle's bomber still hidden amid the builder's spoil. (*Bob Collis*)

Not content with this achievement, Bob established contact with JD Bain, who was fascinated to learn how parts from his Fortress had been found. Never one to make a fuss about his service experiences and unable to make the journey, JD deputized his great-nephew, Jeffrey L. McLaughlin, to act on his behalf. In the summer of 1988, Jeff visited the crash site and was enthralled to discover pieces of the bomber still hidden amid the builder's spoil. Parts were excavated and cleaned for the journey home to an appreciative JD. Bob also sent items to the grateful family of gunner Staff Sgt Clarence V. Baker, who had died some years earlier. Further appreciation was expressed by the Seavert family when contact with his sister assuaged lingering fears about the manner of Doug's death. Dolores F. (Seavert) Moore had for years held horrific images of her brother's last moments, hurtling to earth with a faulty parachute and fully conscious until impact. Bob's research offered the comforting knowledge that Doug would almost certainly have been rendered unconscious after hitting

the bomber's tailplane. From Dolores, Bob learned that her daughter, Carol Yarnall, had followed her uncle into the military. Coincidentally, Carol's USAF training as a communications specialist had taken her to Keesler AFB Technical School thirty-five years after Doug had graduated from the same establishment. Furthering the coincidence, she was posted to Suffolk and was thus able to represent the family with a floral tribute for his grave. Carol also met Bob, her guide for visiting the crash site and the newly occupied Seavert Close. They also spent some reflective moments at the spot in Dell Road where her uncle had fallen.

Carol Yarnall appreciated the honour bestowed by Carlton Colville in naming Seavert Close after her uncle. (*Bob Collis*)

Bob's work on this story attracted media attention, prompting further recognition of the story by two British army veterans. Twin brothers Cyril and Claude Larkin designed a brick memorial and plaque erected on the crash site now hidden beneath Ribblesdale. In 1992, during a service conducted by the Revd Frank Dyson, the memorial was unveiled by Col Walter Berg of the USAF 81st Tactical Fighter Wing with his wife Jeanette. Bob Collis was unable to attend, but Councillor Jim Mitchell read a few words he had written for the occasion:

> The Carlton Colville memorial is a reminder of the price the Allied air forces paid for their victory over Nazi Germany. It is fitting that, at a place which was, in 1945, a scene of devastation after the bomber crash, a monument has been erected to honour the men who died within what is now a new community. This memorial plaque, together with the nearby road-signs, will hopefully perpetuate the memory of the loss of this Flying Fortress and the sacrifice made by two young Americans in the cause of world freedom.

Six years later Bob arranged a further, moving tribute to the fallen fliers during the 1998 Lowestoft Air Show when thousands of people enjoyed powerful performances by examples from the shield of a modern air defence system. The crowds further delighted in the fun of flying illustrated by aerobatic performers. Reminders of our aviation heritage were much in evidence and a star of the day was an elderly but beautifully preserved B-17, the 'Sally-B', Britain's only airworthy example. In tribute to Bob Portsch and Doug Seavert and many others lost in combat, the Fortress altered course to overfly the memorial. As the graceful Boeing banked overhead in her salute to the fallen, Air Show Controller Bernard Bagge was on the telephone to Dolores describing events. Dolores had written a letter to the townsfolk, which was read over the public address system by Airshow Commentator Roger Smith:

Dear Friends at Carlton Colville and Lowestoft. Greetings from across the pond in the US of A! It is with heartfelt gratitude that I write to you and send my warm and loving thoughts to you. My brother, Douglas Seavert, was a quiet, sensitive young man, a quick thinker, dependable and thoughtful. I think it was because of all of these qualities he would have appreciated your remembering him and the others as you are doing today. I do.

I was an immature 14-year-old when my brother died, but I remember reading about the bombing of London and how sad we all felt at the suffering you endured. I know Doug would have felt that way too; he would also have been very angry. Because of that, he would have done all he could to help end the war and being on board that B-17 was the way he chose.

Thank you. I want you to know that we 'Yanks' are deeply appreciative that you remember that we gave our fathers, sons and brothers in the war too. You've touched my heart with this observance today. Sincerely, Dolores F. Moore.

Standing in vigil at the memorial, historian Bob Collis saw Squadron Leader 'Jimmy' Jewell tilt the Fortress westwards, so that it receded towards shimmering clouds, as her sister had intended so many decades earlier. Had that long-ago bomber become a distant speck, with its passing over the town forgotten, there would be no Fortress Road, Seavert Close nor Portsch Close, but a lonely widow might have had the pleasure of grandchildren bearing a now lost family name – but what's in a name?

Had that long-ago bomber become a distant speck, with its passing over the coastal community forgotten, there would be no Fortress Road. The UK's only airworthy B-17 'Sally B' honours a Fortress that failed to make it home. (*Bob Collis*)

CHAPTER NINE

Finding The Falcon

The aviation history of the Second World War may be regarded as 'recent' and ostensibly well documented. One might believe the accuracy of the records is indisputable. Having authored several books on the subject, I would be the first to concede that this is a misapprehension; that evidence supporting facts can be erroneous; that records can be contradictory and that memories can fail. History might be made by gargantuan events with key facts well established – D-Day on 6 June 1944, for example. However, layered beneath such events exists a fascinating sediment containing countless smaller stories. Fact-finding at this level requires persistence, and it was patient detective work by researcher Mike Harris that finally rediscovered the spot where B-24 42-95248, 'The Falcon', fell to earth. On the way, Mike corrected several errors contained in official records and made his own contribution to the history of aviation in East Anglia.

Mike's fascination with The Falcon stemmed from an interest in its parent unit, the 466th Bombardment Group, which, operating from Attlebridge in Norfolk from March 1944 until April 1945, shouldered its fair share of the air war. Post-war, Attlebridge slid into history as an airfield, although a new role emerged when Bernard Matthews occupied elements of the old base for his famous turkey-farming business. Turkey sheds still sit on runways whence the 466th BG flew 231 combat missions, losing nearly 100 aircraft. Mike's parents had moved to the area during the 1980s and, when home on leave from RAF service as an aircraft airframes engineer, he was intrigued by the extensive remains of the old airbase. Listening to local legends evolved into active 466th BG research and a trip to the Second Air Division Memorial Library in Norwich introduced him to the respected aviation historian Tony North. Tony's expertise and knowledge of the B-24 groups based around Norwich further fuelled Mike's enthusiasm. Encouraging the younger man, Tony generously shared his extensive collection of photographs and, concentrating on 466th BG pictures, Mike was intrigued by one aircraft with a very distinctive nose-art. B-24H-25-FO 42-95248 from the 785th Squadron carried the recognition code 2U-S, but this B-24 was further distinguished by its paint scheme. Named The Falcon, this all-silver Liberator sported an excellent rendition of a swooping falcon on both port and starboard sides of its nose. Furthering the theme, the artist had incorporated the perspex navigational viewing blister to create an 'eye' and swept the

Mike was intrigued by one aircraft with a very distinctive nose-art: B-24-25-FO, The Falcon. (*Michael J.G. Harris*)

anti-glare colouring round to imitate a giant bird of prey. The armour-plating on the pilot's side was adapted as a tally board for the bomber's many missions – at least forty-five on one photograph. From a wartime file, 'Aircraft Salvaged by Field Engineering – Aircraft Assigned to 466 BG – Station 120', Mike found that The Falcon's career had concluded on 8 January 1945, when she was declared Category E2 – written off – by a Sgt Gibson, a Field Engineering Inspector. In the 'Remarks' column Gibson noted the aircraft had crashed into two houses at Shipdham in Norfolk. This prompted Mike to investigate. Had there been any civilian casualties? Did the bomber's crew survive? During 1940–5 Norfolk's Civil Defences kept an incident diary featuring aircraft that fell in the county – some 950 in all – but unfortunately the diary revealed no entry for a crash in Shipdham on that date. However, Shipdham, like many East Anglian villages, also hosted a wartime airfield. In this case, Station 115 was home to the famous 44th BG, and the British historian for this unit, Steve Adams, also assisted Mike's investigations.

Contrary to the Civil Defence records, Station 115 control tower did have a crash recorded 'at 1425 hours approximately a quarter of a mile outside this aerodrome'. Other sources indicated the crash site was close to the village of Westfield, so Steve and Mike agreed to visit

The artist had incorporated the perspex navigational blister to create an 'eye'. The armour-plating on the pilot's side was adapted as a tally board for the bomber's many missions. (*Michael J.G. Harris*)

the area to establish the precise location. Further pictures from both Steve and Tony provided dramatic evidence of the aircraft's demise, with one depicting an injured crew member being stretchered away from the wreckage. The rescuers were wading through a track smashed in the ice of a frozen pond. In the background was a thatched cottage, so finding the crash site ought to have been easy, but enquiries in Westfield elucidated only blank stares. No one could recall the crash, not even through handed-down hearsay, nor could they identify the property in Mike's picture. Perplexed, the two enthusiasts retreated to retrench and search for additional evidence. Further delving into Tony's archives unearthed a copy of the Form 14 Report of Aircraft Accident, which gave the location as '1000 yards W. S. W. of Station 115'. This contributed significantly to Mike's knowledge of that last mission and he now compiled all available data into a record of The Falcon's final flight to sift for additional clues indicating the crash site.

On 8 January 1945, the 466th BG committed twenty-three aircraft to participate in attacking a communications centre at Wittlich, Germany. This supported Allied forces now squeezing the 'Bulge' back into line after bitter fighting had curtailed the last major Western offensive launched by the now retreating Wehrmacht. Weather conditions were appalling and

The Taylor crew joined the 466th BG on 8 August 1944 and were assigned to the 785th Squadron. *Rear left to right*: Vernal Dupas (dropped from crew – burst eardrum); William B. Eastman, radio operator; William W. Flack, ball turret; Alfred J. Wilson, top turret; Jerome M. Krzewinski, tail turret; Byron L. Wertz, engineer/waist gunner; Earl Siders, waist gunner. *Front*: Arden D. Mills, co-pilot; Gordon C. Cuneo, navigator; Harry W. Tayler, pilot; Lauren E. Sandborn, bombardier. (*Chris Brassfield*)

aircraft ascending over East Anglia faced ten-tenths cloud, which severely disrupted the cohesion of group formations. Laden with twelve 500lb bombs, The Falcon was piloted by one of the 466th BG's more colourful characters with over twenty missions to his credit. 1/Lt Harry W. Taylor, 'Wiry Willie' to his close friends, drew heavily on experience accumulated since his first operation to Berlin on 1 September 1944. Harry had earned his sobriquet very early in his flying career at the San Antonio Aviation Cadet Classification Center. A rigorous series of medicals eradicating any modesty saw Harry handed a bottle of Blue Vitriol – in essence a mild acid – for the elimination of crab lice, a not uncommon complaint in the 1940s. Unfortunately for young Harry, the affected area was in a somewhat delicate and embarrassing region of his anatomy, but, to the later astonishment of his barrack-room brethren, Harry suddenly stripped from the waist down. Clenching a cigar, undoubtedly intended to add maturity, between his teeth, he proceeded publicly to apply the liquid while uttering a series of profanities to accompany the growing discomfort as the liquid set light to his loins! Frantically fanning himself with a towel, Harry began to remedy a malady that

could have eliminated him from the Cadet programme. Among those witnessing that strange display was Earl Wassom, whose training and combat assignment tracked that of the lad they christened 'Wiry Willie'. This did not reflect anything different about Harry's more intimate regions, simply that the application of his treatment was followed by an impressive workout 'to regain his manly reputation'. A party piece of this performance included single-arm press-ups using either the left or the right arm. This physical prowess earned him his nickname, and, a few months later, his fitness undoubtedly gave him the strength to wrestle with 25 tons of rogue bomber. That day, in one of the bleakest winters on record, their main adversary was again that cold, implacable foe, the European weather.

Harry and his co-pilot, 2/Lt Arden D. Mills, eased The Falcon steadily upwards until the surrounding gloom lightened then burst into the breathtaking brilliance gifted only to those surmounting the heavens. Airmen often paid for their appreciation of such grandeur when ice cheated the aerofoil and deceived the designer's skill to send an aircraft plummeting to oblivion. It had been a long, dangerous climb, but, having broken clear, The Falcon swung towards Germany as part of a seriously depleted 466th BG force. Only fourteen of their aircraft assembled correctly, with the remainder either aborting or tagging onto other formations. Nor were the Group's troubles over. Their H2X lead ship, 'Duffy's Tavern' 42-51699 with Maj Norman R. Crosson as Command Pilot, turned back at the Initial Point when the oxygen system failed and the major suffered anoxia. H2X was an effective ground-scanning radar, colloquially called Mickey, which greatly improved bombing accuracy when overcast conditions prevented visual bombing. However, the Allied armoury now contained a range of electronic aids, and, following problems with their second Mickey ship, the Group resorted to GH. This British-developed radar worked on signalling ground beacons to register the aircraft's position, but, at this stage of the war, was prone to enemy jamming and was engaged today as a last resort. The Group's woes continued when the cohesion of its formation failed at the IP and those aircraft that did bomb simply witnessed their ordnance vanish into the overcast with no opportunity to observe results. At least the weather was impartial and frustrated both enemy fighters and flak. Capt Wellman A. Clark, one of the Group's intelligence officers, noted: 'There was no enemy air opposition nor was any AA fire encountered. No planes sustained battle damage.' That was not how Staff Sgt Alfred J. Wilson, a gunner on board The Falcon, remembered it: 'Our trouble started over the target at Wittlich. Got hit by flack [sic], which caused gas leaks in wing and our bomb bays. Lost power on one engine and started to lose altitude. Came across Channel at about 50 feet. Tossed out anything that we could to lighten the load . . .'

No mention of flak is made in the Report of Aircraft Accident, but Al Wilson's recollections do correlate in other respects and The Falcon's final few minutes can be interpreted from a combination of available evidence.

Harry Taylor was determined to make Attlebridge. He and his crew had kept The Falcon flying but were now desperately seeking an airfield and uncertain of their position. This imperative had been emphasized when, still over the sea, the engineer, Technical Sgt Byron L. Wertz, reported that all his gauges indicated less than 50 gallons each. All on board knew

The Falcon pictured during a daring low-level run earlier in her career. Note the RAF Halifax. Unfortunately its arrival over Shipdham did not coincide with any runway alignment. (*Michael J.G. Harris*)

that death would be the only outcome should they parachute or ditch. They had no option but to pray The Falcon would keep her feathers just long enough and breathed a collective sigh of relief when crossing the coast. The morning's blanket overcast had reduced to scattered low-lying cloud beneath a layer of six- to eight-tenths cloud at 3,000 feet. Visibility was a good 6 miles, but, with no airfield immediately in sight and the fuel situation beyond desperate, Taylor ordered the radio operator, Technical Sgt William B. Eastman, to use 'Darky'. This was an emergency, short-range – only 7–10 miles – radio communication that involved airfields placing a permanent watch on 6,440 kilocycles for lost aircraft seeking help. Anxiously, Eastman transmitted 'Hello Darky, Hello Darky, Hello Darky'. Any aerodrome nearby and equipped for Darky would respond, ascertain the sender's real identity, and then identify itself to confirm the lost aircraft's approximate position. Eastman had barely ceased transmitting when an airfield came into view. They were so close that they overshot and Taylor hastily banked the B-24 to go for the nearest runway with every second now precious.

Watching from the control tower at Shipdham, Maj Clifford T. Lee, Flying Control Officer, saw the B-24 appear to the east on a heading of 360°. They had received the Darky transmission and replied immediately, but had got no response. However, its crew had clearly seen the airfield and those in the tower could see from the stationary No. 4 propeller that the bomber was in trouble. Unfortunately, its arrival did not coincide with any runway

There were two sharp cracks as The Falcon slammed through, severing both wing tips. The starboard wing tip stuck in the trees – note the tail protruding over the distant hedgerow. (*Michael J.G. Harris*)

alignment, so urgent signals told the stranger to use any runway. Lee saw the bomber turn west, evidently trying to swing back for a landing. Its undercarriage descended, they were only a minute or so from safely touching down when it suddenly began to fall earthwards. Some eyewitnesses thought the No. 2 propeller was faltering. Just past the north-west end of the aerodrome, the B-24 was still banking in a tight left turn but was sinking rapidly. If it failed to level off before impact, the crew stood no chance. As its silhouette sank into the skyline, it was clear the race to safety had been lost.

Taylor and Mills saw the airfield's runway reaching like a hand towards a drowning man. Wheels down – flaps next. Things then happened so fast that no flaps were employed; there simply was no time. They stretched, clutching at safety so tantalizingly close it felt like the fingertips must become a secure grasp. They were still at 500 feet when they felt The Falcon fall swiftly away, exhausted – out of fuel – crashing. Their only hope was to level off and avoid cartwheeling to catastrophe in a whirling mass of disintegrating metal, tearing apart the flesh of its crew. As the aircraft levelled, a line of tall trees sprang up directly ahead. There were no gaps wide enough to allow the passage of a 110ft-wing-spanned bomber. Kicking rudder, they gave it their best shot and went for the only space they had enough

energy to achieve. There were two sharp cracks as The Falcon slammed through, severing both wing tips. The port wing, still slightly dipped, struck one tree 20 feet from the ground. The starboard wing hit the other tree a mere 2 feet higher. Striking both trees simultaneously had one possibly life-saving benefit – the bomber avoided slewing and, still upright, slammed heavily on to a frozen field. A small cloud of branches, twigs and aircraft debris showered in their wake as the shorn-off port wing section dropped into the track now being created by an earth-bound B-24 still doing some 100mph. Racing like a runaway train towards some cottages, The Falcon left her severed starboard outer wing section drooping drunkenly from the tree while its erstwhile owner surged uncontrollably onwards.

Somehow, the main undercarriage held as the crop-winged cripple careened over a field towards the next obstacle. Impact this time resulted in total destruction – of a straw stack! Al Wilson recalled:

I'm not sure whether Taylor meant to land at Shipdham or not, but as we made a left turn on the downwind leg, we lost all power. I had just gone back to waist to check gear down and engineer notified me to remain in waist. Just then we hit the first tree. Not much of a hit. Then we hit this huge haystack. I think hitting that haystack saved our necks!

A mass of straw swirled into the aircraft, but the impact barely impeded the bomber's progress, as she burst out beyond the stack in an explosion of straw, bounding on unhindered, travelling fast. Thumping over a drainage ditch, the fuselage slithered across a frozen field until the next contact proved more severe. The Falcon was so close to the aerodrome that she now ran into one of the funnel lights. Mounted on poles, these allowed an aircraft at night to follow an illuminated outer circle indicating the traffic pattern, which led to a funnel of lights pointing at the runway. Closer to touchdown, these lights were colour coded to facilitate night-time alignment with the runway. Making short shrift of this example, the B-24's No. 2 engine smashed it to pieces. The three rotating propellers now cut regularly spaced niches into the landscape, while the feathered No. 4 dragged a continuous groove.

Still moving at speed, they bore down on the dwellings, with Taylor, desperately striving for steerage, doing all he could to divert the aircraft from its headlong impact into the homes ahead. The crash would cause horrendous damage to the buildings and their occupants, quite apart from casualties among his crew. Barely any distance remained when the B-24 cracked across another drainage ditch, which sheared off its nose wheel. Next, it slammed into another tree and this robust representative of England's arboreal heritage stood firm – but not so The Falcon. The aircraft's nose was torn to the left just ahead of the instrument panel. This dragged the port wing into contact with the tree trunk, some 18 inches in diameter, and, as it caught between the port inner and fuselage, the force broke the bomber's main spar. Almost severed, the left wing twisted so violently that it flipped over, with the leading edge now facing backwards and the main undercarriage leg extending gawkily skywards. Caught in a crashing cacophony of noise and violence, both pilots were now in danger of drowning,

because the bomber smashed through ice on a frozen pond and stopped. A deluge of muddy water and chunks of ice almost engulfed them. The jarring halt jerked the No. 3 propeller from its shaft, but, luckily, it fell forward instead of twisting into the cockpit. Both pilots, badly injured, were now trapped, as the bomber settled into water of an unknown depth – had they survived the crash only to drown in a farmer's pond?

Al later recalled those final moments.

The tail and waist gunner and myself all ended up in a big pile at the rear bomb-bay bulkhead all completely covered in straw. All at once we heard a sound like escaping gas and thought she was going to blow up. It's amazing how strong one gets in a situation like that. I literally tore off the plexiglass waist window to get out! The bottom hatch was open only a few inches but two of the gunners got out that! By the time I got out of the aircraft an RAF man came out of the house very near to where we ended up and was trying to help Taylor and Mills. Taylor was cut real bad across the forehead and bleeding very bad. Mills was hanging out the torn fuselage, trapped by his ankles in the twisted rudder pedals. Luckily those two were the only crew that was seriously hurt. One comic part was that a little old lady came walking out of the farm house and said, 'anyone hurt?' . . .

Showing great fortitude, the dazed and badly injured Taylor remained conscious, and his first concern was to ask rescuers whether the houses had been avoided. No properties were damaged, so how the engineering reporting error occurred saying it 'Crashed into two houses' is a mystery. Helpers from nearby homes and Shipdham airbase with uninjured members of the crew worked feverishly in freezing conditions to extricate both pilots. Barely recognizable, the cockpit was a tangle of crushed metal and wires. In addition to his head injuries, Taylor had a broken arm, while Mills had both legs broken, but the two airmen survived. Tragically, the talented Taylor – 'Wiry Willie' – was killed some years later in an auto wreck.

A Board of Inquiry investigated the loss of The Falcon and, after citing the circumstances described earlier, made some additional observations.

Gas tanks were split on the left wing and no gas is believed to have been in them. No. 3 tank was dry; No. 4 had two inches of fuel; the right wing tip tank had 12 inches. Booster pumps off, transfer pump off, No. 1-2-3 fuel switches set 'Tank to engine'. Automatic lean, No.4 not in cut-off position. No. 1 and No. 4 magneto switches were off yet only No. 4 prop was feathered. Superchargers and throttles both off. Gear lever was in neutral position; the engineer stating that the wheels were down and locked. No flaps had been put down.

It is the opinion of the accident board that the aircraft was merely out of fuel. If the engineer had transferred the 12 inches of fuel from the right wing tip to the other engines, the aircraft might have reached the runway. However, the engineer states that all gauges showed less than 50 gallons each when the aircraft was mid-channel, returning from the

Helpers from nearby homes, Shipdham airbase and uninjured members of the crew worked feverishly in freezing conditions to extricate both pilots. (*Michael J.G. Harris*)

continent. It is the opinion of the board that the pilot should have landed at a field near the coast for refuelling rather than attempting to return to base.

Recording Taylor's 294 hours of Liberator flying experience, the report concluded that it was '100% pilot error'. No mention is made of any flak damage and the 'merely out of fuel' seems harsh, given that flak damage was apparently one of the circumstances.

While the report gave Mike Harris a full account, it did not reveal where the bomber actually crashed, simply stating '1000 Yds WSW of Station 115'. Mike now had additional clues, especially reference to the funnel light, so researched maps of the area seeking a farm with a pond, roughly aligned to the east–west runway. Subsequent reconnaissance revealed none with buildings matching those in his photograph. Knowing how the land had been altered, Mike then took his studies into older maps, including tithe maps, and this combination further narrowed his area of investigation. Literally taking to the roads and lanes, Mike eventually found himself approaching Blackmoor Farm Cottages and, while the building had a familiar air, the roof-line did not match that in his picture, nor was there a pond. Further enquiries found the landowner, Mrs Patterson of Grange Farm, Shipdham, and she kindly gave permission for Mike to enter her property and revealed that the cottages had

The roof-line of the buildings did not match Mike's photographs. (*Michael J.G. Harris*)

been altered years ago and a nearby pond filled in by her sons. It all seemed to fit and Mike discerned a darker green line in the crop colouring that matched the shape of the pond in his picture. This had to be it, but there was no visible evidence of The Falcon to prove his point, so I and my trusty C-Scope metal detector were prevailed upon one bitterly cold Sunday in December 2002.

Meeting Mike in Shipdham, I followed him towards the old airfield, where an active airstrip at least hints of its former occupants. Reaching the cottages, then occupied by Keith Barrell and Tina Skipper, we were greeted with the promise of hot tea and home-made cake sympathetically offered to sustain two lunatics. My fingers were so cold I could barely operate the C-Scope, and poor Mike was on tenterhooks. He had convinced himself this was the exact spot where The Falcon had come to rest, but could we prove it? A recognizable piece of the lost bomber would confirm it, but, with easy land access, the USAAF would have thoroughly cleared the site – but hopefully not of every fragment. Grey clouds threatened snow, and frozen soil mirrored the day almost exactly fifty-eight years earlier when a veteran B-24 had ended her last mission on this very spot. At least, we thought so. Tuning the detector, I took about five paces and received a welcoming bleep. There, a few inches down, I found a fragment of grey-painted aluminium. Experience told me it was B-24 – others could argue.

A jubilant Mike Harris holds up a rocker arm from one of the Twin Wasp engines. He had found The Falcon.

A few seconds later, undeniable evidence emerged – a rocker arm from one of the Twin Wasp engines was dug out from the line of the wartime hedge through which the bomber had torn. We soon had a smattering of additional fragments, assorted nails and other farm detritus lost over the years plus an 1861 penny to reward our efforts. There was no doubt now that The Falcon had concluded her crazy journey here, and, using the wartime pictures, we aligned the trees and were rewarded with additional wreckage leading back to the point where the nose wheel had sheared off. This wreckage included part of the cockpit surround, still bearing black paint from the once majestic paint scheme. From this spot, Mike pinpointed the trees where the bomber shed its wing tips. He was jubilant with the day's achievements. The Falcon had been found, and, because of Mike's dedication, her story now takes its place in Eighth Air Force history with fewer errors.

CHAPTER TEN

That Was All

Co-pilot 2/Lt Harold W. Hutchcroft glanced out of the Liberator's starboard cockpit window. The 392nd BG formation was nothing like the charts seen during briefing at Wendling that morning – bad weather had seen to that; it was one of the worst days he had seen so far. The formation scheme presented at the 0300 briefing had looked far less plausible when the twenty aircraft had jostled noisily around the perimeter and commenced take-off into the typically unpleasant overcast at 0545 hr. It was 25 March 1945 and the Group's 270th mission, to an underground oil storage depot at Hitzacker. The end of the European war was tangibly close and this mission would continue pulverizing the remnants of Hitler's oil supplies inside his shrivelling Third Reich.

Even with the assistance of their CO aloft in a P-47 to radio in clear patches when he found them, they had only just finished group assembly. Several altitude changes had been signalled, as they had first tried at the planned assembly altitude of 12,000 feet and then descended to 9,000 before some semblance of a formation began. Now, behind planned times, they set course for the Wing assembly point. Instead of a 576th Squadron sister-ship, the B-24 closing in from their right was a 578th Squadron aircraft, but the 'guy was doing a real good job' and soon formated. Hal had the controls – his aircraft was leading the high element of the Lead Squadron and they managed to climb laboriously to 12,500 feet, trying to locate clearer weather. Had he felt so inclined, Hal might have admired the beauty in England's cloud assortment – stratocumulus, altocumulus and altostratus, layered in patches from 4,000 feet to peaks at 16,000 feet – brilliant white mountains in cerulean blue. However, Hal was flying his thirty-fourth combat mission and had grown weary of English weather. Another wall of cloud confronted them and the loosely held line of B-24s vanished again. On many occasions his aircraft had thwarted this relentless opponent and he thought today would be no different – he was expecting to emerge, annoyed but untroubled. How wrong. Visibility had been vanquished and his pilot, 1/Lt C.O. Markuson, took the controls, but they had lost sight of the squadron. Glancing right, Hal could see the 578th ship through the murk and it skilfully held the vacant slot in their formation. Checking the altimeter, Hal noticed their ship was gently descending and Markuson clearly had his hands full, so Hal clicked onto the interphone and advised his pilot that he would hold altitude and lead. This allowed

Markuson to search for the main formation. They worked well together and, team-working the controls, Hal flashed a quick glimpse up to his right and noticed their companion B-24 had disappeared in the gloom. Hal made a further quick check on the instruments, but then heard a thump and felt the B-24 lurch as if struck by something unseen but very solid. Looking out, the mystery was answered – he was horrified to see their wing-man banking away, with his starboard outer engine completely missing. Turning to Markuson, Hal simultaneously reached to employ the C1 autopilot. It was on and set up; he yelled at Markuson – should he engage it? Sometimes the autopilot compensated for damaged controls, and, if necessary, it might also give them just enough time to bail out . . .

On 30 October 1999, it was one of those balmy autumn days when working outside was a pleasure. The field near the Norfolk village of Skeyton was on set-aside, so fresh grass was cheerfully overtaking old stubble. The JCB Sitemaster had been used to scrape off a layer of topsoil, and the dry, sandy soil beneath was already yielding evidence of a wartime tragedy hidden beneath the innocent landscape. As the machine scoured its first trench, the inevitable rounds of ammunition emerged, plus a substance the digging fraternity referred to as 'Daz' – aluminium corrosion creating blue-white crystals like the washing powder. This is not a good sign for extracting well-preserved finds, but all involved dug enthusiastically, on the basis that even tiny pieces, well presented in a museum, can help relay the story and pay tribute to an aircraft and its crew . . .

Hal now hollered at his pilot over the sound of their engines: did he want to use the autopilot? Markuson, preoccupied, still failed to respond and was clearly fighting the controls to hold the ship straight and level. For a few seconds, the skilled pilot overcame whatever damage their aircraft had sustained in the collision and kept the Liberator holding steady. Again, Hal yelled to get his attention about the autopilot, but Markuson still ignored him. Then the Liberator decided for them both. Its nose dropped sickeningly, and the big bomber torqued right in an ever-deepening spiral. Markuson, still wrestling with the control wheel and rudder pedals, now yelled hard at Hal: 'Bail out!' This was decisive; Hal reached across the control console and repeatedly punched the bail-out alarm button, sending a raucous clamouring from the bells throughout the ship. Waiting a few seconds, Hal heard Markuson yelling even more frantically, 'Bail out. Bail out. BAIL OUT!' Hal struggled to move from his seat – the increasingly deadly grip of centrifugal reaction now made every movement slow motion when his mind was screaming for speed. In this kaleidoscope of events he suddenly realized he had not shut the throttles, so engine power was pulling them down. Suddenly, the Liberator twisted even more violently, thrusting him back into his seat, or maybe it was the cockpit ceiling – his mind was struggling to comprehend a world whirling round faster and faster like a nightmare in a fairground. Grasping handholds in the cockpit structure, Hal forced himself from the right-hand seat. He could see Markuson, giving up hope of recovering the doomed bomber, was now also trying to extricate himself from death's armlock. Using brute strength born from an atavistic instinct to survive, Hal was hauling himself inch by inch up a spinning metal cliff-face using every hand- and foothold he could find. It was every man for himself, and Hal had no choice but to crawl across the legs of the

radio operator, Technical Sgt J.E. Burke, who was pinioned into his compartment just aft of the two pilots. On board that day was Staff Sgt T.J. Hill, a radio countermeasures (RCM) expert who was also apparently trapped. Hal could do nothing to help – each man was fighting for his own survival and Hal again had no alternative but to haul himself over the RCM man's legs, striving to reach the bomb bay. Thankfully, the engineer, Technical Sgt Paul L. 'Sugar' Cain, had been transferring fuel when the two aircraft collided. Standard operational procedure for fuel transfer dictated opening the bomb-bay doors to avoid fuel fumes accumulating and the risk of explosion. When the collision occurred, Cain fully opened the doors and clipped on his parachute. Seconds later, the bomber was spinning and the force was too strong for some of the bomb shackles holding their load of twenty-four 250lb bombs. Cain had pulled the safety pins and now had no time to re-insert them. Pulling himself out by holding one of the bombs, he suddenly found himself being propelled from the aircraft pursued by part of the bomb load torn from the shackles. Cain's action in opening the bomb doors might save his co-pilot's life. Hutchcroft was almost into the bomb bay – presumably others were close behind, but he had no time to check – he could see the earth rotating closer and closer . . .

Rusty bomb fragments were emerging from the soil – their small size indicated a violent high-order detonation. Pete Snowling even found the base plate from one 250lb bomb and sat scraping it clean with his penknife. The aircraft had been blown to smithereens, and complete recovery of every fragment by the wartime authorities would have been impossible. History had now added value to any evidence of that wartime drama. Some discoveries were no more than stains of corrosion or oxidization in the soil, but others were rewarding because they were recognizable and occasionally related to individual crew members. An adjustable wrench from Sugar Cain's toolkit; a navigator's compass from Texan 2/Lt E.B. Maceyra's equipment. This relic had once divided many fraught miles through enemy airspace – Kassel, Hamm, Berlin and some twenty other targets – but now represented a skill overtaken by computers . . .

Hal and Ed Maceyra became friends, with the non-smoking co-pilot frequently sharing his cigarette rations with the navigator. Wartime controls created a currency in tobacco products, and Markuson's crew had rapidly acquainted themselves with local trading arrangements and local girls. Writing to his folks in August 1944, Hal commented:

Met three girls that are the English variety and they look and dress the same as we, I mean our girls do. Sure enjoyed hearing them talk. The Yank boys have been over here so long tho that they [the girls] enjoy using our slang . . . The girls go mad for lipsticks or candy and gum . . . The people treat us very good and seem glad to see us . . . I have tried their tea and their warm beer or bitter as they call it but can't say as I could grow fond of it. I believe Coke and cold has it beat just a bit.

Concentrating on his own survival, Hal had no idea how his friend was faring in escaping from the nose of the aircraft. Hal was almost into the bomb bay, having climbed a vertical wall of airframe and fellow airmen. Never had such a short distance seemed a lifetime, but he

knew that, to have a lifetime, he had only seconds left. They had collided at 12,500 feet. When Hal left the cockpit, the needles on the altimeter were rapidly unwinding and he guessed they had already spun through 7,000 feet. With a final effort, he thrust into the bomb bay then dragged himself clear of the aircraft. Caught in the bomber's slipstream, he somersaulted several times, going head over heels like a spun coin while frantically seeking to grasp his ripcord. Clutching the D-ring, he tugged. Nothing happened for a heart-stopping second, then the parachute snapped open. Pieces of the aircraft were dropping past and he feared one might rip through his parachute. He caught a final glimpse of the aircraft with more bombs stringing out – a brief view of another parachute – then his parachute rotated the vision away. Moments later, the B-24 exploded on farmland below and his next anxiety was to avoid the flames surging skywards. The tendrils seemed to grasp for the flimsy folds now holding him between life and death. Floating over the fire like a dandelion seed, he drifted away with the wind behind him and pitched into a ploughed field a few hundred yards beyond the conflagration. Disentangling himself from his parachute and harness, he turned, staring back over the hedgerows towards the ugly black column pillaring skywards. Smoke and flames convulsed as more bombs detonated and ammunition spat from the wreckage, but Hal was determined to search for surviving friends. He was attempting to get closer when two farmworkers appeared and persuaded him, rightly, that there was nothing he could do. They assisted the airman to a nearby house, where he was given a cup of tea, but shock set in and his hands shook so badly most of it was spilled . . .

We found pieces of wreckage scattered far from the point of impact, but concentrated our efforts following a scar of burnt soil and debris, ultimately creating a shallow trench some 40ft long. The trench was pockmarked with holes yielding finds such as a propeller governor, which had penetrated beneath the layer of burnt detritus. Sieving the soil through a wire mesh framework revealed numerous small finds, while others were carefully excavated from the trench floor. One fascinating fragment was the olive-green plastic base from an Army Air Force regulation flashlight. Not wishing to have it purloined by others, Staff Sgt J.B. Howard had scratched 'Whitey' Howard, which corresponded neatly with the crew list . . .

Hal Hutchcroft was devastated – where were his crew? Whitey, Ed – all the others? It had been Ed's last mission – he had accumulated more than the rest; they had never had any troubles as a crew and were so close to completing their tour. A surviving gunner from the second aircraft was brought to the farm and described how the tail of their aircraft had broken away. He had no parachute on but clutched at one as it floated past. He had only managed to connect one side, but it held as his parachute opened; his face wound had been caused by the other part of the harness slapping him when the parachute popped. Hal, still distraught, left the farmhouse, desperately searching for his friends. Events were a blur – a policeman on a bike – jeeps – anxious faces – finding a body. Hal thought it was Markuson with the familiar green towel around his neck, but it was not. This poor soul's parachute had malfunctioned and, entwining him as he fell, it became his shroud. Hal could not recognize this broken corpse. Where were his crew? Since his first diary entry five months earlier, they had shared many dangers and bonded as a fighting team through 220 air-combat hours in fifteen different

One fascinating fragment was the olive-green plastic base from 'Whitey' Howard's flashlight.

A strip of 'escape' pictures showing the crew in civilian garb. These were intended for use in creating forged documentation should the crew parachute into captivity. It was not to be. *Top left to right*: Harold Wayne Hutchcroft, co-pilot; Warren Gallagher, navigator (not on final flight); Clifford O. Markuson, pilot; Edward B. Maceyra, navigator; Jim B. 'Whitey' Howard, waist gunner. *Bottom*: John K. Horn, tail turret; Elmer R. Hunter, waist gunner; Paul L. 'Sugar' Cain, engineer; Jim Burke, radio operator; Tomyns Monaghan, gunner.

The other aircraft involved was 42-50804 flown by 2/Lt Philip W. Kaiser and crew: 1/Lt R. Parry Jr, co-pilot; 1/Lt J.W. Ott, navigator; 2/Lt J.D. Parrish, bombardier; Technical Sgt S. Louizides, radio operator; Technical Sgt A.R. Slemo, engineer; S/Sgt W.W. Smith, gunner; S/Sgt B.D. Hackins, gunner; S/Sgt K.B. Killea, gunner; S/Sgt W.H. Simpson, RCM operator. The radio call plate was discovered during excavations by Chris Gotts.

aircraft. German flak had shot away their hydraulics, knocked out engines, punched numerous holes through thin aluminium, inflicted wounds. They had been young men acting tough, becoming tough, becoming a crew – but that perpetual enemy, the weather, had achieved what the Luftwaffe had been unable to do: it had destroyed them. Hal's diary entry held no emotions. A simple record of all thirty-four missions. The occasional note of an aircraft lost; that flak had taken out their No. 3 engine over Salzbergen; and that bombs from aircraft above had fallen through their formation, knocking half the tail off another ship in their squadron. With typical understatement, Hal's last entry summed it up: 'Mission 34. March 25, 1945. Ship #340. 1.30 [hours]. Bombs – 24 250lb. Hit plane in clouds. Bailed out. Engineer and myself. That was all.'

The other aircraft involved was flown by 2/Lt Philip W. Kaiser and crew. It, too, had spiralled earthwards so rapidly that only two of the gunners, Staff Sgts W.W. Smith and B.D. Hackins, had managed to bail out. Charles Bird, a 12-year-old schoolboy at the time, had heard the whistle of bombs followed by several explosions near his home village of Oxnead. A column of black smoke on Lodge Farm, Skeyton, pyred the remains of a B-24 north of their cottage, while his father witnessed another Liberator pass low overhead, seemingly trying to crash-land, but it had spun in on meadowland near a small stream on Hall Farm in the village of Buxton Lamas.

Dressing hastily, Charles joined other villagers hoping to mount some form of rescue, but it was tragically apparent that neither wreck, some 400 yards apart, could possibly contain survivors. Several bombs had detonated, ammunition was still exploding, while the early morning air hung heavy with the stench of burning fuel, rubber and human flesh. The aircraft at Lodge Farm had impacted in the middle of a large field, and fire tenders from nearby airfields were swiftly on the scene but could do little. Ambulances from Aylsham and North Walsham were also scouring the nearby countryside seeking further survivors. One incident stayed for ever in the schoolboy's memory. Charles observed one American officer dejectedly leaving the grim remains of Markuson's aircraft on Lodge Farm pause, stoop-shouldered, at the field's entrance, then, turning smartly to face the still-burning wreckage, he stood to attention and smartly saluted his fallen comrades.

The largest recognizable piece extant from either aircraft was the tail section from Kaiser's aircraft lying crumpled in an adjacent field, and this created much interest for Charles and other children. However, the arrival of jeeps full of American personnel sent to begin the grim task of recovering bodies and clearing wreckage prevented close inspection. Dealing with unexploded bombs was a priority, and some had vanished into soft marshland, where rumour has it that a few still rest today. Others had exploded, and the craters they created were in evidence for many years. Recovering the bomber from Lodge Farm was comparatively easy, although widely scattered wreckage made it impossible to retrieve all the pieces, and some buried parts were overlooked. The B-24 at Buxton Lamas was on soft marshland, and much of the debris now lay submerged in a deep, water-filled crater that made extrication of the crew a prolonged and grisly chore. Overhead, heavily laden bombers continued their anxious ascents for a further six weeks, then the skies were suddenly silenced. Peace. At a price. Soon, the surviving American airmen departed and resumed lives interrupted and forever marked by experiences that also became imbued in the rich history of East Anglia.

A fascination with stories of the air war over Norfolk inspired enthusiast Chris Gotts, and he became dedicated to recording and researching incidents in the county. A brief entry in Norfolk's Civil Defence War Diary eventually led to the first of many trips he made to a waterlogged meadow at Buxton Lamas. On 30 April 1972, he invited me to join him for a day's 'fishing'. By then, the crater created in violence had been transformed into a tranquil meadowland pond about 20ft in diameter and deceptively deep. The deception came in the form of a thick mat of weed, which pretended to be the bed of the pond as one stood on it but which, when pulled aside, revealed depths of some 15 feet and was very dangerous. Our only technology was a grappling iron tossed into the depths and dragged ashore. This was a primitive procedure, requiring patience, but, over time, Chris was rewarded with some excellent finds from the sunken wreckage: the remains of a flying helmet, throat microphones, bomb shackles, a split bomb casing and, more importantly, double confirmation of the aircraft's identity. The first item to confirm his wreck was the US Army Air Force Acceptance Plate showing it to be a B-24J, Serial Number 42-50804, manufactured against Order Number W535 AC21216. This find was exciting enough, but Chris could hardly believe his luck when another pull through the crater yielded the brass

The crater created in violence when the bomb load detonated had been transformed into a tranquil meadowland pond. Chris Gotts is fishing for fragments of the lost bomber. (*Chris Gotts*)

The wings once worn by navigator 1/Lt J.W. Ott. (*John Crow*)

radio call plate engraved with the number 250804. These discoveries facilitated his research, which culminated in 1977 when Chris met Hal Hutchcroft, and, although finds on the site of his crash had been poor by comparison, Chris was at least able to take him to the field and later presented the former co-pilot with a bullet from the aircraft he had abandoned three decades earlier. Hal also made a pilgrimage to the US Military Cemetery near Cambridge to honour his friend Ed Maceyra.

In subsequent years, other aviation groups visited the Kaiser site and artefacts found on the crater's edge by the Norfolk and Suffolk Aviation Museum included a set of pilot's wings, those belonging to either Kaiser or his co-pilot, 1/Lt R. Parry Jr. Amazingly, on the same occasion, they found the wings once worn by navigator 1/Lt J.W. Ott and, close by in the soil, a graduation ring inscribed 'Pilot AAF AFS Freeman Field'. It also bore a symbolic eagle and a representation of the P-38 Lightning fighter. The museum exhibited these finds to honour the crew, but, regrettably, the ring was stolen during a burglary some years later and has never been recovered.

In September 1999, a month before we cut our trench on the crash site of his B-24, Hal Hutchcroft died of leukaemia. His family requested pictures of our excavations, led by Nigel Beckett and Simon Dunham, and an interesting display of the discoveries made that day can be seen in the Station 146 Tower Museum at Seething. They may not be large or plentiful, but the men they honour deserve to be remembered, and visitors can reflect on the way a 22-year-old co-pilot played down the horror and loss in his diary: 'Hit plane in clouds. Bailed out. Engineer and myself. That was all.'

The graduation ring inscribed 'Pilot AAF AFS Freeman Field', since stolen from the Norfolk and Suffolk Aviation Museum. (*John Crow*)

CHAPTER ELEVEN

Held in God's Hands

It was a fighter pilot's dream: a formation of unescorted heavy bombers and the sun's brilliance to hide his approach. In classic style, Lt Rudolf Rademacher positioned his small formation of Messerschmitt 262s up-sun of the Liberator formation and concealed himself in its glare. Instinct made him double-check for enemy fighters. Straight and level, his twin-engined jet could outrun any of the now outmoded American piston-engined machines, but they had massive superiority in numbers and, given height, could still catch an unwary jet. To counter the new Luftwaffe machine, the Allies drenched the heavens with fighters and waited over Luftwaffe bases to catch the jets, vulnerable during take-off and landing. Now, there were no fighters, just a tiny flock of bombers, astray and exposed. With nearly 100 kills already accumulated since January 1942, Rademacher understood the brutal simplicity of aerial warfare – kill or be killed. Jet technology was simply a more sophisticated means of delivering the same message and gave Germany the advantage in fighter performance. Since the advent of the ubiquitous, long-range P-51 Mustang, the days of finding unescorted bombers had diminished. Further pressure on the Luftwaffe's weakening resources came when American strategists took the reins off close escort and allowed their fighters to forage the length and breadth of Axis territory. Soon there was no hiding place, and Rademacher witnessed the remorseless erosion of skills when inexperienced German pilots were hunted down during training. In addition, a steady reduction in the training schedule saw men

In classic style Lt Rudolf Rademacher positioned his small formation of Me 262s up-sun of the Liberator formation. (*Gerhard Bracke/Chuck Blaney*)

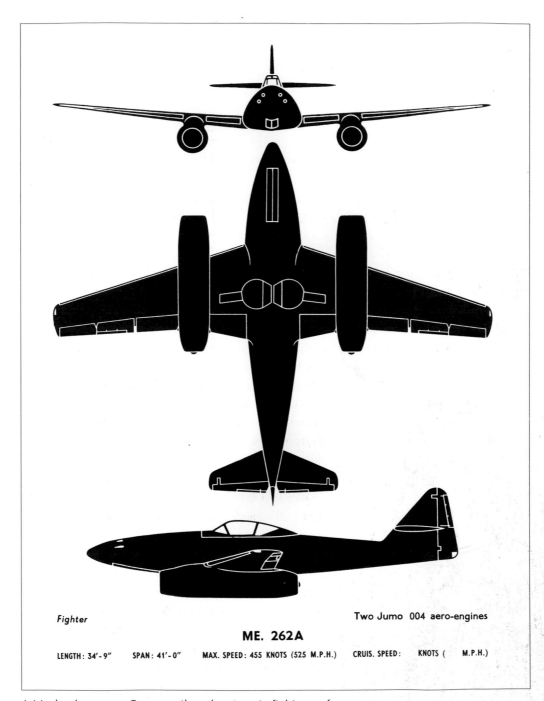

Fighter   Two Jumo 004 aero-engines

ME. 262A

LENGTH: 34'-9"   SPAN: 41'-0"   MAX. SPEED: 455 KNOTS (525 M.P.H.)   CRUIS. SPEED: KNOTS (M.P.H.)

Jet technology gave Germany the advantage in fighter performance.

hurried into conflict against airmen better trained beyond the combat zone and weaned into combat, not thrown in as fighter fodder. The dilution of Luftwaffe skills was relentless, while dwindling fuel supplies further exacerbated the situation. His own service as an instructor with 1 Jagdgeschwader (JG) *Nord* had illustrated the point. Hopes of a Luftwaffe resurgence arose when the Me 262 became part of the Axis arsenal.

First flown in July 1942, the aircraft – later known as the *Schwalbe* (Swallow) – had the potential for wresting air superiority from the Allies, but political interference by none other than Adolf Hitler saw the aircraft's interceptor potential subordinated to adapt it as a 'blitz bomber'. This decision, along with technical difficulties, delayed its introduction until it was too late, and there were never enough operational Me 262s to defeat the Allied bomber offensive and influence the war's outcome. Had the Me 262 been available in quantity, German fighter leaders, including Generalleutnant Galland, believed that the American day-bomber offensive could have been defeated. The Liberators now targeted by Rademacher were about to experience a demonstration of its potency.

On Palm Sunday, 25 March 1945, bad weather and bravery exposed these 448th BG aircraft to Rademacher's assault. The religious festival could not interrupt the war, but inclement weather did, with the First and Third Air Division B-17 force being recalled. However, over 270 Second Division Liberators were already en route, including twenty-six from the 448th BG flying the Group's 244th mission. Having taken off from their base at Seething, Norfolk, they set course for their primary objective, a petroleum storage depot at Buchen, a few miles from the city of Hamburg. Increasingly dense cloud disrupted their formation, and cohesion was broken near the Dutch coast, as aircraft lost visual contact. The 713th Squadron became separated from the main formation but elected to continue, despite trailing some two minutes behind. This fact was not lost on the jets of JG7, and they closed swiftly in from astern. Armed with four 30mm MK108 cannon, the Me 262s were formidable and the sun's glare concealed their ambush until it was too late.

Flying as navigator on board 'Do Bunny', serial 42-95185, 2/Lt Herman Engel noted:

The mission should be a milk run. The usual flack [*sic*] at the Dutch coast and the target. Take off was 0600 and with climb and assembly time we made it to the target on time. Milk run so far although we did see flack and fighters, which were hitting every other bomb squadron (we were in line to be missed). Bombs away at 1133, the last entry in my navigation log for the mission. The Me 262's attacked suddenly and unexpectedly, coming in out of the sun . . .

It seems likely that Rademacher had selected Do Bunny as his victim. Even with conditions in his favour, the Luftwaffe ace had a healthy respect for American gunners, because retaliatory fire had hospitalized him the previous September with serious wounds suffered during an engagement with the 'Viermots' (four-engined bombers). Tactics had been developed for attacking American bomber formations, using a speed of some 550mph to cut through the escorting fighters. This speed had then to be absorbed, in order to avoid closing

Crew 7179, 713th Squadron. *Rear left to right*: Alvin Stout, waist gunner; William Wilson, nose turret; Leonard Dailey, top turret; Albert Bentley, ball turret; Edward Danecki, tail turret; Charles Blaney, radio operator/top turret. *Front*: Paul Jones, pilot; James Mucha, co-pilot; Herman Engel, engineer. (*Chuck Blaney*)

so fast that they overshot the target or lacked time to select and sight their victim. To do this, Me 262 pilots went astern and below the enemy, then curved upwards, shedding speed until they levelled with the bomber formation about 1,000 yards behind but with a closing speed advantage still exceeding 100mph faster than the target. This speed provided protection but offered only one opportunity to strike, because there was insufficient time to reselect another target as they closed in. The Rheinmetall-Borsig cannons fired 660 rounds per minute but carried fewer than 300 rounds, so held less than half a minute's firing time. However, even one hit in a vital area could bring down a bomber, and the punishment from several strikes was devastating, with debris from the victim showering back towards the attacker. To avoid this, the Me 262's method was to pull up some 100 yards from the bomber, disengage overhead and arc back for another assault if conditions allowed.

With Do Bunny silhouetted in his gunsight, Rademacher thumbed his firing button and a storm of cannon shells burst upon the bomber like the world's end as he raked across the port wing, instantly setting the No. 1 engine on fire. In the Liberator's cockpit, 1/Lt Paul J. Jones and his co-pilot, 2/Lt James Mucha, hit the fire extinguisher and feathering button with the speed and experience acquired during twenty-two missions. As the propeller juddered to a standstill, the fire was extinguished and Rademacher's jet pulled away, pursued by angry tracers from Do Bunny. Staff Sgt Leonard E. Dailey fired from the top turret and Sgt William J. Wilson from the nose, but the Me 262 swept away, seemingly impervious, before curving round to finish off its crippled victim.

Caught by the jet attack, other 448th ships fared worse than Do Bunny. The Lead aircraft, 42-50646, was lacerated by cannon fire, which fatally wounded the pilot, Lt Knute Stalland, and his co-pilot, Lt Theodore Warner. Other crews saw the B-24 speckled with exploding shells. Flames erupted from its port wing and the bomber staggered like a man being bullwhipped. With both pilots either dead or dying, the aircraft abruptly dropped 50 feet, levelled, then slid off to the right away from the formation, with harsh orange-red flames devouring its life. Beginning a shallow climb, the stricken aircraft tried grasping the element it lived in, then, hesitating, it swung gently towards its companions as if appealing for a mercy none could grant. A figure leapt from the hell on board. As his parachute popped, his boots were jarred incongruously from his feet. There were twelve men on this aircraft. In deceptive slow motion, the noise of its agony drowned in engine sounds from the spectators' own machines, the silent horror continued. No hands can extend to help in this part of heaven. The starboard wing tore away and a violent red-black bile rose when the bomber exploded in an evisceration of cascading debris. The selective hand of chance saved two further survivors and the battle moved on.

Do Bunny held formation, her grip in the air only tentative, as her pilots compensated for the dead engine and the blast of sub-zero air surging through the bomb bay. The attack had left no time to close the doors, and damage now made it impossible. Some seven Me 262s had hit the 448th, but it felt as though it had been many more, and their own assailant was coming back. This time the gunners were ready, and radio operator Staff Sgt Charles W. 'Chuck' Blaney recalls: 'We maintained formation until a second Me 262 pass on the squadron. This time we responded – all four gun turrets blazing .5 caliber bullets . . . Time seemed to stand still . . .'. Despite the ferocity of their reply, Do Bunny took a beating. Cannon shells slammed into the B-24, throwing top turret gunner Staff Sgt Leonard E. Daily from his position to the floor of the flight deck. Perched facing this onslaught, tail gunner Staff Sgt Edward W. Danecki valiantly kept firing until also blasted away from his guns and bowled backwards along the fuselage amid shards of shattered perspex, armoured glass and other bits from his turret. Amazingly, Danecki was virtually unscathed. His goggles had protected his eyes and good luck managed the rest. To Herman Engel, it seemed a recurring nightmare, as further attacks ripped the guts from Do Bunny. Severed fuel lines and punctured tanks bled gasoline into the fuselage to mix with hydraulic fluid, creating an explosive cocktail that somehow failed to ignite as it vapoured

out into the slipstream. The No. 2 engine had been smashed into useless scrap, with one of the propeller blades left hanging by a sinew. On the starboard side, engine No. 3 had also been destroyed, and Herman felt it was incredible that there were no serious casualties and their sieve of a ship was still airborne, if not airworthy. He 'lost count of the number of passes but it seemed that the shells and bullets were hitting or passing through every section of the aircraft'. At one point, Herman released Wilson from his nose turret; the gunner had expended all 800 rounds of ammunition available. Suddenly the attacks ceased. Whether this was due to friendly fighter intervention or the simple fact that the enemy had expended his own ammunition was uncertain. What was certain was the shambles on board Do Bunny. With three engines destroyed, the B-24 stood no chance of reaching England, and, with the aircraft unable to maintain altitude, there seemed no choice but for the crew to bail out. The electrical and communications systems had been torn apart, so intercom instructions from their pilot, 1/Lt Paul J. Jones, for bail-out preparations went unacknowledged. When word of mouth confirmed his intentions, the crew strongly resisted. It was already known that German civilians had murdered Allied airmen unfortunate enough to fall, literally, into their hands, and logic indicated they stood a better chance by remaining together.

There was also the faint hope of reaching Allied lines, and rapid calculations from Herman were relayed to his pilot. A huge pall of smoke ascending from the ruins of recently bombed Hamburg provided a fix for their position and Herman calculated a course towards Wesel on the Rhine as their closest friendly territory. He knew that the British 6th and American 17th Airborne Divisions had parachuted onto the east bank of the Rhine to support the 21st Army crossing in strength. Discarding all unnecessary equipment, Do Bunny sought to reach the sanctuary of this area, some 180 miles distant. Herman realized the hopelessness of the cause as a litter of unwanted apparel and apparatus spilled from the struggling bomber: flak suits, guns, ammunition, anything to save weight and reduce their rate of descent.

Do Bunny was not alone in a desperate struggle for a safe haven. Further detritus was being added to a war-littered landscape from the crew of 'Eager One' – 42-50326. Cannon fire had slashed into the aircraft, destroying some of its starboard control cables and ripping off the right rudder and flap. With other electrical and mechanical systems also inoperative, the crew jettisoned their bombs and kept the aircraft aloft with the skill and sheer strength of its pilot, Lt Frederick Tod, and his co-pilot, Lt Warren Peterson. The stress and physical fatigue on both were enormous, but they remained airborne over the Baltic, heading for neutral Sweden. At last the coast appeared; then, near the village of Falsterbo on the southern tip of the Fenno-Scandinavian peninsula, engine failure forced abandonment of the bomber. Tod and Peterson held the ship steady while their crew bailed out before they swung the B-24 seawards to avoid the dwellings beneath. Peterson was the last but one to leave and, moments later, Eager One spun into the sea. Some of the parachutes landed on-shore while others drifted into the bitterly cold Baltic as local inhabitants rushed to assist. Peterson was pulled from the waves but could not be resuscitated, while the equally heroic Tod had sacrificed himself for his crew and the community of Falsterbo.

In one of its worst air-combat encounters, the 448th BG lost four Liberators. 'Tarfu II' (44-40099), flown by Lt John Steffan and crew, had been struck out of the main formation and exploded moments later. Only the navigator, Lt Gerald Gottlieb, bailed out. The others perished when the aircraft fell on a shoe factory at Schneverdingen. Other aircraft staggered home or landed at forward and emergency airfields with wounded on board and varying degrees of damage.

However, it was not all one-sided, and information from S.E. Harvey, co-author with John Foreman of *The Messerschmitt Me 262 Combat Diary*, shows that JG7 claimed seven Liberators but lost four jets and their experienced pilots. Lt Muller shot down a B-24, presumably Stalland at 1025, but his aircraft was hit and he crash-landed at Stendal in dramatic fashion when his fast-moving fighter ran into a hangar, hitting five Ju 88s. Feldwebel Fritz Taube claimed a B-24 but died when caught by Mustangs of the 352nd FG, Lt Raymond H. Littge being the likely victor – he reported downing an Me 262 after it had destroyed a Liberator. Oberfeldwebel Herman Buchner also claimed a B-24, as did Oberfahnrich Gunther Ullrich, but he was bounced by P-51s while landing and was killed. Oberfahnrich Windisch allegedly destroyed a Liberator but then got on the wrong side of a Mustang and his aircraft was badly shot up. His attacker is believed to be Lt F.W. Salze of the 479th FG, whose compatriot, Lt Eugene H. Wendt, caught another 262 landing at Rechlin. It is thought his victim was Oberleutnant Schatzle, who was killed in action. The 352nd FG Mustang flown by Lt Wesley Roebuck was shot down, but 3/JG7 claimed two Mustangs, and linking events in detail is often impossible in the confusion of fast-moving air combat. After the attack, JG7 was pursued by P-47s from the 56th FG but outpaced their attackers. The experienced ace, Capt George E. Bostwick, decided on another tactic and went stalking over the airfield at Parchim, where his formation was rewarded with one Me 262 destroyed and another damaged. This rare air-to-air victory was achieved without expending any ammunition, as described in Bostwick's Combat Report:

I was leading Daily Squadron on an escort mission in the vicinity of Hamburg. We were on the right and to the rear of our box of bombers when my Red Leader called in several bogies closing rapidly on a small group of 15 bombers at about 8 o'clock to us. They were in good formation but some distance away from the rest of their box. I turned towards them just in time to see two explode.

The Me 262s split up after their attack, most of them heading roughly east. I followed until I lost sight of them and then proceeded to look over all the airfields in the area. I finally found the airdrome at Parchim and orbited it at about 12,000 feet for about twenty minutes. There were between 20–30 aircraft visible on the field. After many wide orbits, my Number 4 man called in a bogie and I directed him to lead off. This enemy aircraft was also an Me 262 and he led us back to the airdrome.

Upon approaching the airdrome I spotted four more Me 262s milling around almost on the deck. I picked out one flying parallel to the landing strip as if he might be going to peel off to land. He did not, however, but flew straight down the runway. As he

reached the end of it he passed over a second aircraft which was taking off and just breaking the ground.

I pulled my nose through to get a shot at it but before I could the pilot apparently saw me and made a tight turn to the left. His left wing dug into the ground and the plane cartwheeled, breaking into many pieces and strewing wreckage for some distance. I then pulled back up to the right and picked up the e/a I had originally attacked. I got in a burst from about 800 yards and 45 degrees and observed strikes on the fuselage near the tail. It then straightened out and I fired several bursts from dead astern without effect as it was rapidly widening the gap between us. I was indicating 460mph at this time. I fired up to my tracers and then broke off and headed out. My wingman, who had followed behind, joined me shortly and a few minutes later my element joined up.

I claim one Me 262 destroyed and one damaged in the air. Aircraft 44-21160 UN-J. Ammo fired 2060 rounds API [armour-piercing incendiary].

Work by Foreman and Harvey indicates Bostwick's victim was Oberleutnant Gunther von Rettburg of 10/JG7, who died in the crash.

Meanwhile, Do Bunny struggled for every foot of distance, every inch of height. With the aircraft running on only one under-performing engine, the crew soon recognized that their endeavour to achieve Allied lines was a forlorn hope. They were descending at 1,000 feet per minute, and simple arithmetic told Herman Engel that they stood no chance of covering the distance. Hostile territory drew ever nearer and the prospect of maltreatment loomed ever larger. Now, their only hope was to use their little remaining altitude to select a field suitable for a crash landing. With no power to go around again, plus the risk of control being lost during any manoeuvre, the only option was to locate a field dead ahead. Herman recalls, 'At 1143 and 2,000 feet of altitude and sinking fast the pilot ordered us to ditching stations and prepare for the inevitable crash landing . . . We had covered about 36 of the 180 miles to Wesel.' Having had a previous experience, the crew were confident in the skills of their pilots, as Chuck Blaney relates:

On our sixth mission we had experienced an emergency landing with skipper at the controls. We had been on a typical bombing mission to Worms, Germany, when we lost a single engine to flak over the target and a second engine became marginal. Jones maintained formation until we were over friendly territory. Rather than risk the 120 miles run to England over an icy North Sea, he elected to make an emergency landing. We landed on the only runway we could find, which was a PSP mesh fighter strip on the outskirts of Brussels, Belgium. Needless to say, we ran out of this runway in a hurry and settled in the Belgian countryside. Our 'Pregnant Lady' was written off as salvage as two engines were completely burned out during landing. The successful emergency landing was a confidence builder for the crew and especially for our pilot. We were grateful for his judgement and piloting skills . . .

Herman's recollection of this incident recalls the 'welcome' they received from their Allies:

The British, who were responsible for providing the base protection, decided they needed some gunnery practice. To our amazement and fright, we were greeted by a series of AA bursts leading our B-24 to the runway. When Paul queried our 'greeting' he was told it was practice and didn't he think it was well done leading us without a single hit.

The answer from their pilot is not on record but his calmness and skill inspired confidence.

These piloting skills were now vital, as Do Bunny swiftly descended towards the chosen field on the northern outskirts of Soltau, close to Harbuger Street. There was no alarm, with each crew member now too busy with his required duties to worry about what sort of reception they would receive. This now depended on others observing their descent. The ailing aircraft had been seen not only by townsfolk but also by soldiers of the Wehrmacht and by members from a unit of the dreaded SS who were resting up on leave from the front line.

Calmly, the crew released emergency hatches then readied themselves for the crash. In the final moments before touchdown, Dailey turned off the fuel sight gauge valves and wing compartment drain line valves located in the forward bomb bay, then quickly assumed his crash position, lying down with feet braced against a step behind the flight deck. Engel, Blaney and Wilson were already there, bracing themselves as best they could and keeping as far from the top turret as possible. An unfortunate feature of B-24 crash landings was the tendency for this to detach because of the jolt on impact and crush crew members, with sometimes fatal consequences. Unlike the low-winged B-17, the high-winged B-24 was a tougher proposition to belly land. The Fortress had a wider platform for absorbing impact and providing stability as it slithered to a standstill. The B-24 fuselage was like a single ski and could twist, which was why the pilot's manual advised strongly against belly landings and warned, 'dirt and sod roll up into balls, fracturing the plane's skin; then the bottom surfaces serve as a scoop . . .'. For Do Bunny, this would be exacerbated by the still-open bomb doors. Both pilots shed as much speed as possible before flaring out, but they were still travelling at some 100mph when they scraped into contact with German soil on a recently ploughed field. As they touched, Mucha pushed the engines settings into idle cut-off and turned off the master switch to cut all batteries and switch connections, reducing the risk of fire. Initially it was textbook, the B-24 skidded on with both wings level and Jones held her steady as long as humanly possible; but then disaster struck. The bomber swayed left; her port wing dipped then dug in, acting like a stick in a bicycle wheel and twisting the fuselage round with such force that the nose section broke at the bulkhead just behind the upper turret. The abrupt halt tore the top turret loose onto the men beneath.

In the few moments that followed, those that could hurried from the wreckage, spurred on by the risk of fire. Jones and Mucha clambered from the crazily contorted cockpit, now broken from the fuselage like a wrung-necked chicken. Tail gunner Danecki with both waist gunners, Sgts Alvin J. Stout and Albert J. Bentley, climbed unscathed from the rear fuselage. Four men were still trapped in the wreckage, but any chance of aiding their comrades was soon lost. Hardly had the airmen taken stock when a hostile crowd of civilians, some

wielding pitchforks, surrounded them. The decision of staying together looked like it now meant dying together, to judge from the anger of the local citizenry, evident in both tone and gesture if not entirely understood. Herman understood German but he was still trapped in the wreckage and the situation looked like developing into a lynch mob.

One of those who saw Do Bunny descend was Wehrmacht officer Oberleutnant Joachim Grauenhorst, who commanded a small riding academy stationed in Soltau. As the stricken bomber passed overhead then went down, Grauenhorst fully expected an explosion and pall of smoke, but neither occurred. He quickly ordered a few of his soldiers to follow him and they were soon at the crash scene. Others present included two young SS soldiers who were inciting the crowd to harm the captives. The Americans who had emerged from the wreck were roughly manhandled and made to run some 500 yards to a town square opposite the Mehr Hotel – during this run, Paul Jones was rabbit punched and had a 'headache for a week' – would there be worse to follow? The situation was growing uglier as Grauenhorst negotiated for control of the prisoners. In his opinion, these prisoners were 'Luftwaffe' and

Oberleutnant Joachim Grauenhorst stood his ground against the SS to save American survivors. (*Gerhard Bracke/Chuck Blaney*)

therefore should be handed to the German Air Force. Many traditional Wehrmacht men had little time for the strutting SS but had to recognize the power and influence represented by these sinister carrion-black uniforms. Crossing the SS could be detrimental to one's career, even life-threatening, and Grauenhorst would have known this only too well. However, his role at the riding academy presumably imbued many more honourable traits from German military tradition, including fair treatment for prisoners. Grauenhorst remonstrated with the SS, but they seemed determined to have these prisoners, and the anxious Americans knew the outcome of this altercation could mean being murdered and the circumstances altered into a cover-up. The Wehrmacht officer understood this but further argued that, because the SS were on leave and he was not, his jurisdiction prevailed until the prisoners could be handed to the Luftwaffe. Tense moments passed, then, surprisingly, the SS backed down, leaving Grauenhorst in control. Not all the onlookers had been supportive of the SS and Grauenhorst's successful stance swayed more decent-minded opinion, and efforts to rescue those still trapped were soon under way. A Lt-Col Hasse supported by the local chief of police soon planned a controlled assault on the wreckage using hacksaws, an axe and crowbars.

Still inside Do Bunny were Blaney, Dailey, Engel and Wilson. Having torn from its mountings, the top turret had dropped into the flight deck well, pinning all four against

The crazily contorted cockpit now broken from the fuselage like a wrung-necked chicken. Note the hole cut beneath the turret to reach survivors. (*Gerhard Bracke/Chuck Blaney*)

the fuselage walls and the flight deck itself. Chuck Blaney had had his leg broken by the turret but was still conscious, as was Wilson, whose right foot had been crushed and was still trapped. Had the aircraft ignited, all four would have been incinerated, but the crew's actions and the earlier loss of fuel from ruptured tanks had reduced this hazard. This was something of a disappointment for their captors, to whom gasoline was now liquid gold. There was no heavy lifting equipment available, so the soldiers and townsfolk decided to chop through the fuselage and extricate the airmen if enough leverage could be applied to the gun turret to pry them free. Those inside felt some anxiety regarding the first cut by the local garage worker with his axe because his first strike would be like puncturing a tin while trying to avoid damaging its contents. Some discussion ensued and a judgement was taken from the outside on where to strike the fuselage. Herman was uncomfortably close when the axe blade sliced through the thin aluminium of the fuselage skin and later recalled:

The engineer, radio operator and the nose gunner were pinned under the upper turret and, after much prying and considerable pain, were removed from the aircraft through the pilot's window. I was boxed in, without room to move, by the upper turret, radio console, bulkhead and right side of the aircraft. The German troops proceeded to cut away the fuselage around me with an axe – fortunately for me they knew how to use their axe and didn't hit me. Once.

Following Wilson's extrication from the wreckage, it was discovered that the length of time and pressure had caused nerve and tendon damage, which made it impossible for him to lift or hold his foot straight – it simply flopped uselessly as he tried to walk.

The four injured fliers were then taken to the hospital by a horse-drawn cart and Herman felt very apprehensive during the journey. Arriving without incident, they received initial treatment, and, after X-rays had been taken, Wilson had a strap added from the toe to the top of his GI boot to support his foot while walking. Blaney's leg was braced and Jim Mucha was treated for a suspected shrapnel wound in the buttock that he had not initially noticed. To the co-pilot's embarrassment, a German doctor's probing confirmed the shrapnel but felt that surgically removing it was unnecessary and, to this day, the co-pilot still sits on this 'souvenir' from their encounter with the Me 262. Following their medical care, they were taken to the Army Riding Academy in Soltau. As Herman recalls: 'Here we were reunited with the rest of the crew and here the interrogation started . . .'.

The questioning at Soltau was limited; it was obviously not a field of expertise for a riding academy, as Chuck relates: 'The next morning troops from the German Luftwaffe arrived from a nearby Me 262 airbase and took over. Lt Grauenhorst . . . was obviously relieved because he had been worried about the SS officers and his confrontation with them the day before. We stayed at the airbase one night and were then transported to Penneberg Interrogation Centre.' During this truck ride, they were transported with what fuel had been salvaged from Do Bunny, a small amount 'sloshing around in the bottom of a 50 gallon drum'. At Penneberg they were placed in solitary confinement and confronted by interrogators more adept in the art. Their treatment was humane if a bit uncomfortable, with Jones and Engel being questioned more closely, Jones because he was the aircraft commander and Herman because he spoke German. Herman's interlocutor was a friendly fellow sporting a wooden leg replacing one he had lost, he said, after crash-landing in England. Following this he was apparently sent to Canada for rehabilitation and was indebted to the Canadians for their good treatment before his repatriation in a prisoner exchange. Herman listened politely but still offered only his name, rank and number. Following further courteous questioning, the German attempted to impress Herman by illustrating the extensive knowledge they had already. He produced a volume of information and pictures appertaining to the 448th BG. They had a list of serial numbers for each ship at Seething and pictures to accompany them – even one showing Do Bunny. This tactic had been anticipated during Herman's training in a pamphlet entitled 'Instructions for Officers and Men of the Eighth Air Force in the Event of Capture'. One section about the interrogator's techniques read: 'He will try to impress you

with his great knowledge about yourself, your plane and the American Air Force in the hope that you will think he knows everything already, and therefore there is no "harm" in talking freely. He may suggest that others have already told everything so your silence is no longer necessary.' Herman stuck to his brief script despite an even stranger development when the German brought out Herman's own .45 automatic and compared it to his Luger. He then proceeded to hand his gun to the American for his opinion on its quality. It was an uncomfortable moment – Herman briefly held the weapon then quietly passed it back. The Germans would get nothing from him. This episode apparently concluded their efforts, and, after four days, Herman found himself with other prisoners on a locomotive bound for Stalag Luft I at Barth. During this journey the prisoners experienced some frightening moments, first when the train stopped at a heavily bombed railroad terminal in Hamburg and they were allowed to exercise their legs. Recognizing them as 'terror fliers' and 'child killers', the civilian populace grew increasingly hostile and threatening, but 'our guards managed to keep the civilians away . . . fortunately the on-time train got us out of the station before anything happened'. At another halt they were observed by an SS officer with a machine-gun-armed contingent from the Hitler Youth and subjected to a tirade of abuse that threatened to worsen, so their guards hastily ushered them back onto the train. At an overnight stop in Rostock, their guards arranged a billet in a shut-down restaurant, but the local mayor would not allow this and all were herded into a single standing-room cell in the town-hall basement. After this, the POW camp seemed a more secure environment in which to spend the rest of the war.

For the survivors of Do Bunny, their time in captivity was relatively brief. After a month, the camp was liberated by the advancing Russians and, a few days later, a deal was agreed allowing American aircraft to evacuate the POWs. Some, like Gerald Gottlieb, sole survivor from Tarfu II, were still recovering from burns; when he was first seen by Herman in the camp, Gottlieb still had his bandages on: 'His head only had eye slits to see, nostril holes for breathing and a space at the mouth for a straw for his liquid diet. After removal of the bandages his face and hands were clear with new skin free of any scars – it looked like the skin of a new baby.' By comparison, Herman had been lucky and his own wound needed no further attention after his release. By 20 May, less than two months after Do Bunny went down, Herman was back home in Brooklyn.

Like many other war veterans, Herman resumed an interrupted civilian life. He obtained an engineering degree and worked for over forty years for the Air Force, becoming an expert in parachute technology. Living in Dayton, Ohio, he became involved with the USAF Museum at Wright Patterson Air Force Base and contributed many voluntary hours in the service of this excellent establishment. In the early 1990s, Herman was contacted by Gerhard Bracke, who, as a 12-year-old, had witnessed the demise of Do Bunny. Decades later, now a university professor at Braunschweig, with an avid amateur interest in aviation history, Gerhard was inspired to research the story of the B-24. This work culminated in an extraordinary gathering on 11 October 1995, when Gerhard joined some of the surviving crew for a reunion at the Air Force Museum. Thanks to Gerhard, many facts about their crash

Twelve-year-old Gerhard Bracke witnessed the demise of Do Bunny and, decades later, researched its history. (*Gerhard Bracke*)

were revealed for the first time. He had even discovered pictures of the wreck, taken by Mr Mundschenk, owner of the local paper, the *Boehme Zeitung*, who kept them in his archives. Had it not been for the courage of Lt Grauenhorst, the pictures might have represented a shameful episode in the history of Soltau, whereas they are now a fascinating link to a time when two nations, now friends, were at war. They also mark a 'might-have-been' in aerial warfare when the advent of new technology was misdirected, ultimately to the world's better fortune. For Herman Engel they illustrate a minor miracle as he recalled the 12 minutes from attack to crash: 'To my dying day there are some things about those 12 minutes I will never know. How, with hundreds of holes in the aircraft, no one received a serious injury? Why didn't the aircraft burn or explode in flight or on crash landing? I always felt that God rode with us on every mission; on this one he must have held us in his hands.'

CHAPTER TWELVE

Hookem Cow

The people paying tribute to Eighth Air Force bomber crews are many and varied. There are historians, museum volunteers, members of the veterans' organizations with friends and associates, aviation archaeologists and those supporting the few remaining warbirds such as the B-17s 'Sally B' and 'Pink Lady'. Noticeably and sadly absent from European skies is an airworthy B-24 Liberator. One man has, in his own way, compensated for this and has combined elements of several enthusiasms to create a valued contribution to the memory of the Eighth.

John Deacon of Aylsham, Norfolk, is a retired electronics engineer and a recognized craftsman of model aircraft. These are not pre-boxed plastic kits but airworthy miniatures – 'miniature' being a relative term when one flies a four-engined scale-model bomber with fully retracting undercarriage and other operational features, not to mention flight characteristics emulating the real thing. Born in 1940, John grew up in Hoddesdon and, of still tender years, became fascinated by model aircraft after observing two enthusiasts stunting with control-line models. His journey to school took him past a model shop and, after saving his pocket money, he bought a balsa wood chuck glider and a lifelong hobby was born. Graduating to ever-more complex models, John liked the challenge of scaling the real thing and it was logical that an interest in the Eighth sponsored models such as a splendid one-sixth scale 4th FG P-47 appropriately named 'The Deacon' by its pilot, Howard 'Deacon' Hively. John's skills were spurred to their toughest assignment following a meeting with fellow modeller Stephen Carr, whose own one-sixth scale B-17, after the famous 100th BG 'Hang the Expense', was a masterpiece. Stephen also started the US Eighth Army Air Force Model Display Team and began choreographing formation flying and air-combat scenes using scale-model Thunderbolts and Mustangs flown by selected 'pilots' including John. Following a demonstration at Thorpe Abbotts, Stephen lamented the lack of a B-24 in their miniature fleet and John picked up the gauntlet. He would build a representative aircraft – but which one?

During the Second World War, America had manufactured over 18,000 Liberators used in all theatres of war. Living near Norwich and having worked in an electronics company

constructed over the former 458th BG bomb dump on Horsham St Faith, John felt an example from this pre-eminent Group would be ideal, but even they had numerous aircraft to choose from. The decision came during 1995 when John was browsing through Roger A. Freeman's superb *Mighty Eighth in Colour*. On page 83 was a close-up of a 755th Squadron B-24 named 'Hookem Cow' and John was suitably hooked. Of additional interest was the caption relating that she had crashed after take-off on 14 April 1945, and an idea dawned – why not locate the crash site and see if any parts remained extant? It would be an ideal tribute to incorporate an item from the real aircraft into his model and use a display board to relate its history. This would honour the crew and remind people of their sacrifice. John's quest commenced and, while the ensuing months challenged his craftsmanship, they also rewarded him with an expanding account of courage, humour and contrasting tragedy. This period introduced him in detail to the final moments of the real Hookem Cow, while one-sixth scale calculations resulted in some demanding dimensions for his model: a wingspan of 18ft 4in, wing area 29.1sq ft, with a fuselage 11ft 3in long. Detailed design work, construction plans and deciding upon power plants were activities soon under way, while parallel research expanded John's knowledge of the original machine.

Before becoming Hookem Cow, his aircraft was a B-24H-25-FO built in March 1944 by the Ford Motor Company at Willow Run, Michigan. Assigned the Army Air Force serial number 42-95120, she was one of the earliest natural metal finish machines, so John needed to simulate this. In its heyday, one Liberator was rolling off the production line every 100 minutes, seven days a week. His own efforts envisaged in excess of 1,000 man-hours – he could build a real one! Following post-production modifications, 42-95120 was ferried to Europe in the spring of 1944 and allocated to the 755th Squadron, 458th Bombardment Group, and coded J3-M. Her early career saw her christened 'Betty', with a leggy lady adorning the starboard nose. In this guise she accumulated missions and survived her fair share of flak, fighters and operational mishaps, including one in May that saw her needing some major repairs. On 27 May 1944, 2/Lt Lyman W. Call was marshalling the aircraft prior to mission take-off when he had a taxiing accident. He had started engines Nos 1 and 4 and had the electric auxiliary pump on as he taxied Betty towards her slot on the airfield perimeter track. To surmount a slight incline, he boosted the engines, only to discover that, as the B-24 rolled over the crest, he had no brakes! With the aircraft fully laden and gathering momentum down the slope, he found himself heading towards four other fully bombed-up B-24s. Call had no choice but to leave the perimeter track and take his chances that the softer airfield terrain would halt the runaway. Having unceremoniously destroyed a fence, crossed a road ditch and two embankments, Betty then demolished a hedge and a farmer's gate before coming to a halt, straddling the road to the village of Horsham St Faith.

A few weeks later, following repairs to the nose wheel, bomb bay and forward fuselage, there occurred a coincidence that coined the name 'Hookem Cow' and converted Betty to a new crew. Two of the men stationed at Horsham hailed from the district of South St Paul, Minnesota: James R. McGinn was a master sergeant and crew chief, while John L. Ollom was a captain and aircraft commander. However, the bond of men sharing the same background

Betty then demolished a hedge and a farmer's gate before coming to a halt, straddling the road to the village of Horsham St Faith. (*Mike Bailey*)

soon broke the barrier of rank. Surveying the bomber new to their charge, both pondered a name change giving it a character to remind them of their home community. St Paul was proud of its association with American beef processing and, during 1916, some citizens involved in the industry formed the Hookem Cow Club to promote South St Paul, its stockyards and meat-packing plants, and to participate in the St Paul Winter Carnival. Over the years, the club sponsored numerous events and functions and featured the film star Sonja Henie as an honorary member. It also supported the renowned Republican politician Harold Stassen when he became Governor of Minnesota. The two St Paulians wanted to recognize these achievements, so their squat, sturdily built B-24 abandoned 'Betty' and became 'Hookem Cow'. To create a suitable nose-art, they called upon the talents of Harold Johnston, a GI draughtsman with the Group who was already well known for his artwork. Johnston created the caricature of a pugnaciously aggressive steer surmounting the port nose. For the starboard side, John Ollom reserved something more personal and persuaded a reluctant Johnston to create, from a tiny snapshot, a large portrait of the pilot's wife to adorn the aircraft. Ollom also insisted on adding an affectionate reference to her nickname, so a stylized

The talents of Harold Johnston (pictured) created the caricature of a pugnaciously aggressive steer surmounting the port nose. (*Mike Bailey*)

'Stinky' appeared, but, perhaps fortunately, it is not on record what Mrs Ollom thought of this publicity.

John Deacon's challenge was to capture Hookem Cow's character, and much discussion ensued within the US Eighth Army Air Force Model Display Team. Stephen Carr shared knowledge gained from his B-17, offering advice on the weight and centre of gravity because these calculations were critical. The Davis wing on the original design had both aided and handicapped Consolidated's product. The B-24 benefited from an ability to fly higher and faster than the B-17 with a bigger payload but was less stable in formation and arguably absorbed less punishment. The merits and demerits continue to be debated, but one feature common to both was undeniable – the courage of their crews. Meanwhile, John's tribute to one crew, representing the many, gradually took shape. Fuselage formers, wing sections and a host more parts accumulated as he reflected on the benefits of bachelorhood, with

John Ollom (pictured) added an affectionate reference to his wife, but what she thought about Stinky is not on record. (*Mike Bailey*)

components spilling remorselessly throughout the house. Conventional balsa structure was complemented with fibreglass spars, spruce stringers, liteply and aircraft-grade plywood components covered with balsa sheeting. Simulation of aluminium was solved by using litho plate, a form of aluminium foil used in the printing industry, and the undercarriage was adapted around wheels from an industrial trolley with main legs created from purpose-built castings. A notorious danger when flying the real aircraft also translated into a threat to his model. Losing an engine at low altitude could yaw or roll an aircraft, with disastrous consequences. Swift action by those on board was essential, but John would not be on board, so he designed a dual electronic synchronization system on the outboard engines, so that the failure of either would put its counterpart to idle and help maintain stability. Cycling his remote throttle stick would regain control of the good engine and give enough power to go around for an emergency landing. No fewer than twenty-four servos were required to operate

engines and flying controls, the undercarriage retraction and steering mechanisms, bomb doors, bomb release and, as on the real thing, the ability to retract the ball turret.

John wanted to learn more about the men who had taken Hookem Cow on her final flight and he gradually established the facts, with hours of model making shadowed by time spent on research, aided by a skilled local researcher, Christine Armes. Both lines of activity had a focal point — first flight, fully researched. Support from the aviation network saw John eventually make contact with two men lucky to be alive. Don C. Neville and Michael C. Laine (formerly Lavonsky) were on board when Hookem Cow took to the skies — but only just — for the last time. Don demonstrated a keen interest in the project and John sought his approval for the incorporation of a piece of the original into his model. In a letter to Don, he explained: 'This would be my tribute to the members of your crew who paid the ultimate price for our freedom.' Having gained Don's blessing, John now had to locate the crash site and search for a suitable part. Don's dramatic description, supported by local accounts, indicated the likelihood of parts still extant and gave John a vivid account of events leading to tragedy that misty morning in April 1945.

Don Neville was a waist gunner on 2/Lt David R. Totten's crew, who were among the last to arrive at Horsham St Faith before the cessation of hostilities. Fate delayed their appearance for several weeks, as if seeking to spare them, but then contorted matters at the last minute. They formed at Westover Field, Springfield, Massachusetts, in October 1944, and were a typical blend of characters from a variety of states: Totten came from Beckley, West Virginia; Flight Off Walter J. 'Bill' Styneski, co-pilot, North Tonawanda, New York; 2/Lt Lewis L. Anderson, navigator, Wichita, Kansas; Flight Off Michael C. Lavonsky, bombardier, Clairton, Pennsylvania; Sgt Thomas F. Seale, engineer, Wilsonville, Alabama; Sgts Charles E. May, radio operator, Union City, New Jersey; Don C. Neville, waist gunner, Huntsville, Alabama; Charles A. Nystrom, nose turret, Willimantic, Connecticut; Donald Orgain, ball turret, Dickson, Tennessee; and Joe A. Galterio, tail gunner, Pittsburgh, Pennsylvania. Westover welded them together as a crew through training missions in the excruciating winter cold over North America and the bleak Atlantic. These exercises tested each man's capabilities and their overall cohesion as they practised pilotage, bombing, navigation, gunnery and emergency procedures. In January 1945, they were pronounced combat-ready and destined for the European Theatre of Operations.

Departing from Westover, they arrived at Mitchell Field, New York, and were allocated a shiny new B-24 to take overseas. Their planned route would be the Northern Run from Bangor, Maine, to Goose Bay, Labrador, followed by Bluie West One in Greenland; Meeks Field, Iceland, and then into the UK. As they left Mitchell Field on 19 February, the sense of home slipped astern as they droned nervously over an increasingly foreboding landscape of ice and snow. Descending some hours later, they found Goose Bay feathered white and submerged in a snowscape in which chimneys poked through like periscopes. Its runways were cut across white wastes, with the elements frequently successful in shutting down the airbase, and Totten's crew found onward movement prevented for four poker-playing days. Then they made a run for Greenland and the dangerously mountainous terrain surrounding

Pictured in February 1945, the Totten crew were a typical blend of characters from a variety of states. *Rear left to right*: Sgts Charles E. May, radio operator; Charles A. Nystrom, nose turret; Don C. Neville, waist gunner; Thomas F. Seale, engineer; Donald Orgain, ball turret; Joe A. Galterio, tail turret. *Front*: 2/Lt David R. Totten, pilot; Flight Off Walter J. 'Bill' Styneski, co-pilot; 2/Lt Lewis L. Anderson, navigator; Flight Off Michael C. Lavonsky, bombardier. (*Don Neville via Chris Gotts*)

Bluie West One. Don peered apprehensively at the jagged peaks nearby as they descended into a dramatically primeval canyon and chased its contours into a cul-de-sac. Totten then turned the B-24 through 360° and dropped skilfully onto a runway running alongside the dark waters of the Tunulliarfik Fjord. A 'follow-me' jeep guided them to a Sommerfield metal parking ramp, and they were advised to tether their ship because storms were once more chasing them in. That night, winds of over 100mph battered the base and damaged all the exposed aircraft to varying degrees. The playing cards reappeared while mechanics toiled in terrible conditions repairing damaged machines. Four tedious weeks elapsed before they again ran before the storm into Iceland and were again grounded for four days. This time, the weather was not the only adversary and they were ordered to roster guard

duty on their aircraft in four-hour shifts against potential saboteurs sympathetic to the Axis cause. A much-relieved crew took off on the last stage of their journey to RAF Valley in Wales, where they touched down on 20 March, over four weeks after leaving America. They had nursed their factory-fresh B-24 to a combat zone, but any affinity was lost when Totten received orders to use a scratch crew and take it to a staging area for onward movement into combat. He returned to collect his crew, and together they travelled to the Combat Crew Reception Centre at Stone in Staffordshire. Here they received essential theatre indoctrination before more orders, and then a train journey and a truck transported them the last few miles to Horsham.

The war was almost over, but they made one apparently pointless patrol over the North Sea before their first penetration into enemy airspace on 11 April. This was an 8½-hour sortie to Regensberg, a target already infamous in Eighth Air Force history. The Second Air Division bombed marshalling yards, oil depots, airfields and munitions dumps further to reduce the remnants of enemy resources. To the neophytes, the flak seemed as formidable as the legend, but they sustained no damage or harm. There were few strategic targets left, but pockets of enemy resistance still existed, and one defiant enclave was in the French port of Bordeaux, now chosen as the crew's second target on 14 April. When the list of those flying was posted, Dave Totten's name appeared, but Bill Styneski had been bumped as co-pilot, and he was hopping mad because this would put him one mission behind his crew. Unable to find the Operations Officer to get the situation changed, Bill was placated when Dave assured him that the matter would be taken up at briefing.

Don Neville was awoken around 3.30 a.m. and informed that a full crew would not be required. The Luftwaffe was all but spent, and no fighter opposition was expected during this mop-up operation. They needed the officers, the engineer and radio operator with one gunner. This automatically included May on the radio and Seale as top turret and engineer. Eager to go, Don now rued a role swap with Seale made earlier in the crew's career. He had flown top turret during training but recognized that Seale's engineering skills required him further forward, so they had changed positions and Don had become left waist gunner. Now, all the gunners wanted to go, so out came the cards once again. As the pack was shuffled, none knew how much would depend on the cut of that deck. Don drew highest. He won. And lost.

Weather conditions continued to deteriorate rapidly and it was confirmed that their co-pilot, Bill Styneski, would be replaced with a more experienced officer, 1/Lt Joseph J. Szoke. Unable to change these orders, the now reduced crew waved to their comrades from the truck taking them to their hardstand. Bill and the others stood dejectedly in fog so thick that it swallowed their comrades in only 100 feet. Some had vanished for ever.

Piling out at the hardstand, they were introduced to an obvious veteran. Showing the wear and tear of over fifty missions but again pronounced combat ready, the B-24 Hookem Cow loomed dark and damp. As his crew bustled on board, Totten began his external pre-flight check, walking from the starboard wing tip on a pattern to encompass all features. This visual verification was essential for spotting external issues and Totten's flashlight probed through

The Totten crew were introduced to an obvious veteran showing the wear and tear of over fifty missions. Hookem Cow (centre) and two companions. (*Mike Bailey*)

the fog examining wing panels, engines for oil leaks, de-icer boots, gun turrets and pitot tubes. Each supercharger bucket wheel was spun to check easy rotation and the waste gates confirmed as open. All tyres were inspected for damage and hydraulic lines studied for leaks. Satisfied, Totten climbed on board to conduct his visual review internally and paid particular attention to the fuel selector valve settings in the bomb bay. A fuel line or cross-feed manifold failure could prove disastrous.

As Totten and Szoke settled into the cockpit to commence their pre-flight checks, the other airmen assumed their take-off positions. It was standard procedure for the nose to remain empty because of risks should the nose wheel collapse, and Mike Lavonsky joined Don in the waist, leaving five crew forward of the bomb bay. No one was allowed aft of the waist gun windows, because this significantly affected the centre of gravity. Don's duty on take-off was to remain on the interphone and advise if any problems arose, but all seemed normal as the Twin Wasps sequenced into life. Moisture, a dormant sheen on the lifeless airframe, was now shaken into merging silvered rivulets, each scurrying into tiny streams and waterfalls as the bomber shook off its last night's sleep. Listening on the interphone, Don heard no indications of

concern from the flight deck and felt Hookem Cow move as the parking brake was released and the pilots applied a burst of power. Moving slowly, she shimmied into her taxi slot and joined the line of gently jostling bombers heading for runway 05. The morning chorus of many radials echoed across the sleeping city on what would be one of the last occasions before the Group went home. Don would not be among those celebrating that occasion.

Hookem Cow lined up for take-off and, final checks completed, Totten clicked on the interphone to confirm all was secure aft. When he received an affirmative, the B-24 began to roll, engines howling in unison as power and speed increased. Hauling seven men and 4,000 pounds of bombs, Hookem Cow broke contact with the runway and Don felt the vibrations ease into those denoting flight. Moving to the left waist window, he could see the landscape illuminated by their powerful wing lights cutting through the fog. Uneasily, he sensed something was wrong – the aircraft was climbing like a geriatric on steep stairs. Then he noticed their port inner engine was 'flaming'. Not on fire but flash-flaming and clearly pulling inadequate power – was this the only one? Still the B-24 did not adopt its normal, sturdily confident climb; trees and hedgerows were not receding as they should. Clicking on the intercom, concerned but not alarmed, Don called 'waist to pilot, waist to pilot'. No reply. He again tried, this time more anxious. Still no response. Were the treetops getting even closer? Unknown to Don, only seconds ahead were power lines stretching like a giant trip-wire. There was a blinding flash and Don's last recollection was of being thrown like a violently discarded doll.

Consciousness returned amid a confusion of darkness, bright billowing lights and tall shadows with new stars floating in front of them. His gathering senses slowly sorted a grotesque and terrifying reality from the confusion. The pulsating light now clear with harsh orange-red flames came from exploding pockets of burning fuel surging over surrounding trees – his tall shadows. The nascent stars were showers of sparks shimmering skywards sliced by meteoric lines of tracer flashing from the debris. Sharp pain pulled his mind into a personal hell from which he could not escape. His brain screamed commands ignored by his limbs; his nostrils caught the stench of aviation fuel; he heard flames gorging on his aircraft and its contents – he felt the heat scorching closer, growing stronger. His eyes registered pure horror and reflected in terror the avaricious advance of surrounding fires. His mind shrieked for activity – move – RUN – but his body ignored it all. Paralysed, he lay on gasoline-soaked soil waiting for immolation to sear away his last agonizing seconds. Nearby, he recognized one main wheel pointing incongruously heavenwards. The tyre was still gently rotating as if bemused by events, its reality inverted. The pain suggested Don had been thrown against the aircraft's interior and then violently expelled as it disintegrated. Was he to die here alone, his charred corpse discovered in the debris? Oxygen bottles exploded nearby, as the fire, seeking new, combustible material, devoured more of the bomber's remains. Somewhere, nearby he guessed, there would be four 1,000lb bombs getting hotter and hotter – perhaps the explosion would beat the flames – a more merciful end.

Then Don detected movement nearby – not wreckage settling into ash – human movement, closer now. Calling out, he heard someone coming in his direction. Crawling,

This brave gentleman was Walter Giles, a Technical Officer with 26 Group, part of the British Air Ministry. (*John Giles*)

injured. His next shout was answered. A familiar voice – Mike Lavonsky. Dragging himself towards Don, the wounded bombardier lay alongside, as if his own flesh afforded protection for his friend. Don was drifting in and out of consciousness. Next came further movement nearby. Positive, uninjured and searching. Through the smoke stepped the figure of a British civilian.

This brave gentleman was Walter Giles, who lived nearby and was actually a Technical Officer with 26 Group, part of British Air Ministry activities supporting vital radar installations countrywide. An aircraft roaring low over the house had startled him and his wife Elsie into frightened wakefulness. It had been so close that Walter felt that it had clipped the roof and hurried from his bed to check. Peering from his window into the darkness and fog, he saw nothing amiss, but, seconds later, they heard another bomber thundering towards the house. Louder and louder – this time even lower. Staring towards the sound, he was startled by two bright lights surging from the darkness directly towards him. He was later told by the USAAF that these were flames from the engines, but they may have been the landing lights. Walter barely had time to shout before the crescendo of engines turned into a tremendous crash close by, as the aircraft ripped into woodland on the Lewins' land in The Grove next door. Dressing hastily, Walter called into his son John's bedroom for him to dress and urged his daughter, Ann, to join them. John was usually abroad as an engineering officer in the merchant navy but was home taking some exams, while Ann's skills as a nurse might be required if there were survivors.

Hurrying out, Walter grabbed John's bicycle and leapt astride. With John and Ann running behind, he pedalled furiously towards the flames flickering in the fog. Covering barely 100 yards, Walter went full tilt into something straddling the road and was pitched over the handlebars. As the children caught up, they heard a burst of expletives from their father and found him sprawled beneath the bike. As Walter disentangled himself, his torch revealed he had ridden headlong into a massive 1,000lb bomb! Dark and sinister, it sat brooding on the road and was clearly a hazard for any emergency services racing to the scene. A few feet further away lay a second of the menacing shapes. Passing the flashlight to Ann, Walter told her to sit on the nearest bomb and warn approaching traffic! Ann had learned that her father was not someone you disobeyed, so she obediently sat on the cold steel casing, torch in hand. None of the family heeded the risk to themselves as Walter and John hastened

Girl on a bomb. Ann had learned that her father was not someone you disobeyed so she obediently sat on the bomb to warn any oncoming traffic. (*John Giles*)

John was usually abroad as an engineering officer in the Merchant Navy but was fortunately on hand to help survivors. (*John Giles*)

to the conflagration, now 'quite a fire'. They entered the Lewins' gateway to discover trees fronting the house were blazing fiercely and preventing access to the wreckage. Running back to the roadway, they planned to get behind the burning bomber and hastened through a field gate, which enabled them to skirt the blaze. As they ran across the field, further evidence of the tragedy littered their path. Dotted among the destruction were bodies, some on fire and each clearly beyond help. Distressed by the ghastly scene, Walter and John searched even more determinedly amid burning patches of debris, quickly getting closer to the core of wreckage. At first it seemed there were no survivors, but, nearing the largest section still on fire, Walter discerned another human form only 15 feet from flames flowing even closer. There, lying helplessly on his back, was an airman. Thank God. Still alive.

As Walter knelt to check on Don, he was startled by a second figure staggering through the smoke. Clearly dazed, the flier asked if they had taken off yet, and Walter called for John to lead the man (Mike Lavonsky) to safety. Mike's recollections are understandably vague.

The first thing that hit my mind was, that we had gotten off the runway sooner than my previous mission, judging from . . . the runway lights. This was somewhat a surprise to me since we used practically all of the runway on my first mission. I could see the glow

through the porthole of No. 2 engine torching and the waist gunner called me to the window to show me. After I had looked I then experienced a tumbling sensation. The next thing I remember was that I was lying next to the waist gunner on the ground. He had said that I had gotten out of the plane and was walking around, apparently in a daze but I don't remember this. I don't know whether the ship exploded or what, since I was undoubtedly at a loss of memory at the time. I judge we were at an altitude of 100 to 150 feet at the time of my noticing the torching.

As John Giles led the concussed Mike Lavonsky away, Walter told his son to fetch something they could use as a stretcher for Don. Walter knew that any movement might exacerbate the man's injuries, even prove fatal, but the fire, singeing still closer, might give them no alternative.

Don, drifting in and out of awareness, had not seen Lavonsky leave and was desperately grateful for the presence of the civilian. It was a strange introduction, but Walter sat down beside him, reassuring the American that, no matter what, he would stay. Walter then calmly queried how many bombs they had on board and Don's reply made him wonder where the other two were, because none had exploded . . . so far. As the flames crackled and hissed close by, edging even nearer, both men waited for assistance. Several minutes elapsed, and Walter, judging that the fire was at last receding, made his companion as comfortable as possible by pillowing his head. Now the stench of aviation fuel had diminished, they shared some cigarettes. John returned with a door on which Don could be transported, but Walter wisely judged that experts must make any movement, even though he grew increasingly concerned by the airman's deteriorating condition.

Further away Ann sat patiently and very bravely on her bomb. Mr Gee, the local Air Raid Warden, hurried into view and asked what she was doing. 'Sitting on a bomb', answered Ann calmly, as if it was an everyday occurrence. She repeated the obvious comment moments later when her mother hastened by with blankets.

Mr Gee soon located Walter and was followed by the local doctor, who injected Don with some painkiller to ease his suffering. Although in pain himself, Don was relieved when the British National Fire Service arrived and he saw Mike taken to safety by firemen adapting a ladder into a stretcher. Don was judged too seriously injured to move just yet and lay sharing additional cigarettes and being given sips of water as a small crowd of onlookers now gathered. The breaking dawn gave features to figures nearby and made it easier for the ambulance to locate the crash. Spectators stood aside and Walter welcomed the sight of an Army Air Force ambulance reversing bumpily between bits of scattered wreckage. Army medics rapidly established a blood transfusion and attached a brace to Don's broken right leg. With continuing swift efficiency, they soon stretchered him into the ambulance and, as it gently moved away, Don embarked on a medical journey extending over 12 months and several hospitals. He had a broken back, a broken right leg above the knee, and a broken left ankle, his left arm had been broken at the shoulder, and he had broken ribs and numerous cuts and abrasions. He and Mike were the only survivors – all those on the flight deck had perished.

Mike Lavonsky was soon released from hospital but returned to visit Don, as did Walter Giles, who, keeping a promise, wrote to Don's parents on 11 May 1945:

Dear Mr and Mrs Neville. I have recently visited your son Don who, you no doubt know, is in hospital a few miles from here and I am very pleased to tell you he is making very good progress and very soon will be on his way home. He gave me the enclosed photograph but I thought, by giving it to you, you will see how cheerful he is. I understand his arms and legs will mend satisfactorily and there should be no disability.

I contacted him due to his machine crashing quite close to our house very early one dark and foggy morning. Fortunately he and another lad got clear of the wreckage and I found them together and stayed until the medical unit arrived. Although he was knocked about, his courage and fortitude was amazing and he is a son of whom you can be very proud.

No doubt you have been worried having his letters written by one of his pals. But, being left-handed, the picture supplies the answer.

If I can, I will call in and see him again before he leaves hospital. I promised Don I would write and I sincerely hope this letter will put your minds at rest.

Don was also visited by Bill Styneski, who, writing home, conjectured about the cause and his account, albeit second-hand, gives another perspective, even if it contradicts Don's later recollections.

Here is what I think happened, from what I got from Mike and Neville, the only two who got out. Before I go on, I will explain something. Prop wash is something all pilots hate, it gives you trouble. It is the wind made by the propellers of the plane when you give it the gas. The turning of the propellers cause the air to move in all directions, something like a cyclone or windstorm. Saturday morning, April 14, there was no wind to blow the prop wash away. The boys were taking off at one minute apart. Dave took off and got 600 feet high. Here is Neville's story . . . 'We got about 600 feet high [sic] when I told Mike our number two engine was throwing a large flame. Mike came over to look at it . . .' They tried to call the pilot but no one answered. After about three tries they gave up. Just about that time there was a flash and an explosion. Neville was thrown back in the tail. Mike must have gotten knocked out because he doesn't remember anything from then. Neville crawled out of the tail and back to the waist. Again there was an explosion and the ship was on fire all over. The ship then hit a row of trees and broke in a thousand pieces or more. All except Mike and Neville were killed instantly and burned pretty bad. Dave [Totten] and someone else were found about one half mile from the ship and Dave's jacket was 500 feet from his body . . . Just what happened we don't know. Maybe the engine caught fire and maybe they hit prop wash. No one knows what the cause was . . . I only wish it never happened . . .

John Deacon also wished it had never happened, but Don's description of events spurred him into finding the site and locating eyewitnesses. Publicity for the planned model helped,

and John heard from Robin Harrison, then a lad of 10 who had come close to being a civilian casualty. Robin had been at boarding school in Wales but came home for the Easter holiday earlier than expected to find his room at home unprepared. Their neighbours, the Lewins, agreed he could stay overnight with them, and all was fine until the early hours, when a terrifying noise frightened the sleeping lad out of his wits. Suddenly the house seemed surrounded in flames and Robin was sure he 'hadn't got a hope in hell'. Instinct and fear took over. He fled. Rushing to the front door, he nearly fell over a huge black fuel tank smouldering ominously on the doorstep. A big black engine lay wreathed in smoke and flames on the tennis court, with another lying behind the house. Racing past, he ran for the loke leading homewards and dashed fearfully on. Tracer bullets scythed through surrounding foliage amid showers of sparks and acrid smoke swirling across the lane. Reaching his front gate, he leapt over a bomb lying in the driveway and shot indoors. His anxious parents were overjoyed, because the explosion and fire next door had convinced them their son was dead and the bomb on the doorstep had seemed irrelevant. Now, they all hurried to evacuate their home, joining other residents from nearby dwellings until the unexploded bombs had been dealt with.

Returning later, Robin surveyed the scene and realized that the presence of a sturdy elm had prevented the plane from crashing into the room where he slept. Deflected by the tree, Hookem Cow had slewed away from The Grove. One wing, torn off on hitting the elm, had spewed blazing fuel across the Lewins' chicken run and charred chickens lay scattered around – 'already roasted', was Mr Lewin's wry observation. The bomber had broken up in woodland both sides of the driveway, with part of the nose still resting in the open. Momentum had carried the bombs from the wreckage, with some ripping through nearby hedgerows and gouging deep cuts in the terrain before coming to rest. Intriguing to wartime youngsters and a mystery to this day was the presence of numerous large slabs of chocolate littering the inside of the tail section. Airmen clearing away the debris later buried these, but the interment was but a brief interlude before local children had a feast. Chocolate was a rare commodity in their rationed community and digging it up from a crash site did not trouble anyone's conscience. Other pieces of the fallen bomber were also buried *in situ*, and, over five decades later, one of them would be resurrected, phoenix fashion, in the skies above its old base.

John's miniature of Hookem Cow was nearing completion. Armed with Robin Harrison's tale and the enthusiastic consent of the landowners, John searched the crash site in the spring of 1997 while the undergrowth was still low. No evidence of any chocolate emerged, but a myriad of aircraft pieces was found beneath the soft woodland soil. A shiny heliograph from the survival equipment, chromed parachute clips, rounds of ammunition and fragments of radio apparatus fascinated the electronics engineer. To represent the original, John chose a piece of aluminium, which he soon crafted into a section for the nose turret.

In June 1999, his Hookem Cow was ready for her maiden flight, and John assembled the sections at RAF Coltishall. He was about to evaluate his efforts, and one mistake might eliminate hundreds of dedicated hours but, as he later explained to the author, 'If you

Like any pilot; John Deacon (right) diligently adheres to his checklist. (*David Boddington*)

John Deacon's Hookem Cow is far more than a scale model aircraft – it is living history communicated to young and old, recalling airmen and a machine that once proudly dominated the skies over eastern England. (*David Boddington*)

design it correctly, you build it correctly, you do all your pre-flight checks and, most important of all, the centre of gravity is in the right place, it can't do anything else but fly!' His original design had required a co-pilot for certain critical tasks, but clever use of technology enabled him to manipulate the control console single-handed. There would be no one else to blame, and, like any pilot, he diligently adhered to his checklist. One mistake and his personal tribute to the men who flew the original would be lost. As he manœuvred for take-off, he thought of that fateful morning. A few weeks earlier he and Christine had visited the graves of those crew members still buried in the US Military Cemetery near Cambridge. Tears had been shed as they reflected on so many lost hopes, and John was determined his own efforts to honour the men represented by his Hookem Cow would succeed. One by one, the four Zenoah 45cc engines were revved up and, after a final pre-flight check, the junior Hookem Cow commenced her inaugural take-off run. Since that occasion, she has thrilled and fascinated many audiences, and the information board taken to every performance not only relates the statistics behind this impressive model but also describes the story she represents. John Deacon's Hookem Cow is far more than a scale model aircraft – it is living history being communicated to young and old in a manner that helps them understand the real aircraft's past and recalls airmen and a machine that once proudly dominated the skies over eastern England.

Bibliography

Bowman, Martin W., *Home By Christmas? The Story of US Airmen at War*. Wellingborough: Patrick Stephens, 1987.

Brett, Jeffrey E., *The 448th Bomb Group (H) Liberators over Germany in World War II*. Atglen, PA: Schiffer Publishing, 2002.

Foreman, John, and Harvey, S.E., *The Messerschmitt Me 262 Combat Diary*. New Malden: Air Research Publications, 1995.

Freeman, Roger A., *The Mighty Eighth*. London: Macdonald, 1970.

Freeman, Roger A., *Mighty Eighth War Diary*. New York: Jane's, 1981.

Freeman, Roger A., *Mighty Eighth War Manual*. New York: Jane's, 1984.

McLachlan, Ian, *Final Flights: Dramatic Wartime Incidents Revealed by Aviation Archaeology*. Sparkford: Haynes Publishing, 1989.

McLachlan, Ian, *Eighth Air Force Bomber Stories*. Wellingborough: Patrick Stephens, 1991.

McLachlan, Ian, *Night of The Intruders*. Cambridge: Patrick Stephens, 1994.

Morris, Danny, *Aces and Wingmen*. London: Neville Spearman, 1972.

Nicol, John, and Rennell, Tony, *The Last Escape: The Untold Story of Allied Prisoners of War in Germany, 1944–45*. London: Viking Books, 2003.

Index

EIGHTH AIR FORCE BOMBER STORIES